GUARDIANS OF THE DYNASTY

A History of the U.S. Created Guardia Nacional de Nicaragua and the Somoza Family

NICARAGUA GUARDIA CADETS ON PARADE

GUARDIANS OF THE DYNASTY

Richard Millett

INTRODUCTION BY MIGUEL D'ESCOTO, M.M.

ORBIS BOOKS 

Manufactured in the United States of America

Library of Congress Cataloging in Publication Data
Millett, Richard, 1938–

Guardians of the dynasty.

Bibliography: p.
Includes index.
1. Nicaragua—Politics and government—1909–1937.
2. Nicaragua—Politics and government—1937–
3. Nicaragua. Guardia Nacional—History.
4. Nicaragua—Relations (general) with the United States. 5. United States—Relations (general) with Nicaragua. 6. Somoza family. I. Title.
F1526.3.M65 320.9'7285'05 76-49499
ISBN 0-88344-169-1

CONTENTS

ACKNOWLEDGMENTS AND DEDICATION

In the fifteen or more years in which I have been studying the Guardia Nacional de Nicaragua I have received aid and cooperation from hundreds of individuals in the United States, in Nicaragua, and in several other nations. While it is difficult to single out any individuals from among this group I should like to give special thanks to Dr. Edwin Lieuwen of the University of New Mexico, who first encouraged me to pursue this topic and who obtained financing for my initial visit to Nicaragua; to Colonel John Morgan, U.S. military attaché to Nicaragua from 1963 to 1964, who opened a host of doors for me in Nicaragua; to Dr. Dana G. Munro, whose friendship and encouragement along with a constant willingness to share his own information and experiences enriched this study greatly; to the late Lieutenant General Julian C. Smith, U.S.M.C. and his gracious and charming wife, whose patience in answering questions and whose contacts with other former Guardia officers opened a new dimension to the entire study; and to Mr. Jack Hilliard and Mr. Charles Anthony Wood of the Marine Corps History and Museum section, who did all in their power to facilitate my research. Of couse, the cooperation of Father Miguel d'Escoto and the entire staff of Orbis Books was vital in bringing this publication to fruition. Scores of Nicaraguans, both within and outside of the Guardia provided invaluable assistance in this project, but because of the current political situation in their nation it is probably best to avoid singling any of them out for special mention. It is to them, however, and to all those, in Nicaragua, in the United States, and throughout the world, who hope and strive for a better future, when Nicaragua's military will no longer be guardians of a dynasty, that this book is respectfully dedicated.

GUARDIANS OF THE DYNASTY

A History of the U.S. Created Guardia Nacional de Nicaragua and the Somoza Family

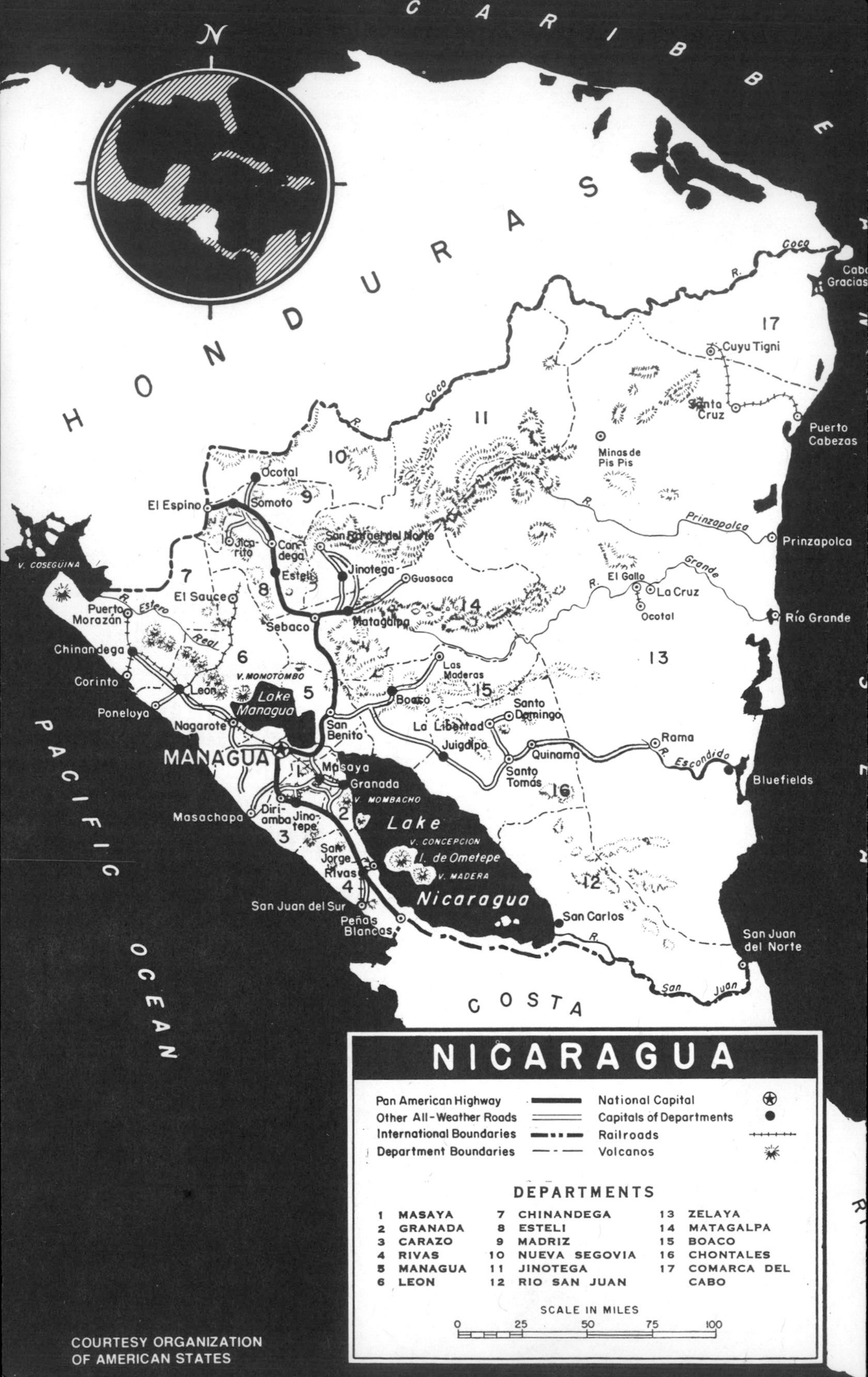

N
CARIBBEAN
HONDURAS
COSTA
PACIFIC OCEAN
Coco R.
Cabo Gracias
17
Cuyu Tigni
Santa Cruz
Puerto Cabezas
Minas de Pis Pis
11
10
Ocotal
9
Somoto
El Espino
Jicarito
Condega
Esteli
San Rafael del Norte
Jinotega
Guasaca
7
El Sauce
8
V. COSEGUINA
Puerto Morazán
R. Estero Real
Chinandega
Corinto
6
V. MOMOTOMBO
Leon
Poneloya
Nagarote
Lake Managua
5
Sebaco
Matagalpa
14
R. Prinzapolca
Prinzapolca
R. Grande
El Gallo
La Cruz
Ocotal
Río Grande
13
Las Maderas
15
Boaco
San Benito
Santo Domingo
La Libertad
Juigalpa
Quinama
Rama
R. Escondido
Bluefields
Santo Tomás
16
MANAGUA
1
Masaya
Granada
V. MOMBACHO
2
Masachapa
Diriamba
Jinotepe
3
Lake Nicaragua
V. CONCEPCION
I. de Ometepe
V. MADERA
San Jorge
Rivas
4
San Juan del Sur
Peñas Blancas
San Carlos
12
R. San Juan
San Juan del Norte
NICARAGUA
Pan American Highway
Other All-Weather Roads
International Boundaries
Department Boundaries
National Capital
Capitals of Departments
Railroads
Volcanos
DEPARTMENTS
1 MASAYA
2 GRANADA
3 CARAZO
4 RIVAS
5 MANAGUA
6 LEON
7 CHINANDEGA
8 ESTELI
9 MADRIZ
10 NUEVA SEGOVIA
11 JINOTEGA
12 RIO SAN JUAN
13 ZELAYA
14 MATAGALPA
15 BOACO
16 CHONTALES
17 COMARCA DEL CABO
SCALE IN MILES
0 25 50 75 100
COURTESY ORGANIZATION OF AMERICAN STATES

INTRODUCTION

MIGUEL D'ESCOTO, M.M.

This is the body, this is the soul of you
Ah, Nicaragua, mother dolorous!
Nor is it lack of love to see you thus–
Were I less sorrowful, my song less true,
I would belie the blood runs in my veins.
My love is savage: I will strip you bare,
And wound you with the sight of your despair,
And whip you with the leash of your own pains.

But when the dawn is red after this night,
When I have beaten you to gestate wrath,
You shall behold your self and test your might,
And through this sad and barren laziness
Shall stretch my passion, your triumphal path,
And you shall weep to know my tenderness.

SALOMÓN DE LA SELVA

The history of Nicaragua is perhaps the saddest history of any country in continental Latin America. This fact alone makes it an interesting and worthwhile object of study. But there is another fact which makes the study of current Nicaraguan affairs even more compelling to Americans—and that fact is that American interference in Nicaraguan political problems is certainly one of the main factors that have contributed to the present condition of the country. American intervention culminated in the enthronement of the Somoza dynasty, which has oppressed the country for the last forty years in total disregard for any value other than the dynasty's own insatiable greed.

The Somoza dynasty has controlled Nicaragua longer than any other family or individual has controlled any Spanish American republic. It has done so by means of coups, electoral frauds, and "free elections" like the one held in 1974 when, disregarding the constitutional prohibition, Anastasio Somoza Debayle ran for reelection against a phantom candidate and "won" after a month's "counting" of nonexisting votes. Flagrant constitutional violations have offered the U.S. many opportunities to withhold the all-important State Department recognition. However, it is most ironic that hypocritical arguments of nonintervention or of the people's right to self-determination should continue to be used to explain American recognition and generous support of a government that is the direct result of United States intervention and that in no way represents the Nicaraguan people.

Among the many causes of the seemingly endless nightmare which Nicaragua has experienced since its independence in 1821, three seem to stand out as the most important. First, the country has from the start been divided by a senseless and destructive type of regionalism. The rivalry between the cities of León and Granada, as well as the hatred and vindictiveness with which the political parties representing each of these two cities treated one another at least up until 1927, is the single most tragic national trait in Nicaraguan history. This exaggerated regionalism and partisanship has been the cause of a continued succession of revolutions and coups, and, in part at least, also the cause of foreign interventions.

Secondly, a unique geography must be counted as one of the most important causes contributing to the current plight of "Muhammed's Paradise," as the conquistadors called Nicaragua. Former *New York Times* correspondent, Harold Norman Denny, was quite right when back in 1928 he wrote: "It has been Nicaragua's fate, often an evil fate like that of a woman too lovely, to be desired by many nations. Geological forces laid out the area which was to be Nicaragua at a point destined to be of enormous strategic importance to the great powers of the world."[1]

Very early in the colonial period Spanish engineers pointed out to the sovereigns that by cutting a waterway through the narrow isthmus not only would they be able to import the products of Peru more easily, but furthermore they might then successfully compete with their rivals for the trade of the Far East as well. Philip II demonstrated his interest by having one of his engineers, Batista Antonelli, conduct the first survey for the Nicaragua Canal. It was only a matter of time before England, France, and the United States would also feel tempted by the idea of controlling an interoceanic canal through Nicaragua. "The construction of the Nicaragua canal," wrote William L. Merry, American Minister to Nicaragua in 1890, "will secure the *domination of the United States over the American Continent,* politically as well as commercially. . . *The nation that with the Nicaraguan Government on a joint agreement, controls Lake Nicaragua, will then control the destiny of the Western Hemisphere.* . . One great advantage possessed by the Nicaraguan canal over any other project of the kind is the *fertility and resources of the territory through which it passes.* . . Nicaragua is one of the *garden spots of the world.*"[2]

President McKinley appointed a commission of experts to investigate all possible sites for the canal in Central America, and although the commission declared itself unanimously in favor of the Nicaraguan route, the canal was built in Panama. Why this happened need not concern us here, but it is important to emphasize that even though Panama got the canal, the Nicaraguan route remained as a potential temptation to some other power, some day, unless the United States kept it in its hands. The future of Nicaragua was thus to become even more inseparably linked with the Colossus of the North. Starting in 1912, the country became virtually a United States colony and all important Nicaraguan political decisions were to be made in the American Legation at Managua or in the State Department in Washington. Nicaragua thus was made to pay dearly for its "privileged" geographic and strategic location.

All this leads us to the third most important fact that helps to explain the present political nightmare of Nicaragua, namely, United States intervention. Regionalism, lack of political maturity, and consequent political and economic instability, combined with the critical strategic location of Nicaragua for United States national defense, made some sort of American intervention practically inevitable. A more enlightened intervention, however, might have had less lasting and damaging effects on the country. But for the United States, the welfare of Nicaragua as such was only of secondary importance. The United States wanted stability because stability in such a strategically located country was deemed necessary for United States security. With the Somoza dynasty, which is the direct result of American intervention, the United States got stability all right—but it is only the deceptive lull that accompanies the death of democratic institutions and portends future revolutions.

Crises, whether individual or collective, have a way of bringing out the best and the worst in people, organizations, or nations. The United States intervention in Nicaragua provoked a true crisis in the Republic's national identity and sovereignty and in so doing it occasioned the most noble, patriotic actions as well as the most base, treasonable opportunism. The first element was represented by Augusto César Sandino, the hero of Nicaraguan patriotism, who courageously and admirably fought the interventionist United States Marines. The second element was represented by Anastasio Somoza García, one of the most charming, most astute, most ambitious, and most amoral public figures Nicaragua has ever produced, surpassed in the last two qualities perhaps only by his son, Tachito, who now rules over the country.

Richard Millett's book, so aptly entitled *Guardians of the Dynasty,* could almost as well have been called "The Fruit of Intervention." The Nicaraguan National Guard, which is the subject of this book, was fathered by arrogant American interventionism and corrupted by the egotistical genius of its United States-picked *Jefe Director,* Anastasio Somoza García. The United States, with the help of its longtime puppet, President Adolfo Díaz, imposed the creation of the National Guard in 1927. The Guard was to be the nonpolitical Nicaragua Army which the United States hoped to use as the main tool for the enforcement of its policy in the country. But there were others whose ambitions were also aroused at the thought of controlling the "apolitical" Guard for their own political ambitions and personal gains. Anastasio Somoza García, a onetime currency counterfeiter, who also had the distinction of being a grandnephew of Bernabé Somoza, Nicaragua's most notorious outlaw, used his great personal charm and undeniable intelligence to marry out of his own social class into one of the most "distinguished" families of the country. Then, in 1932, by ingratiating himself with the American interventionists and deceitfully allaying the suspicions of President-elect Juan Bautista Sacasa, Somoza managed to get himself appointed as the first Nicaraguan Chief of the National Guard. Sacasa actually had little choice in the matter, for pressure from the United States Minister and outgoing President José María Moncada left him almost no option. Of course, the fact that President Sacasa was Mrs. Somoza's uncle did not hurt.

Somoza immediately began his lifelong career of turning the National Guard into his personal henchmen and main instrument to drain dignity, patriotism, and virility from the country he hoped to turn into his personal fiefdom. He began by murdering Sandino, who, as already mentioned, is widely recognized as the greatest hero of Nicaraguan nationalism and patriotism. Then, in the manner so correctly described by deposed President Sacasa, Somoza proceeded to turn the National Guard into his own personal guard:

> The habit of strict subordination to the Jefe Director, to which the academy-trained officers had been accustomed, proved to be a real asset for General Somoza and his political machinations. With flattery and privileges or, on the other hand, intimidation and punishment, he managed to break the upright spirit of the institution entrusted to him. Somoza thus changed the nature of the Guardia from an honorable force committed to the service of Nicaragua into a docile body at the service of his personal ambition.[3]

How all this happened is explained in Professor Millett's objective and unemotional account of the Guardia's history. It was necessary that someone of Professor Millett's academic stature, with the added advantage of not being himself a Nicaraguan, undertake the task of writing the long-awaited story of the institution most responsible for maintaining in power one of the worst and certainly the longest-lasting dictatorships in the history of Latin America.

Somoza García's dictatorial tenure ended in the violent way that it inevitably had to end. On September 21, 1956, he was shot by Rigoberto López Pérez, a patriotic young poet who attempted to liberate his country by a means which did violence to his sensitive soul and ensured his own death. An all-out effort by President Eisenhower's medical mission succeeded only in prolonging the dictator's life for a few days and Somoza died in an American military hospital in Panama on September 29, while Rigoberto López Pérez was riddled with bullets seconds after he had emptied his gun on Somoza. But if United States medical know-how was unable to save Somoza's life, it certainly provided sufficient time for American Ambassador Thomas E. Whelan to help ensure the continuation of Somoza rule. The fact that before his death Tacho had placed his own two sons in key positions was a great help to the Ambassador suddenly turned kingmaker.

Since Somoza García's death in 1956, the country has been increasingly at the mercy of his youngest son Tachito, the West Point graduate who has been described by a former close friend and relative by marriage in the following way:

> People say that he is crazy, and this is not quite true. There is no doubt, however, that he suffers from a progressive psychic imbalance.
>
> Among other symptoms he suffers from a persecution complex. At times he feels that he is being persecuted and at other times he feels the urge to persecute. At times he suspects the loyalty of his most intimate friends without any justifiable cause, or he might confuse the deeds of one with the actions of another, persecuting one for what the other did.
>
> Tachito also has a deformed conscience. It isn't that he does not know how to distinguish good from evil, he had a good education and he is able to do that perfectly well. What happens is that he tries to convince himself, and those around him, that whatever is to his advantage is "good" even though he knows it to be "evil." Since the puppet officers and servile civilians who surround him never dispute him, not even when they clearly see him to be wrong, he gradually comes to believe that whatever he wants to be the truth is actually the truth. Then begins the interminable process of chain reactions in which he becomes more and more confused and removed from reality. Tachito undoubtedly is involved in a fast-moving process of self-exultation, megalomania, and self-deification. Thus he keeps moving further away from his true self.[4]

Fifteen years after this description of Tachito Somoza was written, Jack Anderson wrote the following in his widely read column: "The world's greediest ruler is Anastasio (Tachito) Somoza D., the pot-bellied potentate who runs Nicaragua as if it were his private state. This is no casual observation; we have spent months making the selection. After a thorough study of available evidence, we nominate Somoza as the most grasping of the world's great grabbers. Through his family and his flunkies, he controls every profitable industry, institution and service in Nicaragua."[5]

Without going into a list of the incredible array of the Somoza family's major economic holdings, it is interesting to note that when Somoza García rose to power, he had little more than a ruined coffee *finca.* As Professor Millett points out, in his first three years in office, he accumulated a fortune of $3 to $4 million. By the time he died it was estimated that he was worth some $100 million—some United States sources say $150 million. A recent American report indicated that by 1975 "Somoza businesses *in Nicaragua alone* were estimated at $400–500 million dollars, and constituted a full-blown economic financial group."[6] The family, of course, has most of its ill-acquired fortune securely invested outside of Nicaragua. What the total might be is a matter of conjecture, for the Somozas are not given to disclosures of such "personal" matters.

The scandal of Somoza greed becomes more apparent when we consider that more than half of Nicaragua's 2.5 million population lives in hopeless poverty.[7] Studies show that, along with widespread malnutrition, close to half of the registered deaths are those of children under the age of 5 and that life expectancy is 49.9 years (22 years less than the United States average). A very high unemployment rate of 22 percent is even more serious when one considers that there is a great number of dependents since about half of the country's population is under fifteen years of age. The housing situation, aggravated by the 1972 Managua earthquake, was dramatic even before that date when a study indicated that 73.7 percent of existing housing units were inadequate or substandard.

In spite of such statistics, Tachito once had the audacity to tell this writer that there are no poor Nicaraguans—obviously he must think that only his family and friends are Nicaraguans.

But besides his nomination as "the world's greediest ruler," Somoza should also be awarded some kind of title for repression and cruelty. The cruelties and repression that the Somozas have had to exercise in order to turn Nicaragua into their own family estate, have been amply documented by victims who, having survived the satanic ordeals, dared to write about their experiences. It is interesting to note that Tachito's greatest contribution to the maintenance of dynastic rule in Nicaragua has been his unmatched expertise in the fields of brutality and repression. His West Point education and subsequent advice from American Embassy "experts" have served him in good stead. No need to emphasize that without the Guardia's vested interest in keeping the Somozas in power the latter could not have lasted so long.

The United States ambassadors to Nicaragua, like the pitiful Turner B. Shelton, have at times been impressed "by the *macho* figure of Somoza, who uses American slang and stands solidly with the U.S. both by preference and for survival."[8] Whether or not American policy with regard to Nicaragua will actually change is a matter of conjecture. This book, however, should make it abundantly clear that United States responsibility for the agony which that country has experienced in the last forty years can hardly be overemphasized. It is certainly lamentable that the Central American Peace Treaty of 1923, which called for the nonrecognition of unconstitutional governments, was abrogated just prior to Somoza's seizure of power. As Professor Millett shows, Tachito Somoza is clearly an unconstitutional ruler, for there were and continue to be clear constitutional prohibitions to his 1974 candidacy and his current presidency, to say nothing of the fraudulent nature of the 1974 "elections" and the whole history of the unconstitutionality of the dynasty. Tachito, therefore, should never have been given recognition by the State Department, but since he is an avid anti-Communist and a declared friend of the United States, whatever else he might be seems of no consequence.

The appointment of James D. Theberge in 1975 to replace Turner B. Shelton as United States Ambassador to Nicaragua raised some hopes that Washington might be about to change its policy of complete and unconditional support for the Somoza dynasty. These hopes were founded in the fact that, unlike Shelton, Theberge could at least be credited with intelligence and some knowledge of the area. Unlike Shelton also, Theberge speaks Spanish and thus could talk to someone besides Somoza to learn about what is really happening in Nicaragua. But it now seems unlikely that things will change in spite of the fact that Theberge has made obvious efforts not to project an image of identification with Somoza. This change in style does not, however, appear to signify any basic modification of United States policy toward Somoza, who continues to receive large amounts of material aid and advice. Whether President Jimmy Carter's proclaimed concern for human rights and international justice will have any practical consequences for U.S.-Nicaraguan relations remains to be seen.

Far more significant than Theberge's appointment were the Washington hearings on human rights in Nicaragua, El Salvador, and Guatemala held June 8 and 9, 1976, by the Subcommittee on International Organizations of the House International Relations Committee. Father Fernando Cardenal's testimony helped to bring the horror of the Somoza dynasty before conscientious United States Congressmen and interested American citizens. The hearings also helped Nicaraguans to partly change their view of the United States Government as exclusively made up of discredited State Department officers or the likes of Congressman John M. Murphy (D-N.Y.), a lifelong friend and protector of the Nicaraguan strongman, whom he characterizes as the "civilian leader" of a free and democratic nation.[9] The fact that the hearings were held at all, and the honorable way that they were conducted by Congressman Donald MacKay Fraser (D-Minn.), helped to show Nicaraguans that there are some people in Washington who still hold to the highest traditional ideals of the United States. Finally, the near panic situation created by the Washington hearings on the Nicaraguan rubber-stamp Congress, and government circles in general, helped to underline the fundamental weakness of a government founded on corruption, lies, and repression.

It is ironic that while continued Somoza rule in Nicaragua is the best guarantee for an eventual Communist takeover, the United States will probably continue to support Tachito until it feels sufficiently confident that his successor will maintain the basic Somoza system of capitalist exploitation and doglike docility to the United States. The United States seems ready to make a few cosmetic changes in its relations with Nicaragua, but not to let it decide its own destiny. Again, it is difficult to predict what pleasant surprises President Carter's "New Beginning" might bring in this regard.

When all has been said, it is important to emphasize that the blame for the Somoza dynasty cannot be totally placed on the United States, the Nicaragua rich, or even the National Guard. The Guardia is also a victim of Somoza even though its members have found it necessary to support the dynasty either to survive or to get ahead. On the other hand, the National Guard presently has a historic role to play in the liberation of Nicaragua and without its help that country will inevitably continue under Somoza's heel.

A similar observation can be made concerning the private business and financial sectors, as well as the Church. What Nicaragua now needs least of all is for these different social groups to start placing "greater" blame on one another. The guilt for Nicaragua's history and for its last and worst period, the Somoza dynasty, must be shared by the Guardia and all upper-class Nicaraguans. A joint effort is needed to bring about a long overdue radical change. With Father Cardenal's Washington testimony and the courageous denunciation of the Guardia for murdering, torturing, and terrorizing great numbers of innocent peasants recently made by all thirty-three American Capuchins working in Eastern Nicaragua, it might be said that the Church is moving in the right direction. The statement denouncing torture, rape, and summary executions of civilians which the Nicaraguan bishops published on January 8, 1977, further confirms this thrust. But while the Church is moving it is still quite inhibited by understandable fears of reprisal. Opposition political parties and workers' organizations have been united in a common front to overthrow Somoza. Some like to believe that elements of the Guardia and the private business and financial sectors will also join this opposition front. In the past, however, the Somozas, guided by the conviction that every person has a price, have always been able to divide and conquer the bourgeois political opposition. It remains to be seen whether history will once again repeat itself in this regard.

While all upper-class or "educated" Nicaraguans are co-responsible for the oppression of their country, the United States Government also shares a great part of the blame. The only moral way for the United States Government to act now would be to stop all economic and military support to the despotic and unconstitutional dynasty which it helped to create and has maintained in power for so long. Nicaragua needs aid and should be aided, but Nicaragua is one thing and Somoza is quite another. It would not suffice for Washington to recognize its past "mistakes" in Nicaragua. If the United States does not stop its support of the oppressive Somoza dynasty, then one will have to agree with those who say that far from having been "mistaken," the United States Nicaragua policy has been intentionally consistent and, therefore, simply criminal.

The overthrow of Somoza will not in itself bring about the revolutionary changes that the more socially concerned Nicaraguans would like to see, but it will be an indispensable step in that direction. The work of replacing the ideology of classical liberalism and its unjust social order with a truly democratic order where the rights of persons will be valued above those of capital, can only be done once Somoza is out. However, should Nicaraguans opt for a democratic and anti-imperialist type of socialism, the real question would be whether the United States would, for the first time, respect Nicaragua's right of self-determination.

The Guardia Nacional, the traditional political parties, as well as the powerful local economic groups and all the other pillars of Nicaragua's bourgeois democracy might get together and collaborate with the workers and peasants to overthrow the decaying Somoza dynasty. That would not require much vision or patriotism—it would simply be a case of enlightened self-interest requiring only a little intelligence and some foresight.

The real patriotism of all Nicaraguans, both within and outside the Guardia, would be proven only by their wholehearted collaboration with true representatives of the Nicaraguan people in the construction of a new system after Somoza's downfall. This would certainly require sacrifice. Relinquishing possessions or privileges, even though they do not and never did rightly belong to us, is hard. To go beyond that and actively participate in the construction of a just, noncapitalistic system can only be the result of a moral conversion. If the elite are not up to this kind of patriotic action, then their reluctance will only serve to prove that the Frente Sandinista de Liberación Nacional had been right all along in choosing violence and guerrilla warfare as the only viable strategy to bring about change. Under such circumstances, change, though necessary and ultimately inevitable, will come about in a far more painful way than any decent person may care to imagine. Patriotic and courageous Nicaraguans will continue to be driven to violence as it becomes increasingly obvious to them that there is no other way to obtain justice in their country. Somoza may continue to kill leaders like the Frente's Carlos Fonseca Amador (November 8, 1976) and many, many more, just as his father killed Sandino and hundreds of others, starting 43 years ago. But the spirit of these martyrs will live on as long as there is tyrrany in the land. No matter what Tachito may claim, the Frente is not dead, nor is it about to die, because what causes it to exist is very much alive. These are things that the United States Government and its bourgeois allies in Nicaragua ought seriously to consider.

A closing remark about Professor Millett's book may be in order. Earlier in this introduction, we pointed out that the fact that the author of this book is not a Nicaraguan was an advantage. Not being Nicaraguan, Professor Millett is not as emotionally involved in Nicaragua's tragedy as those whose lives have been directly affected by the Somoza system of government. The book thus presents a type of objectivity that a Nicaraguan author might have found impossible to achieve. On the other hand, the author's scholarly approach to the Guardia's history prevents him from describing many of the blatant evils that are common knowledge in Nicaragua but which cannot be easily documented. A more complete history of the Guardia can be written only when the enemies of truth no longer rule Nicaragua. Our author, of course, is not only not a Nicaraguan, he *is* an American, a fact that should not be ignored. Some may find fault with this book, but no one will rightly be able to say that the book is anti-American or that it exaggerates in what it says about the Guardia and the Somoza dynasty. Without saying it all, this book produces ample and irrefutable evidence to demonstrate the corrupt and oppressive nature of the Somoza dynasty and the Nicaraguan National Guard, and the total bankruptcy of Washington's Nicaragua policy.

NOTES

1. Harold Norman Denny, *Dollars for Bullets: The Story of American Rule in Nicaragua* (New York: Dial, 1929), p. 14.

2. Nicaragua Canal, Reports of the Committee on Foreign Relations of the Senate in the 51st, 52nd, and 53rd Congresses (Washington: Government Printing Office, 1894), p. 126 [author's italics].

3. Juan Bautista Sacasa, *Cómo y por qué cai del poder,* 2nd ed. (León: n.p., 1946), p. 17.

4. Luis Gonzaga Cardenal, *Mi rebelión: la dictadura de los Somozas* (Mexico, D.F.: Ediciones Patria y Libertad, 1961), p. 44.

5. Jack Anderson, *New York Post,* Monday, August 18, 1975.

6. NACLA (North American Congress on Latin America), *Latin America and Empire Report* X (February 1976) 10.

7. Dr. David C. Korten, "Crecimiento de la Población y Calidad de la Vida en Nicaragua," published by the Instituto Centroamericano de Administracion de Empresas (INCAE), Managua, 1973. (All statistics are taken from this study except the one on life expectancy, which is from the *New York Times,* September 28, 1975, Chart: "National Wealth and Its Effects."

8. Jeremiah O'Leary, *Washington Star,* November 28, 1974.

9. Jeremiah O'Leary, *Washington Star,* June 9, 1976, A-4.

I

THE BEGINNINGS OF THE NICARAGUAN MILITARY

Nicaraguan military history had its beginning in 1523 in a battle between the invading army of the Spanish conquistador, Gil González, and an Indian army led by Diriangén.[1] Superior weapons and horses made it possible for Spain to conquer and colonize the territory which now bears the name of Indian Chief Nicaragua. The Indians, however, ancestors of those who in 1927 would follow Augusto Sandino, could never be forced to accept servitude and exploitation. They were so courageous and able in battle that thousands of them were later taken by the Spaniards to help in the conquest of Peru and Equador. Their reluctance to submit to foreign domination, however, made them take advantage of every opportunity to rebel against the Spanish authorities. Gradually, Spain was dissuaded from using Nicaraguan Indians as soldiers.[2]

The colonial period, which for the peasant has never really ended, was initially characterized by repeated eruptions of armed rebellion against oppression. The military superiority of the oppressors and their foreign supporters, both before and after 1821, was and continues to be a major factor in maintaining for more than 450 years the subjugation of the Nicaraguan peasants.[3]

Nicaragua's importance as a route for transisthmian commerce made it subject to repeated attacks by English pirates during the colonial period, but for much of the nation the seventeenth and eighteenth centuries were relatively free of armed struggles with outside powers or between the colonizers.[4] This relative tranquility was shattered in December 1811 when the first armed rebellion against Spanish authority began. Led by Colonel Miguel Lacayo, the insurgents seized control of Granada, but were defeated early in 1812 by royalist forces including 200 men from Costa Rica. The rebellion collasped, its leaders were deported, and Nicaragua settled back into a few more years of uneasy peace.[5]

Independence from Spain came rather peacefully in 1821 and for a few months Nicaragua, along with the rest of Central Americas was united with Mexico as part of the empire of Agustín Iturbide. León took the lead in securing adherence to the empire and this aroused the enmity of its traditional rival city, Granada. The Granadinos declared Nicaragua a republic in 1823 and successfully fought off a 1,000-man force sent against them by León, killing 79 of the attackers.[6] The collapse of Iturbide's empire and the establishment of the Central American Federation later that year did nothing to diminish the conflict between these two cities. Although the Federation endured until 1838, its government was never able to impose complete order upon the Nicaraguans. From 1824 until 1842 Nicaragua witnessed seventeen major battles, lost 1,203 men, and saw eighteen individuals exercise executive authority.[7] Throughout this period control usually resided with the Liberals, centered around Leon. Granada's Conservatives, however, never abandoned their efforts to gain national control. In 1845, with help from Conservative governments in El Salvador and Honduras, they finally managed to drive the Liberals from power and transfer the national capital from León to Masaya, near Granada.[8] Now the Liberals began efforts to topple the government and revolution followed insurrection in monotonous succession. One such uprising, led by a dashing character named Bernabé Somoza, was attributed to the fact that this gentleman "had nothing else to do."[9] Somoza, a very charming and, at the same time, cruel man, was generally regarded as a bandit and was greatly feared in the 1840s throughout the Republic. According to an apologist he was a declared enemy of the English and wanted to get control of Nicaragua so that he could govern with the Americans. His charms were not sufficient to dissuade the Americans from believing that he was really a bandit, and this may be one of the few and most significant differences between him and his more famous or infamous descendant, grandnephew Anastasio Somoza García, with whom much of this book is concerned.[10]

Taking advantage of the country's chaotic state of affairs, the English extended their influence over Nicaragua's disputed east coast. Much of their penetration was accomplished peacefully, but in February 1848, a clash occurred between British and Nicaraguan forces. Nicaragua's "army" in this battle numbered only about 130 men, armed with condemned muskets and old machetes. They proved no match for the 300 British troops who occupied the port of San Juan del Norte and pushed up the San Juan River, defeating the Nicaraguans and killing between fifteen and twenty of them.[11]

In the United States both private and governmental interests felt threatened by this extension of British influence. The discovery of gold in California and the consequent increase in Americans seeking transportation to the Pacific Coast made control of routes across Central America a matter of increasing importance for the United States. In 1849 a group of New York investors, headed by Cornelius Vanderbilt, obtained a charter from the Nicaraguan government for the establishment of "The Accessory Transit Company," a combined stagecoach and lake and river boat transportation system across Nicaragua.[12] Vanderbilt's efforts conflicted with British attempts to control the Nicaraguan route and relations with the United States became rather tense before a compromise settlement was finally negotiated. This was the Clayton-Bulwer Treaty, signed in April 1850. This agreement provided that any future canal or railway across Nicaragua would be under joint American and British control, that tolls would be equal for both nations, and that neither would occupy or fortify the canal route.[13]

It was a revealing measure of Nicaraguan weakness that their government had been totally excluded from the Clayton-Bulwer negotiations. Even if the United States and Great Britain had been willing to include them in the discussions, it would have been difficult to determine who should represent Nicaragua. Throughout the negotiations internal political conflicts had continued unabated, spreading confusion and carnage throughout the land. In March 1851, in an apparent effort to diminish the chronic rivalry between León and Granada, Conservative dictator Laureano Pineda moved the capital to the small city of Managua. A Liberal revolt, supported by his army commander, General José Trinidad Muñoz, briefly returned the capital to León, but when the Conservative President of Honduras sent his army into Nicaragua to support Pineda, this revolt collapsed and the capital returned to Managua where it has remained ever since.[14] Far from ending the León-Granada rivalry, however, this action simply created a new objective for the continuing civil wars.

In May 1854, Liberal troops led by Máximo Jerez made a major effort to overthrow the Conservative government. In retaliation President Fruto Chamorro issued a decree stating that his forces would instantly execute any armed rebels who fell into their hands and Jerez responded by declaring that all those who aided the government were traitors to the nation.[15] Since Honduras now had a Liberal President, their troops fought on the rebel side in this conflict and Jerez' army enjoyed an initial period of success, capturing León and advancing to the outskirts of Granada. The assault on this city failed, however, and the Liberals were forced to fall back on León. The fortunes of war now shifted as Guatemala's Conservative government invaded Honduras, forcing that nation to withdraw its troops from Nicaragua.[16] Facing imminent defeat, the Liberals began to search desperately for aid from abroad. This search soon proved all too successful.

In California, in 1855, lived a young man who, though only thirty years old, had already gained a nationwide reputation for filibustering. His name was William Walker. He was employed as editor of the *Democratic State Journal* in Sacramento when he received the Nicaraguan Liberals' offer of land and gold if he would lead a force of armed adventurers to their aid. Walker accepted and recruited fifty-eight men for his expedition. He sailed from San Francisco on May 3, 1855, arriving off Nicaragua with his small, undisciplined band on June 1.[17] Within a few months this force, strengthened by additional contingents recruited in the United States, routed the Conservatives and captured Granada. Walker now turned on his Liberal allies and within a few months he became, first, as army commander under a puppet president and, later, as president himself, virtual master of Nicaragua.[18]

One of the most significant reasons for Walker's rapid rise to power was the contrast between his "American Phalanx" and the troops of the Nicaraguan armies. Walker's men were undisciplined, but they were heavily armed professionals who fought because they chose to. On the other hand it would be hard to imagine anything less like a professional fighting force than the Nicaraguan armies. Troops were recruited by compulsory dragooning, those who sought to escape being simply shot down.[19] These men received no training, no uniforms, no adequate weapons. Identified only by a ribbon bearing their party's color and armed with antiquated muskets or simply with machetes they were sent into combat.[20]

If the composition of Nicaraguan armies was rather primitive, so too were their tactics. Combat was often hand to hand, consisting mostly of a series of charges by unwilling men driven forward by their officers or of personal encounters between individuals of the opposing sides.[21] Supply and medical services were virtually nonexistent. What supplies there were, accompanied the troops in hide-covered litters and the meager rations were supplemented by looting the countryside. Regard for the rules of war was another notable lack in the Nicaraguan military tradition. No mercy was reserved for a defeated foe. His property was looted, his cities were sacked, and prisoners, wounded or otherwise, were generally shot or bayoneted.[22]

Despite the superiority of his troops Walker's reign in Nicaragua proved surprisingly brief. Alarmed by his rapid success, a host of enemies including the other Central American nations, the British, and the Accessory Transit Company of Cornelius Vanderbilt ultimately combined to bring about his defeat. The Costa Ricans, using weapons supplied by both Vanderbilt and the British, took the lead in military efforts to force out the American filibuster and their troops were later supported by contingents from Salvador, Honduras, and Guatemala. The resultant campaign, which lasted until 1857, devastated much of the country, including the colonial city of Granada.[23] Walker's luck finally ran out in the spring of 1857. His enemies bottled up his army in the town of Rivas and, in order to avoid annihilation, he surrendered on May 1 to Commander C.H. Davis of the United States Navy. Protected by a detachment of Marines, the remnant of his force boarded a ship and returned to the United States. Two later attempts to return to Central America proved unsuccessful and, on September 12, 1860, Walker was executed by a firing squad in Honduras.[24]

The Liberal Party's association with Walker discredited it and his defeat led to a period of 36 years of Conservative rule. While there were some disturbances during this period, most were of minor importance and, from 1867 to 1891, an orderly succession of leaders of the Conservative oligarchy took turns at filling the four-year presidential term, thereby breaking the nation's twin traditions of *continuismo* and revolution. There were even some efforts to reorganize and expand the army, a process which involved the creation of a commissary department, the appointment of a General in Chief, and the levying of a forced loan on the population.[25] Reforms were easier to achieve on paper than in the field, however, and no substantive changes took place in the military.

Ironically, it was a dissident Conservative, General Francisco Gutiérrez, who, on April 28, 1893, began the revolution that would bring to an end the thirty-six years of his party's rule. Liberal forces, led by General José Santos Zelaya, supported the revolt and, following a few brief engagements, drove President Roberto Sacasa out of office. Another Conservative, Salvador Machado, succeeded him, but on July 11 the Liberals staged their own revolt and by July 25 had decisively defeated the divided opposition. José Santos Zelaya became President, inaugurating a new era in the history of Nicaragua.[26]

Zelaya was destined to rule Nicaragua for a tumultuous sixteen years. But this period was also destined to be one of the most important in Nicaraguan history:

> When one considers all the aspects of the 1893–1909 period and when one further compares this period with all that had taken place before and was to come after, then one comes to this inevitable conclusion: Zelaya brought about a more radical change toward the modernization of Nicaragua than any other president. With regard to the lack of multiplier effect, continuity was not able to take place because United States intervention in the last days of Zelaya halted the process. The vast influence of the United States on Nicaragua after 1909 tended to retard the progress initiated by Zelaya.[27]

Shortly after taking power, Zelaya began to arm and equip refugee Honduran Liberals in an effort to overthrow the Conservative government of his northern neighbor. In December 1893, 1,600 of these refugees, supported by a Nicaraguan army of 3,000, crossed the frontier and by March this combined force had installed the Liberal General Policarpo Bonilla in the Honduran presidency.[28]

Having thus secured his northern frontier, Zelaya next turned his attention eastward, to Nicaragua's Mosquito Coast, where British influence still limited Nicaraguan sovereignty. The British initially resisted Nicaraguan efforts in this area, even landing a force of Royal Marines in Bluefields, but continued Nicaraguan pressure, supported by the American Secretary of State, Roger Q. Gresham, ultimately led to a complete British withdrawal from the disputed territory.[29] On January 1, 1895, in his annual message to the Nicaraguan Congress, President Zelaya officially recognized and thanked the United States for its aid and support in the controversy.[30] Relations between Zelaya and the United States, however, were not destined to remain so amicable.

Encouraged by his successes, Zelaya began to transform his regime into an open dictatorship. In order to ensure his continuance in power he began the first serious effort in Nicaraguan history to modernize the nation's armed forces. A military academy, the *Escuela Politécnica,* was established and staffed by a German captain, a Nicaraguan colonel, and several Chilean officers.[31] Within the army separate units of infantry, cavalry, artillery, and sappers (engineers) were organized. The artillery had charge of the machine guns, Nicaragua's being the first Central American army to adopt and make regular use of these weapons. Reforms in equipment extended to water as well as land. Zelaya organized a miniature fleet of five vessels, which were stationed on Lake Nicaragua and in the oceans.[32]

Under the Liberal dictator a detailed set of rules and regulations for the organization and employment of the armed forces was adopted. This *Ordenanza Militar* made all Nicaraguans between the ages of seventeen and fifty subject to military service, provided for military hospitals, and set detailed qualifications for all ranks in the military. Corporals, for example, were supposed to be able to read and write, while generals were required to know mathematics, military statistics, geography, and related subjects. The *Ordenanza Militar* provided for an army of one division commanded by a major general, with further subdivisions into two brigades, each consisting of two battalions of four companies. A brigadier general was to command each brigade and a colonel was to command each battalion.[33]

Zelaya improved the Army's equipment and organization, but the reality of conditions still departed significantly from the ideal. Instead of having 1 major general, 2 brigadier generals and 4 colonels, the Army, in 1908, had 23 major generals, 54 brigadier generals, 174 colonels, and 260 lieutenant colonels.[34] The facility with which these 77 generals handled military statistics and related subjects is certainly open to question, as is the percentage of corporals or even colonels who were able to read and write. Distribution of officers was based on geography with a definite concentration in areas of traditional Liberal strength. Ability to raise a body of armed local partisans seems to have been the primary qualification for appointment to any of these ranks. It was during the Zelaya regime that Nicaragua's classic anecdote concerning recruiting practices evidently originated. While the law provided for universal military service, in reality the ranks were filled by forcibly rounding up members of the lower class, tying them together, and shipping them off to the nearest army camp. A local *jefe político* supposedly sent President Zelaya a telegram which read: "By this morning's train I am sending to Managua three hundred volunteers. Please see that I get the ropes back because there are many more here very anxious to go. There is great enthusiasm among people here."[35]

The reorganized army generally did an efficient job of suppressing opposition. Opponents of the government were exiled, imprisoned, and at times even tortured and killed. Conservative revolts in 1896, 1899, and 1903 were quickly and ruthlessly repressed.[36] Meanwhile, Zelaya perpetuated himself in power through a series of farcical elections. According to one account rural voters were once given their choice of three candidates, "José, Santos, or Zelaya." As expected, General José Santos Zelaya won this "contest."[37] Only force could remove him from office and the improved quality of the army made this increasingly difficult. The next change of administration would require the intervention of a powerful foreign power.

In 1902 the Zelaya administration suffered a major setback when the United States decided to construct its transisthmian canal through Panama. This decision came as a rude shock, since the Nicaraguans had generally assumed they would obtain the canal.[38] Relations between the Zelaya administration and the United States now began to steadily decline, a decline further accelerated by the Nicaraguan dictator's growing desire to play a dominant role in Central America.

Early in 1907 Zelaya used a border incident as a pretext for launching an attack upon Honduras. American and Mexican efforts to prevent this attack were unavailing and the Nicaraguans, making excellent use of their newly acquired machine guns, defeated both the Honduran Army and a force sent from El Salvador to aid them. Superior leadership, provided in part by a South American general, Emiliano J. Herrera, and even the small Navy, which landed troops at the ports of Trujillo and La Ceiba, played a part in the Nicaraguan victory.[39] Alarmed at the prospect of Nicaraguan dominance in the area, the United States and Mexico invited the Central American nations to meet in Washington to resolve their problems. All five republics accepted the invitation and the meeting began on November 14, 1907. A ritual effort to revive the Central American Federation suffered a predictable failure, but the delegates did produce some concrete measures. These included the creation of a Central American Court of Justice to settle disputes among the five republics, an agreement to restrict exile activities, and an agreement not to recognize any Central American government that reached power by revolutionary means. All but the last of these agreements was included in a "General Treaty of Peace and Amity."[40] Unfortunately, signing such agreements soon proved much easier than enforcing them.

When the United States could no longer tolerate Zelaya, it decided to label him a perturber of peace.[41] Gradually the United States conveniently "persuaded" itself that only his removal could bring any hope of stability to the region. The United States' antipathy for Zelaya was strengthened when the Nicaraguan dictator began to turn to other nations, including Japan and Great Britain, in the hope of yet having a canal built through his country.[42] Financial problems further complicated relations. Zelaya cancelled some American concessions, leading to some rather harsh exchanges between representatives of both governments. The American Minister even became convinced that his mail and cable messages were being tampered with. In a final defiant gesture Zelaya, in spite of opposition by Secretary of State Knox, negotiated a loan of several million dollars with the Ethelburga Syndicate of London.[43] The United States was now prepared to see a new government take power in Nicaragua and any major attempt to overthrow Zelaya could count on American support. Given the prevailing traditions of Nicaraguan politics, such an attempt was not long in coming.

In October 1909, the long-awaited revolution finally began. It started in Bluefields, the isolated capital of the Mosquito Coast. The Conservatives played a major part in organizing the uprising, but its nominal leader was the local governor, a Liberal and a Zelaya appointee, General Juan J. Estrada. Estrada's 400 government troops and Bluefield's isolated position were both vital assets for the revolutionary cause.[44] Leading Conservatives in the movement included General Emiliano Chamorro, Nicaragua's perpetual revolutionary, and Adolfo Díaz, a young secretary of the American-owned La Luz y Los Angeles Mining Company.[45]

The United States had advance notice of the revolution, but withheld this information from the Nicaraguan authorities.

Thomas Moffatt, the American Consul at Bluefields, sent a telegram which the State Department received on October 7, 1909, announcing that Governor Estrada would lead a revolution on October 8.[46] Moffatt later reported that rumors of the impending uprising had circulated in the city for some time and that United States Navy officers had been encouraging these plans. He had received definite word of the uprising when someone knocked on the back door of the consulate one night, imparted the information, and then left without being recognized.[47] The fact that special efforts were made to notify the American Consul of the impending revolution indicates that Zelaya's enemies were counting upon at least the acquiescence, if not the active support, of the United States.

Moffatt soon established contacts with Estrada and sent a message to the State Department declaring his faith in the revolution's speedy and popular triumph with many attendant advantages for the United States. These included the establishment of a pro-American regime, reduction of Nicaraguan tariffs, and the "annulment of all concessions now owned by foreigners."[48] This display of premature enthusiasm was too much even for Secretary of State Knox, himself a determined foe of the Zelaya regime, and Moffatt was admonished to "do nothing whatever which might indicate the recognition of provisional administration," only maintaining the informal contacts in regard to local problems.[49]

Reacting swiftly to this threat to his power, Zelaya sent two army corps against the insurgents, one going down the San Juan River to San Juan de Norte, the other going overland from Chontales to the Escondido River. Estrada's expected mass support failed to materialize. What men he had were short on arms and ammunition, receiving only a small amount of supplies sent by Zelaya's Central American rival, President Estrada Cabrera of Guatemala.[50] Having only about 400 armed men to oppose Zelaya's 2,000 to 4,000, Estrada had to confess his inability to protect Bluefields and asked for American intervention. Ostensibly to protect the lives and property of American and other foreign citizens, a force of 400 Marines, commanded by Major Smedley Butler, were landed. Estrada then led his troops out to try to defeat the regular army. He suffered a disastrous defeat and fell back under the protection of the Marines in Bluefields.[51] In a final attempt to save his cause he hired two Americans, Lee Roy Cannon and Leonard Groce, to set mines and blow up the government's troop ships. The mines were laid and exploded, but they failed to prevent the landing of Zelaya's troops, who promptly captured, tried, and executed the two Americans.[52] This action was a fatal mistake by the Zelaya administration.

There is no question about the fact that Cannon and Groce had served the revolution as demolition experts. In a public statement to the Nicaraguan people President Zelaya had this to say about the incident.

> Those individuals could not be likened to prisoners of war taken from the enemy in an international war: they were foreign mercenaries at the service of an internal revolution, hired to destroy and to kill . . . the sentence handed down to them by the war tribunal is in accordance with prescriptions of our code for military justice. . . . Since Cannon and Groce were mercenaries in the revolution, they have forfeited the right to the protection of their government and, that being the case, the United States has no reason to charge that we have done them wrong.[53]

However, the execution of the two American citizens employed by the revolution gave the United States the excuse it wanted to break openly with the Zelaya regime. The fact that Edmund Couture, a French citizen who had served in the revolution as a medic, was given only a one-year sentence by the same tribunal that condemned the Americans to death, simply added fuel to the anti-Zelaya fire.[54] After considerable discussion, including consideration of a proposal for full-scale intervention and occupation of Corinto, and perhaps even Managua, Knox decided to issue a strong statement condemning the Zelaya regime, break diplomatic relations, and set up unofficial contacts with Estrada's forces.[55] A statement to this effect was delivered to the Nicaraguan chargé d'affaires in Washington on December 1, 1909. In extremely insolent language, Knox falsely condemned Zelaya for having "almost continuously kept Central America in tension or turmoil," for "a baleful influence upon Honduras," and accused him of having destroyed democratic institutions in Nicaragua. The note went on to characterize Estrada's collapsing revolution as a movement representing "the great body of the Nicaraguan people" whose "peaceable control" was now "well nigh as extensive as that hitherto so sternly attempted by the Government at Managua." Finally, the execution of Cannon and Groce was condemned, but Knox broadly hinted that the size of the indemnity demanded would be much smaller if a totally different government took power. Diplomatic relations were officially severed and replaced by unofficial contacts with both parties in the civil conflict.[56]

The meaning of Secretary Knox's message was not lost upon Zelaya and his supporters and it soon had its desired effect. On December 17, 1909, Zelaya resigned. In his resignation message, he lashed out against the United States, declaring that only American aid and intervention had prevented his forces from crushing Estrada and adding that one of his reasons for resigning was to halt this intervention by removing the "pretext" for it.[57]

As Zelaya's successor the Liberal-controlled Congress picked a capable and honest Liberal politician, Dr. José Madriz of León. He might possibly have continued the better aspects of the Zelaya administration without repeating the totalitarian abuses and might have become Nicaragua's best president to date. The United States, however, demonstrating a fixed determination to see a totally new administration in power, refused to recognize the Madriz government.[58]

After an initial effort at negotiations broke down, Madriz and Estrada resumed the civil war. The insurgents won a preliminary victory, but in February 1910, they suffered a major defeat and were once again driven back to Bluefields. At this point the American Consul in that city noted that "the revolutionary movement was rapidly disintegrating."[59] This presented the United States with a choice of either abandoning Estrada and trying to reach an accord with the Madriz administration or of intervening much more directly in favor of the faltering revolution. During the early spring the State Department temporized while advice poured in from all sides. The commander of the American naval force in the area recommended recognition of the Madriz government; other officials sought for a way to revive the faltering revolution. Estrada suggested American mediation in the dispute, a suggestion which, given the attitude of the United States throughout the conflict, the Madriz administration was not about to accept.[60]

President Madriz finally broke this deadlock by attacking the last remaining rebel stronghold, the city of Bluefields. An American cruiser, the *Paducah,* was in the harbor at this time and when the government's major warship, the *Máximo Jerez,* prepared to bombard Bluefields preliminary to an all-out land attack, the *Paducah's* captain issued a declaration that no bombardment of or fighting in Bluefields would be tolerated because of the danger to foreign lives and property. Later the American naval commander, acting under State Department instructions, prevented the Madriz forces from halting the flow of ships (and hence of badly needed money and supplies) to the Estrada-controlled customs house in Bluefields.[61]

These actions combined to accomplish what Estrada had, until then, been unable to do. Prevented from crushing his opponents in their now privileged sanctuary, President Madriz was forced to fall back into the interior of the country. Discouragement set in among his followers, thinning his ranks while those of the Conservatives swelled. In a mood of desperation, Madriz sought British intervention on his behalf, offering in return the cession of Great Corn Island. Nothing came of this proposal and, on August 20, 1910, following additional military defeats, he resigned the presidency and fled to Mexico.[62]

General Estrada now took over the office of president and two weeks later applied for recognition by the United States. In his application, Estrada promised to hold free elections within a year, to enlist State Department aid in securing a loan to stabilize Nicaragua's finances, and to punish those responsible for the execution of Cannon and Groce.[63] All threats to American concessions in Nicaragua were also ended, perhaps in return for the reported $1,000,000 which American businessmen had contributed to help finance the revolution.[64]

The patchwork coalition which had brought Estrada to power began almost immediately to show serious signs of strain and the United States hurriedly dispatched a special agent, Thomas Dawson, to assist in efforts to create a stable government. Convinced that any effort to hold immediate elections could only create a crisis, Dawson supported an agreement by President Estrada, Conservative Party leaders Adolfo Díaz, Emiliano Chamorro, and General Luis Mena to call a constituent assembly which would select Estrada as President for a two-year term.[65] Adolfo Díaz was to be chosen as Vice-President and Estrada bound himself not to run for the presidency in the elections to be held in two years.[66] Following State Department approval of this plan, the constituent assembly, on December 31, 1910, obediently "elected" Estrada and Díaz and the United States promptly extended recognition to the new goverment.

The new administration began to disintegrate almost as soon as it took office. President Estrada, heavily dependent upon United States support, backed the proposal of the new American Minister, Elliot Northcott, for the securing of an American loan guaranteed by joint control of customs receipts.[67] Opposition to the loan centered around General Luis Mena, the Minister of War. He hoped to use this issue to elevate himself to the presidency. Mena's bitterest foe in the cabinet was the Minister of Gobernación, José Maria Moncada, an anti-Zelaya Liberal. Another enemy of Mena's was the Conservative military *caudillo,* Emiliano Chamorro, who had gained control over the Constituent Assembly. Alarmed by this development, Estrada dissolved the Assembly and exiled Chamorro.[68]

With Chamorro's departure General Mena represented the greatest threat to the administration. In order to deprive Mena of the support of the Army, Estrada proposed a radical change in the very nature of Nicaragua's armed forces. Admitting that the present Army's major functions were either to attack neighboring states or to use force to perpetuate a government in power, the Nicaraguan President proposed using United States advisors to reduce the military to little more than an internal police force.[69] The United States eventually responded to this request with a project which was, in many ways, a forerunner of later plans for the Guardia Nacional, but before this plan reached Nicaragua, Estrada was overthrown.

Relations between the President and his Minister of War deteriorated rapidly in 1911. In February the main arsenal in Managua exploded, destroying two million cartridges and ten thousand rifles. Fearing a plot by supporters of ex-President Zelaya, Estrada promptly declared martial law.[70] This gave Mena control over all the nation's arms and ammunition. At this same time, Minister of Gobernación Moncada initiated efforts to divide the Conservative Party. The crisis finally boiled over on the night of May 8, 1911. The President had been drinking heavily and Moncada took advantage of his befuddled state to convince him to get rid of Mena. The Minister of War was then arrested on the grounds of "contemplated treason," but army troops responded by marching on Managua to release him. Estrada gave up the struggle, resigning in favor of Vice-President Díaz, who promptly

Adolfo Díaz started out as an employee of an American mining company and twice became Washington's puppet president in Nicaragua.

released Mena.[71] Estrada went into exile, Mena continued as Minister of War, and the United States promptly recognized the Díaz administration.

The new President had little independent support. Plots by Zelaya's supporters continued, the United States exerted constant pressure to complete the loan negotiations, and Díaz found himself a virtual figurehead, "ignored by Mena's followers and [having] no voice in decision on any executive act."[72]

At this point F.M. Gunther, the new American chargé d'affaires, proposed making basic changes in the structure of the Nicaraguan military. In essence this plan called for the creation of "a small disciplined regular armed force, American Army officers to be the instructors." Neither Díaz nor Mena was willing to attempt so basic a reform, but they proposed instead that an American officer supervise the reorganization of the Managua police, a reform which they hinted might eventually be extended throughout Nicaragua.[73] After some effort to persuade the Nicaraguans to accept a more sweeping program of reform, the State Department began to search for a capable individual to train the police. The constitutional barrier against a member of the American armed forces accepting a salary from a foreign government caused the Department to concentrate its search on retired officers. A former member of the "Rough Riders," Greg Scull, was finally selected. A salary of $4,000 was agreed upon and Scull accepted the position in January 1912.[74]

Scull began work on February 5, but it soon became apparent that it was impossible to separate his job from Nicaragua's complex internal political situation. He was appointed Inspector General and instructor of the police, but was given inadequate powers for his assigned tasks. Events reached a ludicrous climax in April when Scull instructed the police to close the Albion Café because of repeated disorders there. Colonel Noguera Mena countermanded the order and the café remained open. Publicly humiliated, Scull resigned in disgust and returned home, ending America's first attempt to reorganize Nicaragua's armed forces.[75] The American Minister noted that had Díaz backed up Scull, giving him the powers needed to carry out his mission, this might well have "precipitated a struggle for the political control of the country." The Minister concluded that "Police reorganization, so far as our participation therein is concerned . . . certainly should not be renewed until political and financial conditions are more decisively settled in Nicaragua."[76]

General Mena's opposition had played a role in the failure of Scull's mission, but the Minister of War's success in this area was not matched in his continuing efforts to secure the presidency. He had a new Constituent Assembly, packed with his supporters, elect him as President for the term beginning January 1, 1913, but the United States refused to recognize this arrangement. Efforts to extort American approval of his election in return for the Assembly's approval of an American loan, customs collectorship, and reorganization of the National Bank only intensified State Department opposition. The return of General Chamorro to Nicaragua led to a further decline in Mena's strength and by June 1912 he had lost control of the Assembly. He still controlled the Army, but due to a lack of funds that body was reduced to 1,600 men.[77]

By July General Mena apparently had decided that his only chance to attain the presidency was to launch a revolution. The major obstacle to this plan was the Managua garrison, whose officers were loyal to the President. In an effort to overcome this, Mena gathered 150 men from his home town of Nandaime and ordered them to replace the garrison in the capital. President Díaz immediately instructed the garrison's officers to obey no orders which did not originate with him, appealing at the same time to his Minister of War not to force the issue. His appeal came too late and on July 29 Mena's troops attacked the garrison on La Loma.[78]

The troops on La Loma remained loyal and their machine guns halted the attack. At this point the American Minister intervened and persuaded Mena to resign as Minister of War in return for a presidential guarantee of his personal safety. A short time later, however, Mena turned off the city's electric lights and under cover of darkness his troops, joined by Managua's police force, fled toward Masaya.[79]

From Masaya the ousted War Minister tried to continue his rebellion. Liberal forces, under General Benjamin Zeledón, joined in the attacks on the government's troops. This alarmed the State Department and when President Díaz asked for American intervention to protect his faltering regime, his request was quickly granted.[80]

On August 4, 1912, a small force of sailors from the *USS Annapolis* landed in Corinto and proceeded directly to Managua. Ten days later an entire Marine battalion, commanded by Major Smedley D. Butler landed at Corinto and shortly thereafter another force occupied Bluefields.[81] Except for a year from August 1925 until August 1926, American troops would remain in Nicaragua until 1933.

While the Marines were landing at Corinto, a rebel force under General Zeledón was bombarding Managua. Their attacks were beaten off, and on the morning of August 15 they fell back on Masaya, ending their bombardment only two hours before the arrival of Butler's Marines in the capital. The course which the American troops were going to pursue in the conflict became quite clear the following day when a young Marine lieutenant arrived in Mena's camp with a demand that he "deliver up his forces to the government," an action which the General naturally refused to take.[82]

Now under the command of Marine Colonel Joseph Pendleton, the American force in Nicaragua increased rapidly, reaching a peak strength of over 2,700 men. Major Butler led part of this force to Granada, where he forced the ailing General Mena to surrender his troops and go into exile.[83] The Marines now turned on General Zeledón's troops, whose position on Coyotepe Hill, outside of Masaya, dominated the railroad line between Managua and Granada. Admiral Southerland, the overall commander of American forces, had no desire to move against this force, but George T. Weitzel, the American Minister, and the State Department were determined to see the rebellion crushed. President Wilson shared this view and ordered the Navy Department to attack Zeledón.[84] On October 3 the Marines sent Zeledón an ultimatum, demanding that he give up his position and allow the Americans to disarm their entire force. If Zeledón failed to yield, he was threatened with immediate attack by American and Nicaraguan government forces and was pointedly informed that no discussion of terms would be allowed.[85] Shocked by this sudden ultimatum, the rebel leader rejected the American demands and prepared to resist. Colonel Pendleton's troops attacked at first light on the morning of October 4 and soon routed the poorly equipped rebels. Zeledón was captured by Nicaraguan government troops as he was fleeing from the battle. The Americans were immediately informed of this fact and asked what disposition they wanted made of the Liberal leader. Major Butler telegraphed Admiral Southerland, asking for instructions. He informed the Admiral that "if you direct I can have Zeledón back here under guard or protected by my men in Masaya," but added that he "personally would suggest that through some inaction on our part someone might hang him."[86] The Admiral's reply to this message had apparently been destroyed, but the final result is quite clear. The next day the Díaz regime announced that Zeledón had been killed during the battle. Peace, enforced by American bayonets, had returned to Nicaragua.

Following the defeat of Zeledón's force the bulk of American troops in Nicaragua were rapidly withdrawn. A 100-man legation guard, however, remained in Nicaragua until August 1925. Small as this force was, its mere presence exercised a major influence on internal politics. Its retention symbolized to Nicaraguans the United States' determination not to allow a revolution. Combined with the experiences of 1912, this served to keep the minority Conservative Party in power and internal disturbances at a relatively low level from 1912 until 1925.[87]

With their security assured by the presence of the Marines, the Conservatives lost much of their interest in developing an efficient Nicaraguan army. As a result the Army declined in both numbers and ability throughout this period. In 1916 its authorized strength was fixed at approximately 2,000 men, but the actual number of regular troops was usually around 1,000. Most of these were concentrated in Managua, which had an authorized garrison of 295 officers and 335 men. The 100-man Presidential Honor Guard was composed almost entirely of officers "in order to give them more pay."[88] In any case, the official pay scale was not designed to promote a high standard of living, even for officers. The daily pay for a brigadier general was $1.40, for a colonel $1, and for a private $.32.[89] Officers took $.20 per day from each enlisted man's salary to buy rations. When an American officer observed that this seemed a rather liberal food allowance by Nicaraguan standards, the Minister of War replied, "Oh yes; they live very well and the commanding officers are still able to make a very nice profit."[90]

Training and equipment also suffered from severe neglect during this period. One account described a typical Nicaraguan Army detachment as: "an armed bunch of ragged men who sat all day long on large wooden benches in front of their cuartel, or went around rural districts terrifying the poor peasants and village people. Practically the only fortunate soldiers have been those stationed at La Loma, Campo de Marte or the Guardia de Honor; they were given three meals a day, uniforms, medical assistance and even shoes, once in a while."[91]

A 1916 report by an American Marine lieutenant confirms the

above account. The lieutenant noted that regulations called for each enlisted man to be equipped with a Remington rifle, shoes, blankets, canteen, dungarees, and a straw hat, but added that only the guard of honor was fully equipped while other units had "a part of the above articles, the amount of equipment and clothing issued apparently in inverse proportion to the proximity to the Capital."[92]

In time of conflict this tiny regular force could be greatly expanded as the government kept a reserve supply of 15,000 rifles on hand. Under such conditions recruitment, as well as the collection of funds to support the expanded Army, was forced. A Marine report noted: "In time of peace they aim to recruit the unemployed, but in time of war they take anyone, beginning with the barefooted classes [the peons], then taking the coatless ones [the artisans], and finally all who have not sufficient influence to escape the recruiting patrols. . . . Occasionally they round up the spectators at a fiesta or a baseball game or a band concert, etc."[93]

In the 1920s another American recorded his observations of this recruiting system in action. The army descended upon a small town on the shores of Lake Nicaragua and rounded up twenty "volunteers," tying each to a soldier and loading them on a ship for Managua. The women of the town stood on the dock "screaming and tearing their hair." Two men managed to escape by jumping overboard, a method which the American described as "the usual method of leaving" the army.[94] Due to the extremely high desertion rate, recruiting parties usually tried to catch four men to fill each vacancy in the ranks, forcing men ordinarily exempt from the military service into the army. A list of thirty-four casualties from one civil conflict included a boy of fourteen and a man of fifty-eight. Three of the wounded were not even Nicaraguans: two were from Honduras and one from Costa Rica.[95] Even cripples were occasionally seen in the ranks.

Perhaps the only redeeming feature of this military system was the rather small proportion of official government revenues assigned to it. In 1919 the regular Army numbered only about 500 officers and men, maintained by an appropriation of $177,136.26, including $1,680.60 designated for the "Navy."[96] The relative stability created by the presence of the Marine legation guard made possible even further reductions in subsequent years. By 1924 the Army had only 37 officers and 329 enlisted men. In addition there were 934 members of the national police, a force used largely to discourage any opposition to the incumbent regime. The nation's military budget throughout this period was the smallest in Central America. In the 1921–1922 fiscal year even Costa Rica, a nation proud of its tradition of small military expenditures, spent four times as much on its Army as did Nicaragua. The total Nicaraguan military budget reached its low point the following year when it was allotted only $132,292.[97]

The Conservative regimes of this period were dependent upon American support for their survival and the United States used this dependence to greatly strengthen their political and economic controls over Nicaragua. In 1914 the Bryan-Chamorro Treaty gave the right to lease a naval base on the Gulf of Fonseca and the exclusive option to build a canal through Nicaragua in return for an American payment of $3,000,000.[98] In 1917 General Emiliano Chamorro became President and his administration soon concluded another agreement with the United States, known as the "Lansing Plan." This involved the establishment of a High Commission, consisting of Nicaragua's Finance Minister, a resident American commissioner, and a third member appointed by the Secretary of State. The Commission controlled all Nicaraguan revenues in excess of $95,999 each month, that figure being all the budget was allowed, and used these funds to pay off foreign creditors.[99]

In 1920 General Chamorro imposed the election of his uncle, Diego Manuel Chamorro, as President. The new President, however, died unexpectedly in 1923 and was succeeded by Vice-President Bartolomé Martínez, a member of the anti-Chamorro wing of the Conservative Party. Martínez hoped to perpetuate himself in office in 1924, but the Nicaraguan Constitution prohibited presidential reelections and the State Department made it clear that it would refuse to recognize anyone who took power in violation of this provision. In order to keep his arch rival, General Emiliano Chamorro, from succeeding him, Martínez then determined to create a coalition of his Conservative supporters with elements of the Liberal Party. In 1924 this political hybrid, known as the Conservative Republican Party, nominated Conservative Carlos Solórzano for President and Liberal Juan Bautista Sacasa for Vice-President. The United States, anxious to withdraw the legation guard and therefore hoping for a free election which would bring to power an administration with popular support, managed to get the Nicaraguans to adopt a reformed electoral code. President Martínez, however, carefully avoided all American efforts to secure effective enforcement of the electoral code and, aided by government force, threats, and some of the traditionally fraudulent vote counting, the Solórzano-Sacasa ticket won an easy victory over General Chamorro in the October elections. The newly elected President soon discovered that Chamorro's efforts to obtain the presidency had been only briefly interrupted by the results of the election.

NOTES

1. Sofonias Salvatierra, *Compendio de Historia de Centroamerica* (Managua: Typografía Progresso, 1960), p. 39.

2. W.W. Cumberland, *Nicaragua: An Economic and Financial Survey* (Washington: U.S. Government Printing Office, 1928), p. 20.

3. Jaime Wheelock R., *Raíces Indígenas de la Lucha Anticolonialista en Nicaragua* (Mexico, D.F.: Siglo Veintiuno, 1974).

4. Franklin D. Parker, *The Central American Republics* (New York: Oxford University Press, 1964), p. 61; Julio N. Guerrero, *Geografía y Historia de Nicaragua* (Managua: Librería Cultural Nicaragüense, 1963), p. 81

5. Salvatierra, *Compendio,* pp. 173–74; Pedro Zamora Castellanos, *Vida Militar de Centro Amierica,* 2nd ed. (Guatemala City: Editorial del Ejército, 1966) I, p. 115.

6. Zamora Castellanos, *Vida Militar,* p. 123.

7. Thomas L. Karnes, *The Failure of Union: Central America, 1824–1960* (Chapel Hill: University of North Carolina Press, 1961), p. 94.

8. Dana G. Munro, *The Five Republics of Central America* (New York: Oxford University Press, 1918), p. 80.

9. Peter Stout, *Nicaragua: Past, Present and Future* (Philadelphia: John E. Potter, 1859), p. 153.

10. Manuel Castrillo Gamez, *Próceres Nicaragüences* (Managua: Talleres Nacionales, 1961), p. 66.

11. Stout, *Nicaragua,* p. 152.

12. For details of Vanderbilt's early operations, see David I. Folkman, Jr., *The Nicaragua Route* (Salt Lake City: University of Utah Press, 1970), pp. 13–42.

13. The best account of these negotiations may be found in Mary W. Williams, *Anglo-American Isthmian Diplomacy, 1815–1915* (New York: Russell and Russell, 1965), pp. 67–109.

14. Salvatierra, *Compendio,* p. 237.

15. Ibid., p. 239.

16. Laurence Greene, *The Filibuster* (New York: Bobbs-Merrill, 1937), pp. 58–59.

17. Ibid., pp. 59–65.

18. For further accounts of Walker's activities, see the previously cited account by Greene and also Albert Z. Carr, *The World and William Walker* (New York: Harper and Row, 1963); William O. Scroggs, *Filibusters and Financiers* (New York: Macmillan, 1916); William Walker, *The War in Nicaragua* (Mobile: n.p., 1859). The Comisión de Investigación Historica dę la Campaña, 1856–187, published in Costa Rica in 1956 a useful series of studies on the campaigns against Walker.

19. James Carson Jamison, *With Walker in Nicaragua* (Columbia, Mo.: E.W. Stephens Publishing Co., 1909), pp. 15–16. (Jamison was a "captain" in Walker's army.)

20. Greene, *Filibuster,* p. 67.

21. Jamison, *With Walker,* p. 40; Greene, *Filibuster,* p. 100.

22. Jamison, *With Walker,* p. 44; Greene, *Filibuster,* pp. 101 and 112–13.

23. The Central American campaign is detailed in Rafael Obreón Loria, *La Campaña del Tránsito* (San José, Costa Rica: n.p., 1954).

24. Greene, *Filibuster,* pp. 291–96, 305–308, and 316–27.

25. "Documentos sobre la revolución de 1869, "*Revista de la Academia de Geografía y Historia de Nicaragua* VIII (December, 1946) 31–38.

26. Juan Simon Padilla Sandres, "Historia a grandes rasgos del General Juan Simon Padilla Sandres," *Revista de la Academia de Geografía y Historia de Nicaragua* XIV and XV (January 1955 to December 1956) 32.

27. Charles L. Stansifer, "Una nueva interpretación de José Santos Zelaya, dictador de Nicaragua, 1893–1909," paper presented to the Congress on the Historical, Economic, and Social Demography of Central America, San José, Costa Rica, February 1973.

28. United States Minister to Nicaragua, Baker, to Secretary of State Gresham, December 26, 1893, *Papers Relating to the Foreign Relations of the United States,* 1894, Appendix I, pp. 441–43. This series of documents, published by the U.S. Department of State, will be cited hereafter as *Foreign Relations;* General José N. Rodriguez, *Estudios de Historia Militar de Centroamérica* (Guatemala City: Tipografía Nacional, 1930), p. 297.

29. Gresham to U.S. Ambassador to Great Britain T.F. Bagard, August 19, 1894, *Foreign Relations,* 1894, pp. 311–12; Pedro Joaquín Cuadra Chamorro, *La Reincorporación de la Mosquitia* (León, Nicaragua: Editorial Hospicio, 1964).

30. Message of President Zelaya to the Nicaraguan Congress, January 1, 1895, *Revista de la Academia de Georgrafía y Historia de Nicaragua* XII (January–December 1953) 132.

31. "The Nicaraguan Army," an anonymous manuscript in the Nicaraguan Records of the United States Marine Corps Historical Archives (Navy Annex, Washington, D.C). Material from this collection cited hereafter as MCHA.

32. Ibid.

33. Nicaragua Ministerio de Guerra y Marina, *Ordenanza militar del*

ejército de la Republica de Nicaragua (Managua: Tipografía Mercantil, 1901), pp. viii, 19, 40, 50, and 75.

34. Nicaragua, Ejército de Nicaragua, Ministerio de Guerra, *Escalafón general de jefes y oficiales arreglado en orden de departmentos,* 2nd ed. (Managua: Tipografía y Encuadernación Internacional, 1908).

35. "The Nicaraguan Army," MCHA. For a later version of this story, see Whiting Williams' article in the *New York Times,* August 21, 1927, Section VIII, p. 5.

36. Zamora Castellanos, *Vida Militar,* II, p. 356.

37. Harold Norman Denny, *Dollars for Bullets: The Story of American Rule in Nicaragua* (New York: Dial Press, 1929), p. 66.

38. Dana G. Munro, *Intervention and Dollar Diplomacy in the Caribbean, 1900–1921* (Princeton, N.J.: Princeton University Press, 1964) p. 38.

39. Zamora Castellanos, *Vida Militar,* II, pp. 356–59; Rodriguez, *Estudios de Historia Militar,* pp. 323–25.

40. Karnes, *Failure of Union,* p. 188.

41. Stansifer, "Interpretación de Zelaya."

42. Munro, *Intervention,* pp. 152–53; Denny, *Dollars for Bullets,* pp.33–35.

43. Munro, *Intervention,* pp. 168–69.

44. Denny, *Dollars for Bullets,* p. 73.

45. Ibid.

46. U.S. Consul at Bluefields, Thomas Moffatt, to Secretary of State Knox, no date (received October 7, 1909), *Foreign Relations,* 1909, p. 452.

47. Denny, *Dollars for Bullets,* pp. 73–74.

48. Moffatt to Knox, October 12, 1909, *Foreign Relations,* 1909, p. 452.

49. Acting Secretary of State Adee to Moffatt, October 13, 1909, *Foreign Relations,* 1909, p. 453.

50. Salvatierra, *Compendio,* p. 277.

51. Denny, *Dollars for Bullets,* p. 77.

52. Rodriguez, *Estudios de Historia Militar,* p. 364.

53. J.S. Zelaya, *La Revolutión de Nicaragua y los Estados Unidos* (Madrid: Imprenta Rodriguez, 1910), p. 125.

54. Munro, *Intervention,* p. 175; Zelaya, *La Revolutión,* p. 138.

55. Munro, *Intervention,* pp. 176–77.

56. Knox to the Nicaraguan chargé in Washington, December 1, 1909, *Foreign Relations,* 1909, p. 455.

57. "Manifesto of President Zelaya to the National Assembly," December 17, 1909, translation in *Foreign Relations,* 1909, pp. 458–59.

58. Munro, *The Five Republics,* p. 229.

59. Munro, *Intervention,* pp. 180–81.

60. Ibid., pp. 181–83.

61. Ibid., p. 184.

62. Denny, *Dollars for Bullets,* pp. 89–90.

63. Munro, *Intervention,* pp. 187–88.

64. Denny, *Dollars for Bullets,* p. 79.

65. Munro, *Intervention,* pp. 187–88.

66. "Translations of Agreements Signed by Provisional President Estrada and Others," *Foreign Relations,* 1911, pp. 652–53.

67. The American Minister to Nicaragua, Northcott, to Knox, February 25, 1911, *Foreign Relations,* 1911, p. 655.

68. Munro, *The Five Republics,* p. 234.

69. Northcott to Knox, February 25, 1911, *Foreign Relations,* 1911, pp. 655–56.

70. Acting Secretary of State Wilson to Secretary of the Navy, February 15, 1911, *Foreign Relations,* 1911, p. 655.

71. Northcott to Knox, May 9, 1911, and May 11, *Foreign Relations,* 1911, pp. 660–61.

72. The American chargé in Nicaragua, Gunther, to Knox, July 30, 1911, *Foreign Relations,* 1911, p. 666. Word in brackets is mine.

73. Gunther to Knox, Decimal Files, Department of State, Washington, 817.1051/0 (General Records of the Department of State, Record Group 59, National Archives, Washington, D.C.). Cited hearafter as NA RG 59.

74. The State Department's decimal file 817.1051 contains numerous items relative to Scull's selection.

75. U.S. Minister to Nicaragua George T. Weitzel to Knox, April 10, 1912, NA RG 59, 817.1051/20.

76. Ibid.

77. Munro, *Intervention,* pp. 200–205; Gunther to Knox, January 6, 1912, *Foreign Relations,* 1912, p. 1013.

78. Weitzel to Knox, July 31, 1912, *Foreign Relations,* 1912, p. 1025. La Loma is a hill dominating Managua. For decades whoever held this hill ruled the nation. Early in this century a fort stood there; later it was the site of the Presidential Palace and La Curba, General Somoza's palatial residence and headquarters for the Guardia Nacional. A volcanic crater, filled with water, lies directly behind La Loma, making it virtually impossible to attack from the rear. The 1972 earthquake destroyed the Presidential Palace and La Curba and evidently left La Loma unsuitable for future major construction.

79. Weitzel to Knox, July 31, 1912, *Foreign Relations,* 1912, pp. 1027–32.

80. Knox to President Taft, August 5, 1912, *Foreign Relations,* 1912, p. 1032.

81. Bernard C. Nalty, *The United States Marines in Nicaragua,* Marine Corps Historical Reference Series, No. 21, rev. ed. (Washington: Historical Branch, G-3 Division, Headquarters, U.S. Marine Corps, 1962), p. 7.

82. Weitzel to Knox, August 30, 1912, *Foreign Relations,* 1912, pp. 1040–41.

83. Nalty, *Marines in Nicaragua,* p. 9.

84. Munro, *Intervention,* p. 209, Weitzel, the American Minister, seriously considered having the Marines capture and hang both Zeledón and Mena. See Weitzel to Knox, September 17, 1912, NA RG 59, 817/00/1988.

85. Colonel Joseph Pendleton to General Benjamin Zeledón, October 2, 1912, in Major General Smedley D. Butler, USMC, Papers (Marine Corps History and Museums Division, Navy Yard, Washington, D.C.) Cited hereafter as Butler Papers.

86. Telegram from Major Butler to Admiral Southerland, October 4, 1912, in Major General Joseph Pendleton, USMC, Papers (Marine Corps History and Museums Division, Navy Yard, Washington, D.C).

87. Munro, *Intervention,* p. 216.

88. "Military Report of First Lieutenant Ross E. Rowell, USMC, to the Secretary, War College Division, War Department," 1916, Naval Records Collection of the Office of Naval Records and Library, Subject File, 1911–1927, Box 642, National Archives, Record Group 45. Cited heareafter as Rowell Report. Documents from this collection cited hereafter as NA RG 45.

89. Nicaragua, Ministerio de Hacienda, *Presupuesto suplementario del ramo de guerra, 1916–1917* (Managua: Tipografía Nacional, 1917) pp. 3–4.

90. Rowell Report, NA RG 45.

91. "The Nicaraguan Army," MCHA.

92. Rowell Report, NA RG 45.

93. Ibid.

94. Major Calvin B. Carter, "Kentucky Feud in Nicaragua," *World's Work* LIV (July 1927) 317.

95. List of Military Casualties in the Hospital de Sangre, León, Nicaragua, October, 1912, Records of United States Marine Corps Units Abroad, Records of the United States Marine Corps, National Archives, Record Group 127. Hereafter cited as NA RG 127.

96. Captain James Underhill, USMC, to Major General Commandant, USMC, 1919, NA RG 45, box 642.

97. Major Keyser, Commander of Managua Legation Guard, to the Major General Commandant, USMC, August 26, 1924, NA RG 59, 817.1051/38.

98. For details of these negotiations, see Munro, *Intervention,* pp. 400–406.

99. Ibid. pp. 413–17.

II

MAJOR CARTER'S CONSTABULARY

Carlos Solórzano took the oath of office as Nicaragua's President on January 1, 1925, and almost immediately asked the United States to suspend its plans to withdraw the legation guard.[1] This request was quite understandable. Solórzano's army was small and disorganized, his party an uneasy coalition already showing signs of strain, and his disgruntled electoral opponent was a man with a reputation for leading more revolutions than anyone else in Nicaraguan history. Rumors of impending upheavals were widespread and it was widely felt that if the Marines left, a revolution would "be inevitable."[2] While unwilling to abandon the plan to withdraw the Marines, the State Department was willing to agree to a postponement provided that the new administration took immediate steps to create an American-trained, nonpartisan constabulary. The creation of armed forces of this type had become a pet project of the Department. In the words of Dr. Dana G. Munro, former United States chargé d'affaires in Nicaragua and later Minister to Haiti:

> The establishment of non-partisan constabularies in the Caribbean states was one of the chief objectives of our policy from the time it became clear that the customs collectorships wouldn't assure stability by themselves. The old armies were or seemed to be one of the principal causes of disorder and financial disorganization. They consumed most of the government's revenue, chiefly in graft, and they gave nothing, but disorder and oppression in return. We thought that a disciplined force, trained by Americans, would do away with the petty local oppression that was responsible for much of the disorder that occurred and would be an important step toward better financial administration and economic progress generally.[3]

In 1923 the State Department had pressured the governments of all the Central American republics into signing a treaty pledging themselves to create such National Guards, and using "suitable instructors" with "experience gained in other countries in organizing such corps."[4] This last phrase was obviously meant to suggest the United States, which was currently engaged in creating just such forces in the Phillipines, Haiti, and the Dominican Republic. The American experience had been far from satisfactory in these cases; in the Dominican Republic the American Minister had commented that the Marine-trained Guardia Nacional Dominicana was "in no way fitted to insure law and order if our forces should retire."[5] Still the State Department remained anxious to create this type of military force in other Caribbean area nations.

Prior American efforts to get the Nicaraguans to implement the constabulary provision of the 1923 treaty had been unsuccessful, but Solórzano's military weakness gave the United States new policy leverage. In February 1925 the State Department submitted to the Nicaraguan government a detailed plan for the organization of a constabulary. Although limited to 23 officers and 392 men, this force was eventually supposed to replace the entire "national police, navy and army of Nicaragua." A separate training branch, made up of American officers, was to have complete control over the organization of the constabulary and was not to be under control of the Minister of War. Furthermore, it was to have total control over supplies, accounts, and enlistments.[6]

Solórzano disliked this plan, but continued threats to withdraw the legation guard forced him to take some positive action toward creating a constabulary. Chamorro's supporters, however, were determined to prevent the plan from being put into effect, and when the Nicaraguan Congress discussed the proposal, it found itself threatened by a mob that promised dire vengeance upon anyone voting to create a Guardia Nacional.[7] The reason for this opposition was made clear to the American Minister, Charles C. Eberhardt, by a supporter of Chamorro's. The Nicaraguan asked the Minister "if, in case of revolution, the constabulary might be expected to take the field against the revolutionists." When Eberhardt responded in the affirmative, the Nicaraguan declared that he was "unequivocally opposed to the Constabulary since it was only by revolution that a party opposed to the government might hope to gain proper recognition."[8] Despite such opposition the bill to create the constabulary was finally approved by the Nicaraguan Congress in May, but it differed considerably from that proposed by the United States. The power of the training branch was curtailed and it was placed under the authority of the Minister of War. Control over the supply system, with its lucrative opportunities for graft, was given to the Minister of Police. Finally, the functions of the Guardia were defined as those of "an urban, rural and judicial police force" and nothing was said about its replacing the regular Army.[9] This was considerably less than the United States had hoped for, but it was evidently accepted as the best possible solution under the circumstances and no real effort was made to have the Nicaraguan government alter it.

The next problem was that of finding an American to command the National Guard. The search was undertaken by the State Department, which finally selected Major Calvin B. Carter, United States Army retired, who had experience in training native troops for the Philippine Constabulary. On June 10, 1925 Carter signed a one-year contract with the Nicaraguan government. He was appointed "Chief of the Constabulary and of the School of Instruction of the National Guard" and was paid $600 per month. An additional $1,000 per month was allotted to pay for four American assistants.[10]

The proposed new National Guard differed from the old Nicaraguan Army in many ways. It was to be recruited voluntarily and was to include regular complements of noncommissioned officers and company grade commissioned officers. Recruits were to have uniforms, regular pay, training, and discipline. The Guard's loyalty was supposed to be to the nation, not just to its leader, and recruits were to be drawn from all segments of the population, not just from partisans of the party in power. Unfortunately, it soon became obvious that the various Nicaraguan political factions were determined to transform the Guard into an instrument to advance their own political fortunes.

On July 16, 1925, Major Carter arrived in Managua to begin his duties. He had hoped to find a force waiting for him, but was badly disappointed. The Nicaraguan government had sent out a circular to local *jefes políticos* asking their help in finding "suitable persons" for the constabulary, but since these officials were usually extreme political partisans this proposal did not help to establish the non-partisan character of the new force.[11] Plans had also been made to have the legation guard begin the training of the constabulary, but by the time details were worked out, Carter had already arrived in Nicaragua and the Marines were preparing to depart. The State Department was determined to withdraw the Marines at the end of July, leaving the Nicaraguans to their own devices. All that Carter found waiting for him were 200 raw recruits who had been living on an administration food allowance of thirty centavos a day.[12] They were quartered in one section of the Campo de Marte, Managua's central army barracks. The rest of the Campo was still occupied by the regular garrison and by the Nicaraguan Army's arsenal.

Carter and his American assistants immediately began efforts to improve this situation. Carter had originally planned to train the initial recruits for two years, then send them out to the provinces to train similar units to replace the police in each area.[13] It soon became apparent to the Americans, however, that such long-range plans would have to be abandoned to meet more immediate needs.

Ninety of the original two hundred recruits failed the physical examination. The remainder lacked arms, ammunition, and uniforms, and the force had no machine guns. The budget was also totally inadequate and Major Carter soon found himself exceeding it just to purchase basic supplies, including "mahogany boards for the men to sleep on." In addition, the infant organization was given the task of forming the Presidential Honor Guard and also of patrolling the streets of Managua.[14]

Despite efforts by the President's two brothers-in-law, General Alfredo Rivas, commander of the fort on La Loma, and Colonel Luis Rivas, commander of the Campo de Marte, to subvert the Guard for their own political ends, Carter did make some progress in creating a professional, nonpartisan force. The government began seeking additional recruits, promising $30 a month to each enlistee.[15] The force soon expanded to 18 officer cadets and 225 enlisted men and a genuine effort was being made to recruit men without regard to political affiliation.[16] Had the political situation remained stable, this little force might eventually have fulfilled some of the hopes held for it, but less than two months after the Major's arrival, political violence again broke out in Nicaragua.

The last Marines sailed from Corinto on August 4, 1925. Three weeks later President Solórzano found himself facing a serious political crisis. It began at a party held on the night of August 25 in Managua's International Club. The American Minister, the High Commissioner, Roscoe Hill, and most of the Nicaraguan cabinet, including Liberals Victor Román y Reyes, Minister of Finance, and José María Moncada, Minister of War, were present. Even the President and his wife put in a brief appearance.

Suddenly a ragged force, dispatched by General Alfredo Rivas, rushed into the Club announcing that they had come to "liberate President Solórzano from the Liberal element in his government," an objective they achieved by arresting Moncada, Román y Reyes, and several other Liberals.[17] General Rivas then sent the President an ultimatum, demanding that he purge his cabinet of its Liberal members. Major Carter urged Solórzano to crush the revolt, offering to "shoot Rivas if he misbehaved," an offer which the President declined on the grounds that Rivas was his brother-in-law.[18] Instead Solórzano gave in to the demands.

General Chamorro always denied any involvement in the International Club incident, but immediately after it, he returned to Managua to take advantage of the altered political situation.[19] He saw the Guardia as the major obstacle to his drive to gain power and launched a campaign of opposition to that force in the Conservative press. By October 25 the General felt enough confidence in his own strength and the Guardia's weakness to move directly against the government. At two o'clock in the morning he led a force up La Loma, where the doors to the fort were opened to him by its commander. Two hours later Chamorro phoned the old Presidential Palace in downtown Managua, and informed the surprised President that he had occupied the fort and would meet any attempt to dislodge him by opening fire on Solórzano's quarters.[20] Taken by surprise, Solórzano pursued his usual vacillating course. Major Carter offered him the support of the Guardia and he repeated this stand when Chamorro phoned to ask if he would obey a Presidential order to attack La Loma. Chamorro's only response to this was a laughing request that Carter phone him before he attacked.[21] Since the Guardia had only thirty rounds of ammunition per man, such good humor was quite understandable. Carter begged for additional arms and ammunition, but the President was afraid to resist Chamorro.

Up on La Loma things were going quite well for the General. Commander of the Campo de Marte opened his gates to Chamorro and all but one of the regional military commanders agreed to obey his orders.[22] With Solórzano's decision not to resist, the success of the virtually bloodless coup seemed assured.[23] In a conference the following day the President agreed to Chamorro's demands that all remaining Liberals be removed from government posts, that Chamorro be made Commanding General of the Army, and that the government grant an amnesty to all his followers and pay all the expenses of the uprising.[24]

Carlos Solórzano remained President, but control of Nicaragua was now in the hands of General Emiliano Chamorro.

Following his agreement with the President, Chamorro's attitude toward the National Guard underwent a striking reversal. Shortly after assuming his post as Army commander, he visited the Guard compound and promised full rights and privileges to the 140 Liberals in the force. At the same time Major Carter made it clear that troops who were members of that party could resign and seventy-three took advantage of this.[25] Chamorro now began building up the Guard with the same zeal he had earlier exhibited in trying to tear it down. This seeming paradox was explained by Minister Eberhardt in a message to the State Department:

> Logically enough the Ins are usually in favor of a well-trained Constabulary. Such was the case recently with the Liberals who wanted the Constabulary placed in command of La Loma. The Chamorro elements were opposed. It is doubtful if in these countries such an organization, free from politics, is ever wanted, but rather one made up largely of men of the same political faith as is held by those in power. Thus General Chamorro and the Conservatives as a whole, who formerly opposed strengthening the organization, now recommend its increase by several hundred men and their continued training under Major Carter.[26]

Solórzano's days as President were now numbered. Following the October coup, Vice-President Sacasa had fled the country. Congress, now purged of most of its Liberal members, obediently declared the office of vice-president vacant, banishing Sacasa for two years for alledgedly buying arms in Guatemala to use in a revolution.[27] Congress then selected General Chamorro as first *designado,* putting him directly in line to succeed Solórzano. All of this alarmed the State Department, which was committed to a policy of nonrecognition of Central American governments that took power by violent or other extraconstitutional means. The Department made repeated efforts to persuade the General not to replace Solórzano, but they were ignored. On January 6, 1926, Secretary of State Kellogg told Minister Eberhardt to make it clear that any government headed by Chamorro would not be recognized.[28] Chamorro remained determined. On January 16, for reasons of "health," Congress granted Solórzano an indefinite leave of absence and General Chamorro assumed the executive power.[29] On January 22, Secretary Kellogg informed both Eberhardt and the Nicaraguan minister in Washington that the United States would not recognize the new administration now or in the future.[30] Having gained power, however, the General was determined to retain it as long as possible. On March 13 the Nicaraguan Congress accepted President Solórzano's resignation and Chamorro formally replaced him. His term as President was destined to be brief and violent.

For months the American legation in Managua had been predicting that the Liberals would soon resort to force to regain their position in the government. Their uprisings finally began on May 2, 1926, when an exile force seized Bluefields. Chamorro responded rapidly to this threat to his regime. He expanded the regular Army to over 5,000 men and sent them, along with 200 members of the National Guard, against the Liberals.[31] This combined force soon crushed the uprising but this initial setback failed to dampen the Liberals' determination to overthrow the government.

In his effort to retain power, General Chamorro was counting heavily upon the support of the Guardia. All pretense of nonpartisanship in that force was now abandoned and new recruits were screened to ensure their total loyalty to the Conservative *caudillo.*[32] By March 1926, the American Minister reported that the Guard was "fast disintegrating into a politically controlled machine of the present regime" and, in early May, he added that "hopes for an efficient organization under American ideas and ideals are fastly disappearing."[33] Eberhardt, who admired Major Carter and sympathized with his efforts, blamed all of the Guard's problems on "divided authority and political intrigue," then summed up the entire situation by writing:

> It is very apparent that the time has not yet come, if it ever will, when a nonpartisan constabulary or National Guard, organized and maintained under American ideas and ideals, will be a success in Nicaragua. *It is not wanted.* Just as the President may be Conservative or Liberal, so will he insist that the organization be made up of men of his following. General Chamorro is doing this at present. The future of the organization will depend largely upon the extent to which an American instructor, like Major Carter, assisted by other Americans can contend against this condition and the tendency of a President and his advisors to interfere with the interior administration of the organization.[34]

The sending of the Guard into battle against the Liberals was simply the last in a long series of events which ended the high hopes once held by the United States for this force. Its creation, nevertheless, signaled a turning point in Nicaraguan military history. Nonpartisan it was not, but it was better disciplined, better trained, and better led than any previous Nicaraguan force. The importance of its contribution to the crushing of the initial Liberal uprising was clearly reflected in the casualty figures from that campaign. The regular Army lost only 12 men out of a force of 5,000, but Guardia casualties were between 13 and 26 out of approximately 200 engaged.[35] This meant that the Guard's casualty rate was between twenty-seven and fifty-four times as high as that of the rest of the Army. Malaria also took a heavy toll of the Guard and, until it was totally reorganized by the Marines in 1927, it would never again be as effective a fighting force.[36]

In June the American Minister was recalled from Nicaragua and a young legation secretary, Lawrence Dennis, became chargé. Since the United State would not recognize Chamorro, Dennis decided that it was his task to remove the General from office. To facilitate this, Dennis urged that revenue from customs be denied to the government and that all American officers be removed from the Guard.[37] The State Department, however, limited its response to authorizing Dennis to tell Major Carter and his aide, Major Rodriquez, that "if they take an active part in the political affairs of Nicaragua their action will not meet with approval of the Department of State."[38]

Lawrence Dennis, like Chamorro, was a very stubborn man. During the next few weeks he sent a barrage of cables and letters to the State Department, detailing his efforts to oust Chamorro and making numerous requests for stronger American action. He also put direct pressure on the Nicaraguan President, phoning him every day to ask when he was going to resign and missing no opportunity to make clear the Department's position that he could never hope for American recognition.[39]

While the American chargé was trying to persuade Chamorro to resign, the Liberals resumed their use of military force to achieve the same end. On the heavily settled West Coast a rebel force cut the railroad line between Chinandega and León. On August 20 this Liberal force, now numbering 900 men, reached the port of Tamarindo where they expected to find arms being shipped to them from Mexico. Instead they found a government Army led by General Alfonso Estrada which attacked and routed them, capturing their commander.[40] Another Liberal force succeeded in briefly capturing the town of San Marcos, but it too was easily scattered when government troops arrived in force.[41] The commander of this force was an American-educated former toilet inspector and used-car salesman named Anastasio Somoza García. Known to his friends simply as Tacho, this erstwhile revolutionary fled into hiding after the defeat of his force, but emerged after a few days to accept a government pardon in return for his promise "not to join any other subversive activities."[42] Despite this rather ludicrous climax to his first military venture, "Tacho" Somoza was destined to become the dominant figure of twentieth-century Nicaraguan history.

A few days after Somoza's defeat a much more serious uprising occurred on the East Coast. Liberals seized Rio Grande, north of Bluefields, and would probably have captured Bluefields as well if Marines from the *USS Galveston* had not landed and declared the city a neutral zone. Undaunted by this setback, the Liberal troops, commanded by former War Minister José María Moncada, extended their control over other areas of the east coast, capturing Puerto Cabezas and driving the government's forces inland to Rama. The strength of the Liberal attack produced consternation and divisions within the Conservative Party with demands that General Chamorro step down and that some accommodation be sought with the Liberals. The revolution was spreading, the regime was bankrupt, and negotiation seemed to offer the only way out.

Even General Chamorro was forced to admit that his regime's financial situation could hardly be worse. By September the conflict had already cost the government more than a million dollars and revenues were falling as costs soared. The General tried to sell the National Bank and the National Railroad, but he could find no buyers, perhaps because former Vice-President Sacasa, the Liberals' political leader, declared that any such sale would not be recognized if he should attain power.[43] The financial problems, the Liberal revolt, splits within his own party, and determined American opposition, personified in Lawrence Dennis, finally proved too much even for Chamorro. Early in September he asked for a truce conference under American supervision, following which, regardless of the results obtained, he agreed to turn over the presidential power to a designate selected by Congress.[44]

It took almost a month to make preparations for the conference, but on October 15, 1926, a fifteen-day truce was declared and representatives of both sides began discussion on board the *USS Denver* in Corinto harbor. All factions soon agreed that

Chamorro must go, but no agreement could be reached on his replacement or on the division of government positions between the two parties. Adolfo Díaz, whom the Conservatives, with support from Dennis, advocated as interim President, was unacceptable to the Liberals, while the Liberals' insistence that Sacasa be recognized as legal President was rejected by the Conservatives. With the Liberals expecting aid from Mexico and the Conservatives hoping for American support, the conference became deadlocked and, on October 24, broke up without ending the war.[45]

Chamorro now resigned the presidency to the Congressional Designate, Senator Sebastián Uriza. At the urging of Dennis and the State Department the Nicaraguan Congress went through the motions of reinstating its twenty-one Liberal members expelled by Chamorro, but since most were in exile or engaged in the fighting, only three members and six alternates took their seats.[46] Still following Dennis's recommendations, which were strongly supported by Secretary of State Kellogg, this reorganized Congress then selected Adolfo Díaz as First Designate and Uriza promptly turned over executive power to him.[47] Díaz was inaugurated on November 14, with Dennis playing a conspicuous role in the ceremony, and was granted formal recognition by the United States three days later.

American support for Díaz failed to curb the Liberals' determination to drive the Conservatives from power. Sacasa landed at Puerto Cabezas and proclaimed himself "Constitutional President" of Nicaragua. His government was promptly recognized by Mexico.

In an effort to halt the Liberal advance, President Díaz turned to the United States, requesting a loan, supplies, and a military mission to rebuild the National Guard.[48] While unwilling to send a military mission in the midst of a revolution, the State Department did agree to consider granting to private dealers licenses for the shipment of arms and munitions to the Díaz government, a break in the earlier embargo policy, and expressed willingness to try to find another instructor for the Guard.[49]

Internally, Díaz moved quickly to consolidate his control over the government. General Chamorro had taken command of the Army when Díaz became President, but he and Díaz soon quarrelled and the President, supported by Dennis, pressured him into diplomatic exile as Minister to France, Great Britain, Spain, Italy, and the Vatican.[50] Díaz also removed Major Carter

Lt. Col. Elias R. Beadle, USMC, Commander of the Guardia Nacional de Nicaragua, established the pattern of the American development of the Guardia.

and several other American instructors from the Guard because of their suspected pro-Chamorro views.[51] Finally, the Nicaraguan President requested the return of an American legation guard to Managua. When Minister Eberhardt, who returned to his post at the end of 1926, and the British and Italian governments joined in this request, Secretary Kellogg gave his assent. A landing party from the *USS Galveston* arrived in the capital on January 6, 1927, and were welcomed by the Nicaraguan government as deliverers from the threat of a Liberal victory.[52]

The American decision to support the Díaz regime was justified in part by repeated State Department charges of Mexican and Communist support for Sacasa and the Liberals. On January 2, 1927, using phrases strikingly similar to those advanced in later years to justify American intervention in Vietnam, Under-Secretary of State Robert Olds wrote a confidential memorandum summarizing American policy goals in Nicaragua. Olds argued as follows:

> The Central American area down to and including the Isthmus of Panama constitutes a legitimate sphere of influence for the United States, if we are to have due regard for our own safety and protection. . . . Our ministers accredited to the five little republics stretching from the Mexican border to Panama . . . have been advisors whose advice has been accepted virtually as law . . . we do control the destinies of Central America and we do so for the simple reason that the national interest absolutely dictates such a course.
>
> There is no room for any outside influence other than ours in this region. We could not tolerate such a thing without incurring grave risks. At this moment a deliberate attempt to undermine our position and set aside our special relationship in Central America is being made. The action of Mexico in the Nicaraguan crisis is a direct challenge to the United States . . . .
>
> . . . We must decide whether we shall tolerate the interference of any other power (i.e., Mexico) in Central American affairs or insist upon our own dominant position. If this Mexican maneuver succeeds it will take many years to recover the ground we shall have lost. . . . Until now Central America has always understood that governments which we recognize and support stay in power, while those which we do not recognize and support fall. Nicaragua has become a test case. It is difficult to see how we can afford to be defeated.[53]

While determined to prevent a Liberal victory, Secretary of State Kellogg still hoped to avoid full-scale intervention. Nonmilitary efforts to end the revolt took many forms. President Díaz attempted direct negotiations with the Liberals. Sacasa seemed willing to allow the presidency to go to some third party, but this conflicted with the State Department's insistance on retaining Díaz in order to prevent "a Mexican triumph."[54] The Department did manage to assist Díaz in obtaining two loans, totaling $1,300,000, from American sources, but money alone could not save the Conservative cause.[55] As a last resort, the Nicaraguan President suggested a formal treaty of alliance between his government and the United States, but the State Department wanted nothing to do with this idea.[56]

On the military front Conservative fortunes continued to decline. Early in February a Liberal army occupied the west-coast city of Chinandega. Government troops, aided by two American aviators, eventually drove them out, but much of the city was destroyed in the process. Meanwhile the American force in Nicaragua was rapidly built up and the number of "neutral zones" in the country was greatly increased. By March 15, 1927, there were over 2,000 sailors and Marines on duty in Nicaragua. They controlled not only the port cities of Bluefields and Corinto, but also the Liberal centers of León and Chinandega, the highland city of Matagalpa, and had 12 officers and 141 men occupying La Loma in Managua.[57] A sailor on duty in Nicaragua summed up the situation by stating, "It was obvious that had we not arrived to declare the various towns neutral, the Liberals would have swept the Conservatives out of control in short order."[58]

Early in March a final effort to negotiate an end to the war failed, foundering on the perennial issue of the retention of Díaz in office until after the 1928 elections. The country headed toward near anarchy with armed bands of deserters from both sides terrorizing the population.[59] The prolonged fighting had led to an abandonment of the fields, and the crops, which had to be in by the end of June, would be lost if the war did not end by then.[60] The United States decided, at this point, to send a special presidential representative to Nicaragua to attempt to resolve this situation. For this vital mission the President selected former Secretary of War Henry L. Stimson, who had previously served on special missions to report on the Tacna-Arica dispute between Chile and Peru and to observe conditions in the Philippines. His experiences with the Tacna-Arica issue had convinced Colonel Stimson that only outside supervision could ensure a fair election in much of Latin America, while in the Philippines he had been impressed with the creation of a native constabulary force, trained and led by American officers.[61] These experiences helped shape his approach to the Nicaraguan situation.

On April 7, 1927, President Calvin Coolidge and Secretary of State Kellogg met with Stimson to discuss the Nicaraguan mission. Coolidge refused to negotiate the retention of Díaz as President, but was willing to risk a Liberal victory in American-supervised elections in 1928. Stimson was given wide authority to negotiate a settlement. If his efforts failed and Sacasa could not be stopped in any other way, it was agreed that the United States would then undertake full-scale intervention,[62] primarily to save face by not letting the world think that Mexico had been more influential in deciding the outcome of the revolution.

Stimson sailed from New York on April 9, arriving in Nicaragua six days later. He immediately began a rapid round of conferences with all those he felt might shed some light on the Nicaraguan situation. In his first conference Admiral Latimer, commander of the Special Service Squadron, the naval unit stationed in the area, told him that he saw only two possibilities acceptable to the United States, a victory for Díaz, which he felt quite unlikely, or open intervention.[63] Stimson, however, was determined to find another alternative and began conferring with leaders of both Nicaraguan political parties.

The subject of a reorganized National Guard was a major theme in many of his conversations. Dr. Enoc Aguado, a leading Liberal, approved the idea of an American-officered constabulary. L.S. Rosenthal, the American manager of the National Bank, advocated the creation of a force led by American officers on active duty and the stationing of this force in small detachments throughout the country. Stimson also met with Major Rodriguez, the American who had succeeded Major Carter as commander of the National Guard. Rodriguez told Stimson that a force of at least 1,500 men, costing $1,000,000 annually, was necessary to maintain peace in Nicaragua.[64]

By April 21 Stimson had drawn up what he felt would be acceptable peace terms. These included: (1) immediate peace; (2) a general amnesty; (3) inclusion of Liberals in the cabinet; (4) disarmament of both sides with the arms turned over to the Americans; (5) retention of the Marines in Nicaragua until a new National Guard was formed to replace them; (6) the organization of a nonpartisan National Guard under American officers; and (7) American supervision of the 1928 elections.[65] The following day President Díaz signed a peace agreement incorporating these points.[65]

The government was now definitely committed to an American-supervised peace, but getting the Liberals to agree remained a difficult task. Stimson concentrated his efforts upon General Moncada and his officers and generally ignored the Sacasa government. Among those who met with Stimson was General Anastasio Somoza García. Somoza's suggestion that Solórzano be returned to the presidency made no impression on Stimson, but the personality and fluent English of the young Liberal evidently did. The Colonel noted in his diary: "Somoza is a very frank, friendly, likable young Liberal and his attitude impresses me more favorably than almost any other.[67] As a result of this favorable impression Stimson took Somoza with him for a few days to assist in interpreting for his other meetings.[68] This would not be the last time that "Tacho's" command of English and his ability to ingratiate himself with influential Americans would serve him in good stead.

In final preparation for his talks with General Moncada, Stimson obtained State Department permission to use American military force to prevent Moncada's troops from crossing the Tipitapa River.[69] This served final notice on the Liberals that the United States would not allow them to defeat Díaz, leaving them only the choice of defeat or accepting American terms.

Moncada and Stimson met under a large blackthorn tree on May 4, 1927. The American representative carefully separated the Nicaraguan General from Sacasa's political representatives, who were still steadfastly opposed to the retention of Díaz, and conferred with him in private. Given the choice of agreeing to the proposed terms or fighting the United States, Moncada agreed to recommend that Sacasa yield to "avoid bloodshed." At the time of this meeting Moncada did manage to persuade Stimson to agree to the appointment of Liberal *jefes políticos,* some of whom were to be former officers in his army, in the Liberal departments.[70] On May 5 Moncada told his troops that he had agreed to Stimson's terms and the same day President Díaz proclaimed a general amnesty. It seemed as if Stimson's mission had succeeded in restoring peace to Nicaragua.

Government forces soon retired to the south and the Americans occupied a line along the Tipitapa River, placing themselves in a position to disarm both sides. Admiral Latimer announced that his forces would collect the rifles and machine guns held by both armies and that the Nicaraguan government would pay ten córdobas for each serviceable weapon turned in. Those not turning in their weapons voluntarily would be forcibly disarmed.[71] Stimson sent Moncada a personal letter, pledging American supervision of the 1928 elections and the assignment of "American officers to train and command a national constabulary."[72] On May 12 Moncada and all but one of his generals signed Stimson's peace terms and agreed to disarm. General Augusto César Sandino denounced the agreements, but Stimson attached little importance to his opposition, noting it in a message to the State Department, but concluding that the agreement of the other generals marked "definitely the end of the insurrection."[73] The American representative had badly underestimated the courage and determination of General Sandino.

With the disarmament proceeding rapidly and smoothly, Stimson took leave of Nicaragua on May 16, noting in his diary for that date his belief that the Marine force in the country could be safely reduced to 1,000 men. These, he believed, would have to remain until after the 1928 elections, but by then the new Guardia Nacional should be fully organized and functioning, eliminating any possible reason for their retention beyond that date.[74] Minister Eberhardt also felt that peace had been restored. On May 26, he cabled the State Department, praising Admiral Latimer and General Feland, the Marine commander, for "having effected a wonderful disarmament with a minimum of bloodshed or friction."[75] A total of 11,600 rifles and 303 machine guns had been turned in, but General Sandino refused to surrender his arms. He was, however, reported heading for the Honduran border with only 200 men.[76] The major tasks now facing the United States in Nicaragua seemed to be supervising the 1928 elections and reorganizing and training the new National Guard.

NOTES

1. Thurston to Hughes, January 3, 1925, *Foreign Relations,* 1925, II, p. 618.

2. Thurston to Hughes, January 7, 1925, *Foreign Relations,* 1925, II, p. 619.

3. Letter from Dr. Dana G. Munro to author, February 14, 1965.

4. Marvin Goldwert, *The Constabulary in the Dominican Republic and Nicaragua: Progeny and Legacy of United States Intervention,* Latin American Monographs, No. 17 (Gainesville: University of Florida Press, 1961), p. 12. For descriptions of the Haitian and Dominican forces, see Goldwert and James H. McCrocklin, compilers, *Garde d'Haiti, 1915–1934* (Annapolis, Md.: United States Naval Institute, 1956).

5. Goldwert, *The Constabulary,* p. 12.

6. "Plan for the Establishment of a Constabulary in Nicaragua." February 17, 1925, *Foreign Relations,* 1925, II, p. 624.

7. Thurston to Kellogg, April 6, 1925, NA RG 59, 817.1051/61.

8. The United States Minister to Nicaragua, Charles C. Eberhardt, to Kellogg, October 2, 1925, NA RG 59, 817.1051/87.

9. Thurston to Kellogg, May 15, 1925, *Foreign Relations,* 1925, II, pp. 628–30.

10. Transcript of Contract between Major Calvin B. Carter and the Nicaraguan Government, NA RG 59, 817.1051/81.

11. *La Noticia* (Managua), June 13, 1925, p. 1.

12. Carter to Eberhardt, September 30, 1925, NA RG 59, 817.1051/87 (enclosure).

13. Calvin B. Carter, "Kentucky Feud in Nicaragua," *World's Work* LIV (July 1927) 317.

14. Carter to Eberhardt, September 30, 1925, NA RG 59, 817.1051/87 (enclosure).

15. *La Noticia* (Managua), July 19, 1925, p. 1.

16. Anonymous manuscript on Major Carter's constabulary, p. 4, MCHA.

17. Harold Norman Denny, *Dollars for Bullets: The Story of American Rule in Nicaragua* (New York: Dial, 1929), pp. 203–204.

18. Carter, "Kentucky Feud," p. 318.

19. Interview with General Chamorro, Managua, November 21, 1963.

20. General Emiliano Chamorro, "Autobiografía," *Revista Conservadora* II (August 1961) 146.

21. Carter, "Kentucky Feud," p. 319.

22. Chamorro, "Autobiografía," p. 146.

23. There is some dispute as to the actual amount of fighting that occurred. Harold Norman Denny of the *New York Times* mentions a battle between Chamorro's troops and the National Guard, producing eleven casualties (Denny, *Dollars for Bullets,* p. 210). Chamorro, in his "Autobiografía," claims his men only fired once, at a group near the Presidential Palace. Eberhardt, in an October 25, 1925, telegram to Secretary Kellogg reporting on this incident fails to mention any battle between Chamorro's and Carter's forces. Carter's article in *World's Work* LIV (July 1927) also omits any mention of such a conflict, but in a February 24, 1927, dispatch to the Secretary of State (NA RG 59, 817.1051/135) the Major claimed that his men killed fifteen of Chamorro's troops and lost two of their own.

24. Eberhardt to Kellogg, October 25, 1925, *Foreign Relations,* 1925, II, p. 640.

25. Carter to Kellogg, February 24, 1927, NA RG 59, 817.1051/135.

26. Eberhardt to Kellogg, November 3, 1925, NA RG 59, 817.1051/88.

27. William Kammen, *A Search for Stability: United States Diplomacy toward Nicaragua, 1925–1933* (Notre Dame, Ind.: University of Notre Dame Press, 1968), p. 190.

28. Kellogg to Eberhardt, January 6, 1926, NA RG 59, 817.00/3376. For further details on United States efforts, see Dana G. Munro, *The United States and the Caribbean Republics, 1921–1933* (Princeton, N.J.: Princeton University Press, 1974), pp. 189–93.

29. Eberhardt to Kellogg, January 16, 1926, NA RG 59, 817.00/3398.

30. Kellogg to Eberhardt, January 22, 1926, *Foreign Relations,* 1926, II, pp. 784–85. Munro, *The United States and the Caribbean Republics,* p. 193.

31. The American chargé in Nicaragua, Lawrence Dennis, to Kellogg, June 18, 1926, NA RG 59, 817.00/3667.

32. Eberhardt to Kellogg, February 18, 1926, March 14, 1926, and May 20, 1926, NA RG 59, 817.1051/96, 817.1051/98, and 817.1051/106.

33. Eberhardt to Kellogg, March 14, 1926, and May 11, 1926, NA RG 59, 817.1051/98 and 817.1051/103.

34. Eberhardt to Kellogg, April 8, 1926, NA RG 59, 817.1051/99.

35. Dennis to Kellogg, June 18, 1926, NA RG 59, 817.00/3667; Carter to Kellogg, February 24, 1927, NA RG 59, 817.1051/135. Carter puts the Guardia's losses at twenty-six; Dennis lists them as thirteen.

36. Carter to Kellogg, February 24, 1927, NA RG 59, 817.1051/135.

37. Dennis to Kellogg, June 10, 1926, NA RG 59, 817.00/3617.

38. Kellogg to Dennis, June 12, 1926, NA RG 59, 817.00/3616.

39. Denny, *Dollars for Bullets,* pp. 221–22; interview with Lawrence Dennis, New York, October 1965.

40. Chamorro, "Autobiografía," pp.149–50. Dennis to Kellogg, August 25, 1926, NA RG 59, 817.00/3769.

41. *La Prensa* (Managua), August 20, 1926, p. 1, and August 21, 1926, p. 1.

42. Ternot MacRenato, "Anastasio Somoza: A Nicaraguan Caudillo" (M.A. thesis, University of San Francisco, 1974), pp. 65–67.

43. Denny, *Dollars for Bullets,* p. 226.

44. The dominant role of Dennis at this time can be seen in messages from Dennis to Kellogg on September 6, 8, and 10, 1926, NA RG 59, 817.00/3759, 817.00/3767, and 817.00/3777.

45. Most of the important messages relating to this conference are printed in *Foreign Relations,* 1926, II, pp. 796–802.

46. U.S. Department of State, *A Brief History of the Relations between the United States and Nicaragua, 1909–1928* (Washington: U.S. Government Printing Office, 1928), p. 37.

47. Dennis to Kellogg, November 1, 1926; Kellogg to Dennis, October 30, 1926; NA RG 59, 817.00/3997, 817.00/3992. Dennis to Kellogg, November 11, 1926, *Foreign Relations,* 1926, II, p. 806.

48. Dennis to Kellogg, November 15, 1926, NA RG 59, 817.00/4063 and 817.00/4097.

49. Kellogg to Dennis, November 22, 1926, NA RG 59, 817.00/4087.

50. Ibid.; La Prensa (Managua), December 10, 1926, p. 1.

51. Dennis to Kellogg, November 12, 1926, NA RG 59, 817.1051/113.

52. Dom Albert Pagano, *Bluejackets* (Boston: Meador Publishing Co., 1932), p. 76.

53. Confidential memorandum by Under Secretary of State Robert Olds, January 2, 1927, NA RG 59, 817.00/4350.

54. Eberhardt to Kellogg, January 23, 1927, NA RG 59, 817.00/4456.

55. Roscoe R. Hill, *Fiscal Intervention in Nicaragua* (New York: Columbia University Press, 1933), pp. 48–49.

56. Eberhardt to Kellogg, February 20, 1927, NA RG 59, 817.00/4604; *La Prensa* (Managua), February 22, 1927, p. 1, and February 26, 1927, p. 1.

57. U.S. Department of State Press Release, February 21, 1927, *Foreign Relations* 1927, III, pp. 312–13.

58. Pagano, *Bluejackets,* p. 133.

59. Henry L. Stimson, *American Policy in Nicaragua* (New York: Charles Scribner's Sons, 1927), pp. 51–53.

60. The Diary of Henry L. Stimson, Vol. VII, April 10, 1927, in Yale University Library, New Haven, Connecticut. Cited hereafter as Stimson Diary.

61. Henry L. Stimson and McGeorge Bundy, *On Active Service in Peace and War* (New York: Harper and Brothers, 1948), p. 110; Stimson, *American Policy,* p. 60; Stimson Diary, Vol VII, April 22, 1927.

62. Stimson Diary, Vol VII, April 7, 1927.

63. Ibid., April 17, 1927.

64. Ibid., April 18 and 20, 1927.

65. Ibid., April 21, 1927.

66. Ibid., April 22, 1927.

67. Ibid., May 3, 1927.

68. MacRenato, "A Nicaraguan Caudillo," p. 71.

69. Eberhardt to Kellogg, April 26, 1927, and Kellogg to Eberhardt, April 27, 1927, *Foreign Relations,* 1927, III, pp. 328–29 and 331.

70. Stimson Diary, VII, May 4 and 5, 1927.

71. Notice Issued by the Commander of the Special Service Squadron, *Foreign Relations,* 1927, III, pp. 334–45.

72. Stimson to General José María Moncada, May 11, 1927, *Foreign Relations* 1927, III, pp. 345–46.

73. Eberhardt to Kellogg, May 12, 1927, *Foreign Relations,* 1927, III, p. 347.

74. Stimson Diary, VII, May 16, 1927.

75. Eberhardt to Kellogg, May 26, 1927, *Foreign Relations,* 1927, III, p. 349.

76. Ibid., pp. 349–50.

III

THE GUARDIA REBORN

The first commander of the new *Guardia Nacional de Nicaragua* was Colonel Robert Rhea of the United States Marine Corps. His first task was to decide what to do with the 295 enlisted men, 65 of whom were absent without leave, who still remained in the old constabulary. In order to prevent any complications that might arise from previous political ties, that body was disbanded and all of its men discharged.[1] Several immediately enlisted in the new Guardia Nacional, thereby providing a certain measure of continuity between the two organizations.[2]

Recruiting for the Guardia began on May 24, 1927. Within a month three companies had been organized. At this point Colonel Rhea, who was in poor health, was replaced by Colonel Elias R. Beadle, who was given the Nicaraguan rank of Brigadier General and the title *Jefe Director de la Guardia Nacional de Nicaragua.*[3]

During its first months it is difficult to determine under what authority the Guardia operated or from where it obtained its funds. The conscious effort of the United States to separate the new Guardia from the former constabulary made the laws relating to that body of doubtful application. The Stimson agreements, signed by Díaz and Moncada, did provide for the creation of a constabulary under American officers, but furnished no guidelines as to the size, budget, regulations, or organization of that body. Finally, there was a memorandum sent by President Díaz to President Coolidge on May 15, 1927. This stated, in part, that "the function of preserving law and order throughout the country shall be assumed by a National Constabulary to be organized under the instruction and, so far as possible, the direction and command of American officers now in active service and detailed to this duty by the President of the United States."[4] The memorandum also discussed future relations of the Guardia Nacional with election officials, but failed to include any guidelines for the day-by-day functioning of the organization. On May 8, President Díaz had requested Coolidge to allow an American to be appointed as commander of the Guardia. The officer appointed by Coolidge was to select additional instructors. Díaz evidently expected that these would include both Nicaraguans and Americans.[5] The Nicaraguan President also preferred Army to Marine instructors. At first Stimson expressed some support for this position, but both Admiral Latimer and Brigadier General Logan Feland, Commander of the Marine Brigade in Nicaragua, strongly opposed such a course, with Latimer reportedly declaring that this would reflect upon the honor of the Marine Corps.[6] Stimson decided not to press the point and the Marines began to assign officers to the Guardia. The ease with which Díaz's wishes were ignored clearly illustrates the complete control that the United States had assumed over the Guardia's development. For several months the Nicaraguan government's role was limited to issuing decrees requested by the United States and paying the Guardia's bills.

The amount which the Nicaraguans had to pay was increased by the Marines' insistence that officers detailed to the Guardia receive a salary from the Nicaraguan government in addition to their regular Marine pay. The American Minister, Charles Eberhardt, objected to this proposal, arguing that any extra compensation should come from American sources, a position which General Feland dismissed as "absurd."[7] Ultimately the Marines' position, which was supported by both Stimson and Admiral Latimer, won acceptance. Officers received a salary from the Nicaraguan government corresponding to their rank in the Guardia. Nicaraguan salaries were lower than those in the Marine Corps, but since most Americans held a rank in the Guardia one or more grades above their rank in the Corps, this extra compensation often amounted to nearly double pay.

On June 18, 1927, President Díaz issued his first decree relating to the Guardia Nacional. This established a pay scale for officers ranging from $250 per month for the *Jefe Director* down to $60 per month for 2nd Sub-District Commanders.[8] On July 8, Díaz authorized the Guardia's Marine commander to increase his force's strength to 600 men and to appoint Navy and Marine officers and noncoms as officers in numbers up to 7.5 percent of the enlisted strength.[9] It was not until July 30, 1927, that a detailed decree covering Guardia duties, obligations, and legal procedures was issued. This document included a provision for the gradual replacement of all police by the Guardia. Local authorities were to have no control over the Guardia, which was to be "subject only to the President of Nicaragua." Except in purely civil cases Nicaraguans in the Guardia could be tried only by court-martial and the decisions of these courts were subject only to a limited review by the Supreme Court. American officers would be subject to American, not Nicaraguan, court-martial for any offenses they might commit.[10] Until the signing of a formal agreement between the United States and Nicaragua in December 1927, this decree provided all the official authority that the Guardia had.

The continued presence of Sandino's armed band in the mountains of western Nicaragua brought the Guardia into military action long before its legal status was resolved. Until his decision to resist the American intervention Sandino had been virtually unknown outside of Nicaragua and not too well known within that nation. He was born in Nicaragua in 1895, the illegitimate son of a local landowner and a young Indian girl.[11] In 1920, following a fight in which he wounded a man, he fled the country, eventually arriving in Mexico. He worked in the oilfields around Tampico, became a Freemason, and was impressed by the nationalism of the Mexican Revolution and its glorification of the nation's Indian heritage.[12] He returned to Nicaragua in 1926, just before the Liberal revolt against Chamorro began. In the ensuing conflict Sandino rose rapidly, becoming one of Moncada's leading generals. He was, however, still only one of many Liberal generals, most of whom returned to relative obscurity after the Stimson agreements.

Sandino's motives for defying the United States were not due to anti-Americanism (often he expressed respect for the American people). He came from a strong Liberal background and was extremely irritated to see a Conservative puppet imposed on the people by American intervention. The Marines, for obvious reasons, characterized him as a bandit, but Nicaraguan and Latin American intellectuals in general looked upon him as a noble patriot fighting against "Yankee aggression."[13] Sandino's first public proclamation of his decision to continue fighting was directed much more against Díaz and the Conservatives than against American intervention.[14] He even suggested what Moncada had previously suggested, namely, that, as an alternative to keeping Díaz in office, the United States should establish an American military government in Nicaragua until the 1928 elections.[15] The Americans were in fact dominant and Sandino was against the hypocrisy of hiding this behind a puppet president. When this proposal was rejected, Sandino began publicly to

Nicaraguan Liberal troops halted by United States Marines and disarmed in 1927. Typically the intervention only led to American armed involvement and more bloodshed.

denounce the American presence in Nicaragua. This is not to imply that strong patriotic sentiments did not influence Sandino's actions. It is only to suggest that while Sandino had in the last few years become aware of the threat of imperialism, at the time of his rebellion he still was more of a Liberal fighting the Conservatives for the constitutional rights of his party. The change to a patriot fighting for the sovereignty of his country came gradually. Since the Americans helped keep the hated Conservatives or, after 1928, the Liberal "traitor" Moncada in power, Sandino had to fight the Americans. The experience of years of guerrilla conflict led him to believe that the greater problem was American imperialism and he was eagerly seized upon as a symbol of the anti-imperialist cause throughout Latin America.[16] Sandino's motives, however, came much more from understanding the Nicaraguan situation than from any a priori commitment to an international, anti-imperialist movement.

Following the Stimson agreements, Sandino retired into the

isolated, mountainous, and thinly settled Department of Nueva Segovia. Shortly thereafter the first Marine detachment, commanded by Major Harold Pierce and Captain Gilbert Hatfield, entered the department, escorting the newly appointed Liberal *Jefe Político* to the departmental capital of Ocotal. They reached Ocotal on June 9 and quickly disarmed both the Liberal garrison and a Conservative force which had been operating in the area.[17]

Pierce intended to spend only a few days in Ocotal, but the new *Jefe Político,* who was terrified of Sandino, vowed that if the Marines pulled out, he would leave with them. The Marines were therefore ordered to remain and were kept supplied by aviators operating out of Managua. On June 13, Major Pierce and most of his men left Ocotal for Matagalpa, but Captain Hatfield and ten enlisted men remained behind to garrison the town.[18] Sandino and Hatfield now began exchanging telegraph messages, alternating insults and challenges with political philosophy from Sandino and offers to negotiate from Hatfield. In his final message, promising to attack Ocotal, Sandino signed himself "your most obedient servant who ardently desires to put you in a handsome tomb with beautiful bouquets of flowers."[19]

In between telegrams Sandino found time to issue his first political manifesto. In this document he denounced Moncada as a traitor, vowed to drive the Americans out of Nicaragua and the Conservatives out of power, then threw in a plea for Latin American construction of a Nicaraguan canal.[20]

By late June the inability of the Marines to disarm Sandino began to alarm some American officials and plans were hurriedly made to reinforce the Ocotal garrison. On July 1, the three American officers and fifty Nicaraguan enlisted men of the newly created lst Company of the Guardia Nacional left Managua, arriving in Ocotal a few days later.[21] That same week Feland sent Major General Lejeune, the Marine Corps Commandant, his proposals for dealing with Sandino. While still entertaining hopes that the rebel leader was only trying "to accumulate as much money as possible and then slip out of the country," he also noted that Sandino gave "every appearance of a fanatic." Referring to the dispatch of the Guardia to reinforce Ocotal, Feland noted that his force contained "a good proportion of old men," probably a reference to veterans of the original constabulary.[22] A force of "Provisional Guardia," made up largely of veterans of the old Conservative army, had also been enlisted for the task of patrolling Nueva Segovia until more regular Guardia were trained. Feland expressed confidence that these preparations would allow the withdrawal of the Marines to proceed as planned, but he admitted there was a "very unlikely possibility that Sandino might infect the entire country and cause serious trouble."[23] Eight days later Sandino began transforming this "unlikely possibility" into a most unpleasant reality.

The five-and-a-half-year conflict between Sandino and the Guardia Nacional began on July 16, 1927, when Sandino attacked the garrison at Ocotal. The battle lasted from 1:15 in the morning until after 5:00 the following afternoon. After their initial charge was repulsed, the Sandinistas surrounded the city hall and Guardia barracks, where the defenders had barricaded themselves, and kept up a steady exchange of rifle and machine gun fire. Strafing attacks by a Marine patrol plane, followed by further attacks by five De Haviland bombers sent from Managua, finally broke the back of the attack and drove the remnants of the rebel force back into the mountains.[24] Only one defender, a Marine, was killed in the engagement. One Marine and three Guardia were wounded and four Guardia had been captured. Captain Hatfield estimated Sandino's losses at 300.[25] His first attack had resulted in a costly defeat, due largely to two important factors. First, the Sandinistas were poorly trained and equipped, with only sixty of the men reportedly being armed with rifles. The other factor was the activity of Marine aircraft, something which Sandino, admittedly, had completely omitted from his prebattle calculations.[26] The defeat was costly, but the guerrilla leader learned from his mistakes. After Ocotal he concentrated on ambushes and sudden raids instead of open attacks on a strong and fortified enemy.

The attack on Ocotal and a July 29 presidential decree, ordering the Guardia to assume police duties throughout the nation, created an urgent need to recruit and train additional troops.[27] Several factors, however, including disbelief, based on long experience that a Nicaraguan government would pay soldiers a regular salary, political pressures in some areas to discourage prospective enlistees, and the high wages available during the coffee harvesting season, combined to hamper recruiting efforts.[28] Many of those who were recruited failed to meet Guardia standards. Out of one group of twenty recruits in early August only eleven passed their physical examinations.[29] Since traditionally any male with two arms, two legs, and a warm body was considered suitable army material, the idea of rejecting men who wanted to join represented a definite break with earlier Nicaraguan military practices. Despite such problems the Guardia grew steadily, and by August 22 two additional companies had taken up posts in Chinandega and Estelí.

Lack of funds was a continuing problem. Budgetary provisions for the Guardia did not begin until July 1, 1927, when the *Jefe Director* was given $75,000 from a $1,000,000 loan Nicaragua had obtained from an American banking firm and $40,000 from the surplus of official revenues collected by the High Commission. An additional $60,000 was allotted to the Guardia from the regular War Department budget, giving it a total of $175,000 to cover its expenses from July 1, 1927, until January 1, 1928.[30] This sum could not support a force large enough to replace the regular Army and also take over all police duties even without the added costs of combat operations against Sandino.

Continuing funding problems for the Guardia increased American concern over the prospects for successfully supervising the 1928 elections. The intricacies of Nicaraguan politics made it apparent that while Marines could maintain order, they could not "prevent abuses of power and intimidation by the local police authorities during the campaign."[31] To remedy this situation it was necessary to replace all local police with Guardia units. By October 1927, it appeared that only $200,000, providing for a force of 600 men, would be available for the first six months of 1928.[32] Adequate electoral supervision would require a force of at least 1,100 Guardia supported by an annual budget of $689,000. To raise this money, Dana G. Munro, the American chargé, suggested another loan to Nicaragua and a revision of the 1920 financial agreement to allow the government to increase its budget.[33] Sandino's activities, however, soon made even this sum entirely too small and for years the State Department struggled to obtain additional funds. This issue was further complicated by the conflicts over ratification of a basic agreement for the establishment of the Guardia Nacional.

Although the treaty formally establishing the Guardia was signed by Dana Munro and Carlos Cuadra Pasos, the Nicaraguan Foreign Minister, neither of these individuals played a major role in determining the terms of the agreement. This was done largely through correspondence between Generals Lejeune and Feland of the Marine Corps. By the end of July 1927, General Feland presented a draft of the treaty to President Díaz for his approval.[34] Meanwhile, the State Department had obtained a copy from the Navy Department and, finding it satisfactory, authorized the American Minister to sign it if the text remained basically the same.[35]

While the State Department found the treaty satisfactory, the Nicaraguans did not and in late summer the Díaz administration proposed several major changes in the agreement, affecting the very nature of the Guardia. The Nicaraguans proposed to fill the ranks through compulsory military service rather than voluntary enlistments, arguing that failure to do so might contribute to the rise of a professional military caste, and to create separate forces for military and police functions. The American legation rejected both of these proposals, claiming that both voluntary enlistments and combined military and police functions were necessary to create a nonpolitical force and prevent intimidation and fraud in the 1928 election.[36] On both these points the legation's view prevailed, providing another illustration of the final control exercised by the United States over the development of the Guardia Nacional.

After further discussions with the Nicaraguan government and minor changes in the wording of the treaty, portions of the completed, but as yet unsigned document were published in Nicaragua's leading Conservative newspaper.[37] The "National and Legal Directorate of the Conservative Party" quickly approved the proposed agreement, but General Chamorro and his supporters within the Party did everything they could to prevent ratification by the Nicaraguan Senate. The objective of these efforts was to prevent the Guardia's replacing all local police forces, thereby allowing Conservative-controlled police to influence the results of the 1928 elections.[38] In order to muster support for his efforts, General Chamorro concentrated his criticism on the clause exempting American officers from the jurisdiction of Nicaraguan courts. Munro repeated American insistence upon this point, adding a scarcely veiled threat of "disastrous consequences to the Conservative Party of any open conflict with the Government of the United States over measures considered necessary to make good our promises to both parties here."[39]

While the Conservatives were divided over the issue of the Guardia, most Liberals, led by General Moncada, supported the proposed treaty. They recognized that their hopes for victory in the 1928 elections depended upon Marine and Guardia supervision to prevent the traditional frauds practiced by the party in power. The Liberals even suggested that the Guardia agreement run for a period of twelve years, with American training and leadership continuing throughout this period.[40] Secretary of State Kellogg rejected this request, pointing out that such a long-range commitment did not conform to American policy in Nicaragua. Explaining this position, he wrote:

> The Guardia agreement has for its sole object the creation of an efficiently organized Nicaraguan constabulary, primarily to insure supervision of the forthcoming election and secondarily to guarantee general order and stability for the future. It looks to the establishment of a strictly Nicaraguan constabulary as soon as such a result can be accomplished with the aid and advice of American officers detailed for the purpose, these officers to be withdrawn as Nicaraguans are trained to take their places. The idea of any permanent American officering of the constabulary is quite foreign to the fundamental objective of the agreement and is indeed inconsis-

> tent therewith. To fix any definite period of long duration as is now proposed would simply encourage critics of both governments to claim that something in the nature of a military occupation of Nicaragua by the United States is in contemplation.[41]

The signing of this long, detailed, and controversial document finally took place on December 22, 1928. It provided for American organization of a force of 93 officers and 1,136 enlisted men with an annual budget of $689,132. Recognizing that Sandino's activities might make this force totally inadequate, provision was made for possible future increases in both strength and budget, noting that the figures specified in the agreement "shall be regarded as the minimum requirements for the Guardia Nacional de Nicaragua." In line with American demands the Guardia Nacional was declared to be "the sole military and police force of the Republic" and was given control of all arms and ammunition in Nicaragua. It also inherited control of "all fortifications, barracks, buildings, grounds, penitentiaries, vessels, and other government property" controlled by the old police or armed forces. Great powers were given to the *Jefe Director,* who, subject to presidential approval, controlled "recruiting, appointment, instruction, training, promotion, examination, discipline, operation of troops, clothing, rations, arms and equipment, quarters and administration" and who also issued all Guardia rules and regulations. Other sections of the agreement exempted American officers from the jurisdiction of Nicaraguan courts and provided for the appointment, by the President of the United States, of American officers to serve with the Guardia until Nicaraguans were trained to replace them.[42]

The signing of the Munro-Cuadra Pasos Agreement failed to bring an end to the controversy surrounding the organization and legal status of the Guardia. While ratification was easily achieved in the Nicaraguan Senate, a dispute in the Chamber of Deputies tied up the bill for the remainder of the Díaz administration. When the Liberals assumed power in 1929, their attitude toward the Guardia underwent a striking change and the United States found itself faced with another, even more complex set of problems concerning its role in the creation of that force.

While the failure to complete formal ratification bothered the State Department, it had little effect on the Marine's day-by-day development of the Guardia. They continued to recruit and to spend funds as if the legal basis for such actions was fully established. On October 1, 1927, the Guardia had 47 officers and 438 men stationed in four departments, Estelí, Nueva Segovia, Chinandega, and Managua.[43] Spurred on by the fighting against Sandino and by the pressure of preparing for the 1928 elections, recruitment and training went rapidly in the following year. By September 30, 1928, there were 173 officers and 1,637 enlisted men, a force already nearly 50 percent in excess of that provided for in the Munro-Cuadra Pasos Agreement, and this force was distributed throughout virtually every department in the nation.[44]

The organization and training of the new Guardia Nacional produced a wide variety of problems for the Marines. The first problems came with the quality of the recruits. Guardia regulations provided that all recruits, except for apprentice musicians, had to be at least eighteen years of age, pass a physical examination, and, except in "exceptional cases," be able to read and write.[45] Since literate Nicaraguans were rarely interested in enlisting as privates, this requirement soon had to be waived. Schools for illiterate soldiers were set up at some of the larger posts and instructors were hired with the rank and pay of a corporal. The instructors did not have to wear uniforms and could quit after giving fifteen days' notice, a right naturally not extended to other enlisted men, who served a term of three years.[46]

For several years almost all the Guardia's commissioned officers were Americans assigned to that duty by the Navy Department. The Nicaraguan government had virtually no voice in the selection of these men, who were shuttled in and out of the country as the interests of the Navy Department dictated.[47] While some of the Marines had previous experience training constabulary forces in Haiti or the Dominican Republic, few spoke Spanish, and had therefore to rely on interpreters or gestures to get their instructions understood.[48] Officers assigned to Nicaraguan duty were rarely, if ever, given any prior orientation as to the culture, political situation, or even United States policy goals in the nation.[49] Despite such handicaps, as well as the limitations on training time imposed by the demands of the campaign against Sandino, the Marines did suprisingly well, transforming their raw recruits within a few months into the best trained, disciplined, and equipped force in Nicaraguan history.

While most of the Marines assigned to the Guardia had some previous experience in training troops, few had any background in directing the police functions which the Guardia was expected to undertake. Language and cultural barriers were also greater in this sensitive area, leading to a host of problems and, at times, rather ingenious solutions hardly imagined by the statesmen and generals who drew up the original Guardia agreements. Some of these problems were described by the first Marine to serve as Managua's Chief of Police:

> The first few days were spent getting in touch with the old police force. . . . Well it was run mostly by graft. . . .
>
> I went to the Jefe Político and told him that I had to have forms and police blotters and showed him by keeping an up-to-date record of offenses that I could get more money on fines for repeaters as the old records were impossible. . . .
>
> We had to study up on existing police laws and how to cut thru red tape to get convictions. I had four junior officers assigned who could read, write and speak Spanish. . . . To get the office going we had to borrow, bum and swipe what we needed.
>
> We were soon getting crowded for room. So I spoke it over with the Police Director. Well he had to use what he had. I asked the Jefe Director for some intelligence money and was allotted $30.00 monthly. I first got to work on the Police Director to see if I could get something on him officially or socially. Well I got the goods on him that he was padding the pay roll by pocketing the money that was for people who were supposed to work in his office, but they did only on paper. I called him in my office and we had a nice talk. The result was that he wrote a letter to the Minister of Police stating that he had discharged certain people (the ones on paper). I then proceeded to take more room. . . .
>
> I immediately started schools and had the lieutenants go over with the men the police laws then in force. The policeman was taught first to know what is wrong and then to know what to do about it. Their idea of the job was to lock up everybody they had a grudge against or who would not turn over to them a little graft. Well we had to weed out the undesirables at the start before we got a write-up in the papers. I held office hours each morning for the newspaper men at 10:00 A.M. We worked on the newspaper men and got something on them and they left us alone. . . .
>
> In the beginning the police force was armed with the rifle and bayonet. We immediately discarded that because we had several policemen cut by their own bayonets as other people would interfere with the arrest, take his weapon as his both hands were busy holding the rifle and attack the policeman when his back was turned. We then had several cases where the policeman was justified in shooting his rifle, but the bullet after hitting the fugitive would continue on and hit an innocent by-stander or continue on in its flight and hit

somebody sitting in his adobe house. We then turned to and armed them with clubs and pistols. . . .

I hope it is possible that you can put it across to have the Marine Corps get up a pamphlet in practical police work. . . . I believe it should be made part of the law course in the Marine Corps Schools in Quantico. It is very important that when the Marines capture a place for the Navy in a foreign country that we have officers competent to handle one of the most important functions of getting in touch with the natives. Also, in taking over a foreign city allowance should be made for differences in race, customs, laws, language and habits of the natives, until they get used to us. . . .

The people were against our methods at first because they could not bribe us to look blind or the other way. I used the lady next to the police station (Mrs. Irene vd. de Pasos) to present our case to the President (Díaz) whenever we had to lock up some prominent Conservative or once in awhile his nephew or brother or his secretary. . . .

I had a complaint by some of the citizens one morning that there were no policemen on the streets at night. Well my officers claimed that they had inspected the police force once every hour from midnite until 6 in the morning. So I told that to the people and they replied it could not be true as if the policemen were on the job they would blow their whistles all nite and let the people know they were on the job. Well I had to explain to the people that the police had orders not to blow their whistles until something happened that they needed assistance. Well one can not satisfy all the people. Some like to sleep.[50]

In outlying areas the police also acted as judge and jury, combining police and judicial functions. They also exercised control over the *Jueces de Mesta,* a rough equivalent of American justices of the peace, and over the *Jueces'* assistants, the *Jefes de Cantón.* Even Indian chiefs came under the Guardia's jurisdiction as they traditionally exercised certain police and judicial functions. Other police duties included the control of all traffic in arms and explosives, the enforcement of sanitary regulations, the suppression of contraband, and the control of all traffic in liquor and tobacco.[51] These last functions led, in September 1928, to the Guardia's replacing the Hacienda (Treasury Department) Guards. These Guards were described as "very bad characters" and as "more of a menace to peaceful communities than the outlaws they were supposed to operate against," and their elimination evoked no recorded protests.[52]

By taking over police functions the Guardia also gained responsibility for all prisons in Nicaragua. Old prisons, such as the National Penitentiary in Managua, served as places of confinement and little else. Criminals, political prisoners, and the insane were locked up together under miserable conditions. Under the Marines an effort was made to teach prisoners a trade. A furniture factory was established in the prison, cattle raising was introduced, and the institution became virtually self-supporting. Prisoners were allowed visitors on weekends and church services were conducted. As part of the campaign to renovate the National Penitentiary the entire building was painted green. Since green was the official color of the Conservative Party and the painting was done after the Liberals' victory in the 1928 elections, this paint job produced a bumper crop of political jokes in Managua.[53]

In replacing the police, the Guardia Nacional assumed an immense task, one that inevitably led to mistakes, political involvements, and virulent criticism, but considering the handicaps under which they operated, the Guardia's Marine officers probably carried out their police duties as well as could reasonably be expected. In fact, much of the criticism of their activities may have been due as much to the new efficiency which they introduced as it was to any failures in police duties. In Managua the amount collected in fines jumped from $40 per month to over $500 when the Guardia replaced the municipal police.[54] In Chontales the local police made fourteen arrests and collected $30.80 in fines from September 1927 through February 1928. They were later replaced by Guardia who, from September 1928 to November 1928, made 334 arrests and collected $717.60 in fines, along with confiscating 132 rifles, 42 pistols, 53 shotguns, and 193 cutting weapons.[55] Obviously, such increased efficiency did not make them popular with all segments of the population.

The assumption of police duties influenced the Guardia's development in many ways. In order to carry out those duties and continue to combat Sandino, it became necessary to create a much larger force than originally anticipated. Ordinarily, Guardia assigned to police duties were not used on combat patrols and those assigned to combat patrols were not used on police duties.[56] There was some rotation between these duties, but no fixed system in this regard. The assumption of police duties also complicated training procedures, since the same training did not fit a recruit to carry out both police and combat duties.

Original plans contemplated establishing a recruit depot in Managua to train all enlisted men, but this soon proved impractical. One of the first exceptions was made for the isolated Atlantic Coast, where it soon became obvious that recruits would have to be raised and trained locally.[57] Eventually it became necessary to extend local recruitment and training to most areas of the nation, a development which made a good part of each local garrison natives of that area. Some rotation of troops from post to post did take place, primarily because enlisted Guardia, following the Nicaraguan tradition of *personalismo,* often became too attached to their immediate Marine commander. Transfers were therefore instituted to get the rank and file used to serving loyally under different officers.[58]

Training was by no means the only area of traditional Nicaraguan military practice that was radically changed by the Americans. Exhibiting a typical American drive for efficiency and modernization, the Marines made massive alterations in the areas of supply and communications. A Quartermaster's Department was established and made responsible for introducing standardization of arms, organizing a rudimentary system of motor transportation, creating formal disbursing and accounting sections, and establishing a regular system of uniforms. These efforts often encountered serious obstacles. For example, the horrible condition of Nicaraguan roads limited the use of motor transport, at times forcing the Guardia to rely upon pack animals and oxcarts. The Americans' lack of experience in handling transportation of this sort provided more than its share of headaches while Marines commanded the Guardia Nacional.[59]

While bull carts, native dugouts, and other primitive methods supplied much of the Guardia's transport capability, a vital contribution was made by the most modern means of transportation, the airplane. In August 1928 alone, 130,905 pounds of human and material cargo were flown from Managua to outlying Guardia posts.[60] Even entire units were occasionally moved by air. Perhaps the best example of this was the airlifting of the entire cadet corps of the Nicaraguan Military Academy, in November 1931, from Managua to Estelí to combat a threatened attack by Sandino's forces.[61]

Establishing a functioning communications system brought another major problem. The existing Nicaraguan postal and telephone systems were bluntly described as "unsatisfactory" and the telegraph service as only "slightly less so."[62] The only advantage of these systems was that they were all government-owned and could therefore be used without having to expend additional funds from the constantly strained Guardia budget.[63] The limitations of traditional communications systems, including Sandino's constant destruction of telegraph and telephone lines, led to Marine efforts to establish a complete radio system between Guardia posts. On December 22, 1931, this network, known as Radio Nacional, began the first transcontinental radio service in Nicaraguan history with the inauguration of a station at the American-owned mining center of Bonanza.[64] In September 1931 twenty Nicaraguan enlisted men were enrolled in a Guardia school for radio operators. Eight months later fifteen of them graduated and were assigned to duty as radio operators.[65] Lack of time before the final Marine evacuation prevented organization of a second class, but while this left the Guardia a bit shorthanded in experienced radio operators, the Marines had laid the basis for the most efficient communications system Nicaragua had ever known. Unfortunately, they had also left a heritage of military control over communications, a heritage which has continued up to the present.

Not all the Americans attached to the Guardia were Marines. In the same way in which they provided health services for the Marines, officers of the Navy's Hospital Corps developed medical services for the Guardia Nacional. Commander J.B. Helm, the Guardia's first Medical Director, ran into a host of problems. Nicaragua was hardly famous for its healthful climate or high morals. Syphilis was rampant; malaria, typhoid, dysentery, internal parasites and tropical infections, combined with casualties suffered in combat with Sandino's forces, posed tremendous challenges for the Navy doctors.[66] Much of Nicaragua was virtually devoid of doctors, hospitals, and sources of medical supplies. When he first took command of the Medical Department, Commander Helm tried to interest the Red Cross in Nicaraguan conditions, but got no response. Efforts to obtain supplies from the Navy's Bureau of Medicine and Surgery gained no more success. Ultimately Helms obtained $1,500 worth of goods from the Medical Supply Depot in New York and received an additional $250 worth of medical supplies from the commander of the New York Naval Hospital.[67]

When Commander Helm took office, there were three Navy officers and one Nicaraguan doctor working with the Guardia.

Three more medical officers, a Chief Pharmacist's Mate, and seventeen other pharmacist's mates were added before the end of 1927. A school to train Nicaraguans as corpsmen was established and, by October 1, 1928, had graduated twenty-nine enlisted men from its three-month program.[68] Those who completed the course received the regular private's pay plus an additional $2 a month, no small sum in Nicaragua.[69] The medical personnel operated two hospitals, one in Managua and another in Ocotal, center of the most active combat area, and operated six infirmaries and numerous dispensaries throughout the nation.[70] While these facilities were limited and often inadequate, they were far better than anything Nicaraguan soldiers had known before.

Control of venereal disease was one of the most difficult tasks confronting the Medical Department. The rate of infection among enlisted men was extremely high and lectures on morality and the danger of infection did nothing to reduce it. Even handing out prophylactic kits did not reduce the rate of infection, a failure which the Guardia's Medical Director attributed to the fact that the enlisted men were using the contents to polish their shoes. The Medical Director further noted, however, that even the most virulent infections didn't bother the Nicaraguan soldier, who seemed to accept them as a matter of course.[71]

In an effort to control this problem, control over prostitution was vested in the Guardia by a presidential decree, issued on July 3, 1928. Prostitutes were required to register and were given weekly inspections. Four special venereal hospitals were established and by early 1929 officials claimed a drop of over 80 percent in the venereal disease rate among Guardia personnel. In addition sixty-eight prostitutes were reportedly cured.[72] This report, however, was apparently overly optimistic. In 1932 the Medical Department reported prostitutes were no longer being treated and that 487 new cases of venereal disease had been contracted by enlisted men in the past year. Only malaria, with 804 cases, presented a more serious health problem.[73]

Efforts to aid nationwide immunization campaigns against smallpox and typhoid were considerably more successful. General Order 43-1929 ordered the Guardia to cooperate in a national smallpox vaccination campaign, adding: "The Guardia will not use physical force to compel any person to be vaccinated, but those who refuse vaccination will be taken before the director of police."[74] With this inducement refusals were probably quite rare. For a while Guardia doctors and corpsmen also made free medical treatment available to civilians in remote areas. From September 1927 through October 1928, 1,147 Nicaraguans received this free care, but shortly thereafter lack of funds brought this program to an end.[75]

Regular pay, improved equipment, and medical care combined to make conditions for Guardia enlisted men much better than those of the average Nicaraguan, but despite these advantages, efforts at organization were constantly hindered by desertions and even occasional mutinies. From October 1, 1928, through September 1929, 480 men deserted and 387 others were discharged out of a total force of 1,846.[76] As organization and discipline within the Guardia improved, this problem declined. From October 1, 1931, to September 30, 1932, the size of the Guardia remained fairly constant, increasing only from 2,234 to 2,307 enlisted men. In this time 580 men were discharged, but only 116 deserted, making the desertion rate only a fifth of what it had been three years earlier.[77]

From time to time mutinies flared up in outlying posts. These never occurred in major centers and no unit ever mutinied during combat with Sandino's forces. Neither was there any conspiracy uniting mutinies in more than one area.[78] There were a total of eleven mutinies during the years Marines commanded the Guardia Nacional. The first occurred on January 8, 1928, at Somotillo. Nine of the post's fifteen enlisted men participated in the effort to kill the three officers, all Marines, stationed there, following which they planned to join Sandino. Their plan misfired and four mutineers were killed in the ensuing fight while the rest scattered.[79] A more successful mutiny occurred in 1929 at Telpaneca. Following the murder of an American officer by an enlisted man, most of the garrison deserted, kidnapping two other Marine officers, both of whom eventually escaped, and fleeing to Honduras.[80] From April to June 1932, three major mutinies occurred, resulting in the death of several American officers and, in at least one case, providing recruits and weapons for Sandino. The last of these was led by a Nicaraguan officer, the only case in which an officer participated in a mutiny.[81] These uprisings probably reflected tensions building up within the Guardia over the continuing failure to eliminate Sandino, the upcoming presidential elections, and the subsequent withdrawal of all Marines from the Guardia and from Nicaragua.

Despite syphilis, mutinies, desertions, and Sandino, the

Marines managed by 1932 to develop an effective, disciplined armed force in Nicaragua. The great burden of this task fell upon junior officers and enlisted men of the Marine Corps and most performed their duties remarkably well. After a period of service with the Guardia, most Marines developed a genuine respect for the fighting qualities of the Nicaraguan soldier and even something of an affection for the men serving under them.[82] This attitude contributed to the relatively high morale among the Guardia's enlisted men. Their life was hardly easy, but a private's pay of $12 a month was higher than that of a laborer in Managua.[83] The addition of uniforms, medical benefits, and food allowances made enlistment even more attractive. Compared to the majority of his countrymen, the lot of the average Guardia was not bad at all and he knew it. After its first year, the force never lacked recruits and the clause in Nicaragua's Constitution establishing conscription became a dead letter.

The United States had three basic objectives in creating the Guardia Nacional. The first was to replace the former army and police with a disciplined, adequately trained and equipped constabulary. The Marines made great strides in this direction in the five-and-a-half years they directed the Guardia. Had the achievement of technical and organizational improvements been the sole objective, the Guardia's creation would have to be rated, with some qualifications, a major success. There were however, two other objectives. The most pressing of these was establishing internal order by suppressing all uprisings directed against the government. From 1927 through 1932 this meant defeating Sandino. The final objective, and from the State Department's point of view the dominant one, was to transform Nicaragua's armed forces into a nonpolitical force, dedicated to defending constitutional order and guaranteeing free elections. On these last two objectives the American record was to fall far short of success. Fighting Sandino or finding itself involved in a snare of political disputes, the Guardia encountered frustration piled upon frustration in the 1927–1933 period, frustrations which ultimately spelled failure for American policies in both these vital areas.

NOTES

1, Captain Evans F. Carlson, "The Guardia Nacional de Nicaragua," *Marine Corps Gazette* XXI (August 1937) 9.

2. Interview with Colonel Salvador Mendieta, Managua, December 1963.

3. Carlson, "The Guardia Nacional," p. 9.

4. President Díaz to President Coolidge, May 15, 1927 (enclosure), *Foreign Relations,* 1927, III, pp 351–53.

5. Eberhardt to Kellogg, May 8, 1927, *Foreign Relations,* 1927, III, pp. 433–34.

6. Carlos Cuadra Pasos, "Apuntes del Dr. Carlos Cuadra Pasos," in Adolfo Reyes Huete, *ETAPAS del Ejército* (Managua: Talleres Nacionales, n.d.), pp 31–32; Brigadier General Logan Feland to Major General John A. Lejeune, Commandant, U.S. Marine Corps, June 6, 1927, Microfilm of Documents concerning U.S. Marine Corps Operations in Nicaragua, Reel 1, MCHA.

7. Feland to Lejeune, May 24, 1927, Nicaragua Microfilm, Reel 1, MCHA. For a full exposition of the Marines' views on this dispute, see the unsigned and undated memorandum from Headquarters, U.S. Marine Corps, on "Extra Compensation for Officers and Enlisted Men Detailed to Assist the Governments of Latin American Republics in Military and Naval Matters," NA RG 45, Subject File, WA-7.

8. Major Julian C. Smith et al., *A Review of the Organization and Operations of the Guardia Nacional de Nicaragua; by Direction of the Major General Commandant of the United States Marine Corp* (n.p.; n.d.), p. 205. Cited hereafter as Smith et al., *Review.*

9. President Díaz to the Jefe Director of the Guardia Nacional, July 13, 1927, printed in Smith et al., *Review,* p. 207.

10. President Díaz, "Presidential Decree," July 30, 1927, printed in Smith et al., *Review,* p. 207.

11. Gregorio Selser, *Sandino, General de los hombres libres,* Vol. I (Buenos Aires: Editorial Tríangulo, 1958), p. 159; Gustavo Alemán-Bolaños, *Sandino el Libertador* (Mexico, D.F.: Ediciones del Caribe, 1952), p. 19. Anastasio Somoza García, *El verdadero Sandino o el Calvario de las Segovias* (Managua: Tipografía Robelo, 1936), p. 19, gives 1893 as the year of Sandino's birth.

12. Neill Macaulay, *The Sandino Affair* (Chicago: Quandrangle Books, 1967), pp. 50–52.

13. For a more complete discussion of this issue, see Joseph O. Baylen, "Sandino, Patriot or Bandit?," *Hispanic American Historical Review* XXXI (August 1951) 394–419.

14. Selser, *Sandino,* I, pp. 228–29.

15. Colonel L.M. Gulick to General Feland, May 30, 1927,

Nicaraguan Records, Box 10, Folder 3, MCHA; Harold Norman Denny, *Dollars for Bullets* (New York: Dial, 1929), p. 292.

16. The best account of Latin American reactions to Sandino is found in Lejeune Cummins' *Quijote on a Burro* (Mexico, D.F.: Impresora Azteca, 1958).

17. Major Edwin North McClellan, "He Remembered His Mission," *Marine Corps Gazette* XV (November 1930) 30–32.

18. Ibid., pp. 32 and 51–52.

19. Sandino to Captain Hatfield, June 29, 1927, Nicaraguan Records, File on Sandino, MCHA.

20. Selser, *Sandino,* I, pp. 248–51.

21. Smith et al, *Review,* p. 9.

22. Feland to Lejeune, July 8, 1927, Nicaraguan Microfilm, Reel 1, MCHA.

23. Ibid.

24. Aircraft Squadron, 2nd Brigade, "Record of Events for Week Ending July 16, 1927," Nicaraguan Microfilm, Reel 10, MCHA.

25. Hatfield to Feland, July 20, 1927, Nicaraguan Microfilm, Reel 10, MCHA.

26. Selser, *Sandino,* I, p. 254.

27. President Diaz to General Elias Beadle, July 29, 1927, printed in Smith et al., *Review,* p. 206.

28. Smith et al., *Review,* p. 10.

29. *La Noticia* (Managua), August 6, 1927, p. 1.

30. Munro to Kellogg, October 15 and 17, 1927, NA RG 59 817.00/5074 and 817.00/5121.

31. Ibid.

32. Munro to Kellogg, October 17, 1927, NA RG 59, 817.1051/5121.

33. Letter from Dr. Dana G. Munro to author, November 24, 1964.

34. Ibid.

35. Kellogg to Eberhardt, August 20, 1927, NA RG 59, 817.1051/159; letter from Dr. Dana G. Munro to author, November 24, 1964.

36. Carlos Cuadra Pasos, "Introdución a la historia de la Guardia Nacional," *Revista Conservadora* II (August 1961) 8.

37. *La Prensa* (Managua), November 20, 1927, p. 1.

38. Dana G. Munro, *The United States and the Caribbean Republics, 1921–1933* (Princeton, N.J.: Princeton University Press, 1974), p. 240.

39. Munro to Kellogg, December 7, 1927, NA RG 59, 817.1051/185.

40. Munro to Kellogg, December 2, 1927, NA RG 59, 817.1051/178.

41. Kellogg to Munro, December 8, 1927, NA RG 59, 817.1051/178.

42. "Agreement between the United States and Nicaragua Establishing the Guardia Nacional de Nicaragua," December 22, 1927, *Foreign Relations,* 1927, III, pp. 434–39.

43. "Annual Report of the Guardia Nacional de Nicaragua for the Period from 10/1/27 to 10/1/28," Nicaraguan Records, Box 10, File 3, MCHA.

44. Ibid.

45. "Guardia Nacional Personnel Manual," Nicaraguan Records, Box 9, File 14, MCHA.

46. "Annual Report of the Guardia Nacional de Nicaragua for the Period from 10/1/31/ to 9/30/32, "Nicaraguan Records, Box 10, File 14, MCHA; "Guardia Nacional Personnel Manual," Nicaraguan Records, Box 9, File 14, MCHA.

47. For an example of this shuttling back and forth, see Burke Davis, *Marine! The Life of Lt. Gen. Lewis B. (Chesty) Puller, USMC (ret.)* (Boston: Little, Brown 1962).

48. Interview with former Guardia Lieutenant Stanley Haggard, Corinto, Nicaragua, December 1963.

49. This lack of preparation became clear from interviews with numerous Marines who had served with the Guardia.

50. Captain Herbert S. Keimling to Major Fleming, March 11, 1933, NA RG 127, Entry 198, Papers of the Jefe Director of the Guardia Nacional de Nicaragua.

51. Smith et al., *Review,* pp. 48–49.

52. Memorandum by Major Victor Bleasdale, October 3, 1928, Nicaraguan Records, Box 10, File 3, MCHA.

53. Interview with Colonel James Denham (USMC, ret.), former commander of the National Penitentiary, Managua, Washington, May 1964.

54. Captain Herbert S. Keimling to Major Fleming, March 11, 1933, NA RG 127, Entry 198, Papers of the Jefe Director of the Guardia Nacional de Nicaragua.

55. Division Commander, Chontales, to the Jefe Director, February 13, 1929, Nicaraguan Records, Box 12, File 19, MCHA.

56. Interview with Lt. Gen. Julian C. Smith (USMC, ret.), former Chief of Staff of the Guardia Nacional, Alexandria, Virginia, May 1964.

57. Smith et al., *Review,* p. 12.

58. H.C. Reisinger, "La Palabra del Gringo, Leadership in the Nicaraguan National Guard," *United States Naval Institute Proceedings* LXI (February 1935) 216.

59. Major Roger W. Peard, "Bull Cart Transportation in the Tropics," *Marine Corps Gazette* XV (February 1931) 29–30 and 47–49.

60. Lt. Col. Charles R. Sanderson, "The Supply Service in Western Nicaragua," *Marine Corps Gazette* XVII (May 1932) 42.

61. Smith et al., *Review,* p. 105.

62. Munro to Kellogg, November 11, 1927, NA RG 59, 817.00/5165.

63. Smith et al., *Review,* p. 91.

64. H.J. Phillips, "Sistema de comunicaciones," in Reyes Huete, *ETAPAS,* p. 77.

65. Smith et al., *Review,* p. 93.

66. Lt. W.T. Minnick, U.S.N., "Medical Difficulties Encountered by

Combat Forces Operating in Nicaragua," *United States Naval Medical Bulletin* XXVI (October 1928) 884–88.

67. "History of the Medical Department of the Guardia Nacional de Nicaragua, 1927," Nicaraguan Records, Box 10, File 4, MCHA.

68. Ibid.

69. Ibid.

70. Smith et al., *Review,* pp. 88–89.

71. Commander J.D. Helm to Jefe Director, Guardia Nacional, November 13, 1930, "Annual Sanitary Report of the Guardia Nacional de Nicaragua for the Year Ending September 30, 1930," Records of the Guardia Nacional, NA RG 127.

72. Captain Fred G. Patchen to the Jefe Director, February 28, 1928, Nicaraguan Records, Box 10, File 14, MCHA.

73. "Annual Report for the Medical Department, Guardia Nacional de Nicaragua, for the Period October 1, 1931, to September 30, 1932," Nicaraguan Records, Box 10, File 14, MCHA.

74. General Order 43-1929, April 10, 1929, Nicaraguan Records, Box 9, File 15, MCHA.

75. Smith et al., *Review,* p. 89.

76. Raymond Leslie Buell, "Reconstruction in Nicaragua," *Foreign Policy Reports* VI (November 12, 1930) 332.

77. "Annual Report of the Guardia Nacional de Nicaragua for the Period from 10/1/31 to 9/30/32," Nicaraguan Records, Box 10, File 14, MCHA.

78. Smith et al., *Review,*. p. 109.

79. B-1 Journal, 2nd Brigade, USMC, January 15, 1928, Nicaraguan Microfilm, Reel 4, MCHA.

80. Smith et al., *Review,* pp. 111–115.

81. Ibid., pp. 119–22.

82. Interviews with Stanley Haggard, Corinto, Nicaragua, December 1963, and Lt. Gen. Smith, Alexandria, Va., May 1964; Tape-Recorded Conversations with Lieutenant General Lewis B. Puller, USMC, and Colonel William Lee, USMC, U.S. Marine Corps Museum and History Office, Navy Yard, Washington, D.C.

83. Marvin Goldwert, *The Constabulary in the Dominican Republic and Nicaragua: Progeny and Legacy of United States Intervention* (Gainesville: University of Florida Press, 1961), p. 38.

IV

CHASING SANDINO

The story of the military campaign conducted by the American Marines and the Nicaraguan Guardia Nacional against Augusto Cesár Sandino has been recounted, in considerable detail, several times.[1] This chapter will not attempt to duplicate accounts already available, but will focus on the impact of the campaign on the development of the Guardia.

Following his attack on Ocotal, Sandino and his men were denounced as bandits by the Americans and by the Díaz administration, and an effort was made to convince the public that they were mere thieves or wandering adventurers who would easily be eliminated.[2] Other attempts sought to link Sandino with the Communists or to dismiss him as a somewhat unbalanced fanatic.[3] Simultaneously, State Department officials were privately reassuring themselves that the Ocotal fiasco had finished Sandino and he would "not offer much further serious resistance."[4] These attempts to dismiss Sandino as a bandit or a lunatic and the wishful speculation that his movement would soon evaporate proved grossly inaccurate.

A strong Marine Patrol sent into Nueva Segovia to "crush" Sandino did succeed in driving him out of all the towns he held, but was unable to force a decisive battle. In contrast to the optimistic reports circulating around Washington, Major Oliver Floyd, the patrol's commander, reported that the population seemed generally friendly to Sandino, his men appeared determined to resist, and eliminating him would require a major campaign and many casualties.[5] Under such circumstances the Marines could not confine their duties to police and security measures and the Guardia's plans for a slow expansion to a force of only a few hundred men no longer appeared feasible.

Sandino, meanwhile, had regrouped his troops on an inaccessible mountain, which he called "El Chipote," and prepared to use guerrilla tactics to oppose the Marines and the Guardia. He also had his men sign a lengthy document, recognizing his leadership, denouncing the United States and the Díaz regime, and pledging themselves to fight to defend Nicaraguan sovereignty and dignity.[6] After remaining relatively quiet throughout August 1927, Sandino resumed his attacks in September with an unsuccessful effort to overrun the combined Marine and Guardia garrison at Telpaneca. Once again the Guardia performed well in combat despite their brief period of training.[7]

Sandino's continued activity produced consternation in Washington, where American policy in Nicaragua was already under strong attack. As early as July 27, Secretary Kellogg had been complaining that "we have been led to believe that armed opposition to the existing program would rapidly disappear and that we need anticipate no serious complications on that score." As the situation developed it seemed that this assumption might well prove false.[8] The State Department urged immediate action to eliminate Sandino, but the Marines replied that operations during the rainy season, due to end in November, were very difficult and any major effort would have to wait until the weather improved.[9] The Marines did undertake a series of bombing raids against El Chipote, but the total effect of this effort seems scarcely to have been worth the cost of the bombs.[10]

Before the Marines and the Guardia could undertake a joint offensive against Sandino it was necessary to establish principles that would govern relations between the two forces. On December 9, 1927, the Navy Department decided that, except in emergency cases, the Guardia and the Marine's Second Brigade, the unit stationed in Nicaragua, would function independently. Overall responsibility for coordinating their operations was given to the Admiral commanding the Special Service Squadron. If combined operations were necessary, they would be directed by the commander of the Second Brigade.[11] These provisions further weakened the Nicaraguan government's theoretical control over the Guardia, since the Special Service Squadron's commander, whenever he felt an emergency existed, could take direct control of Guardia operations without the necessity of even consulting the Nicaraguans.

The long-delayed combined offensive finally began on December 19, 1927. Two columns, with a total of 174 Marines and Guardia, were involved, making this by far the largest force yet sent against Sandino.[12] The guerrilla leader quickly ambushed both columns, slowing the offensive to a crawl. When El Chipote finally fell on January 26, 1928 Sandino had already evacuated his forces.[13] In February he began raiding coffee plantations around Matagalpa, acquiring funds and supplies in the process. He also ambushed a patrol of the newly arrived 11th Marine Regiment which had been rushed into the area, killing five Marines and wounding eight. Sandino had raised a force of several hundred men for this attack, including numerous local citizens who joined up for the ambush, then returned to their civilian pursuits.[14] Far from eliminating the guerrillas, the combat operations seemed to be gaining them increased popular support.

Attempts to negotiate with Sandino proved as unsuccessful as efforts to subdue him by force. A delegation from the Fellowship of Reconciliation failed in an effort to obtain a direct interview with the guerrilla leader, and an American civilian employee of the Marines who attempted to initiate private negotiations lost his life in the process.[15] The Marine commander at San Rafael del Norte, Lieutenant Wilburt Brown, also tried to initiate direct negotiations, but Sandino politely replied that he could not guarantee the officer's safety and, in any case, could think of nothing Brown could say that would interest him. Brown next obtained permission to appoint Sandino's wife as telegraph operator in San Rafael, hoping to open up negotiations through her. He had her tell her husband that he had given her the job "to give her some means of livelihood when she became a widow." Sandino replied with a final expression of appreciation and an expression of regret that he would be unable to do anything for the Lieutenant's widow.[16]

A more official effort to open negotiations was made by the Special Service Squadron's commander, Admiral David F. Sellers, who wrote Sandino on January 20, 1928, to try to persuade him to surrender. Sellers was only willing to discuss ways in which the rebel leader might come to accept the Stimson agreements, but in his reply Sandino demanded American withdrawal from Nicaragua, the removal of Díaz as President, and supervision of the 1928 elections by Latin American nations instead of by the United States.[17] Since none of these points was deemed negotiable by the United States, efforts at finding a peaceful settlement collapsed.

Frustrated by American inability to dispose of Sandino, Secretary of State Kellogg sought the advice of Brigadier General Frank R. McCoy, the Army officer in charge of the American Electoral Commission in Nicaragua. In a letter that could as easily have referred to Vietnam in the 1960s as it did to Nicaragua in the 1920s, Kellogg noted:

> There is a great deal of criticism in this country about the way in which these operations are being dragged out with constant sacrifice of American lives and without any concrete results. So far as anybody here can see, what is now taking place can and will go on indefinitely. People cannot understand why the job cannot be done and frankly I do not understand myself. There is an uneasy feeling that there may be something wrong with the plan of campaign or the leadership. Inquiries at the Navy Department invariably elicit the response that the situation is entirely satisfactory, but neither the Congress nor the public can be expected to be satisfied with these general statements and criticism in the face of continuous losses and lack of any indication of a definite conclusion of the operations is certain to become more and more insistent.[18]

General McCoy's reply did little to relieve Kellogg's anxiety. Noting that he too was "seriously concerned over the military situation," the General detailed what he felt were some of the problems plaguing the efforts to eliminate Sandino:

> Sandino's forces have the advantage of local language, thorough familiarity with the terrain, of the assistance, particularly as regards information, of elements some of which are in sympathy with Sandino while others either consider the continuance of his operations favorable to their immediate political purpose or else do not dare to incur the hostility of the outlaws by giving information or assistance to our forces. . . .
>
> Failure of the Nicaraguan Government to pass to date legislation appropriate for the development of the electoral and Guardia programs has given encouragement to Sandino and his sympathizers and has prevented the full potential use of the Guardia to take over responsibilities incident to ordinary police functions so as to release for field operations the maximum Marine strength.[19]

The pressures caused by the upcoming 1928 election supervision led to a general adoption of General McCoy's suggestion that the Guardia concentrate on police duties while the Marines pursued Sandino. The rest of 1928 was spent in continued scattered contacts with Sandinistas, most of which involved ambushes of Marine patrols. From May 30, 1928, till the end of the year most Guardia were fully occupied with supervision of the campaign and election. During this period Guardia patrols reported only two minor contacts with "bandit" forces and suffered no casualties.[20]

Following the 1928 elections American military policy in Nicaragua underwent a significant change. The object now was to withdraw the Marines from combat, replacing them with Guardia units as rapidly as possible. The new Nicaraguan President, Liberal General José María Moncada, also favored a change in tactics. He hoped to use the conflict with Sandino to develop a military force loyal to himself, something that he could not do within the framework of the Guardia.[21] This effort would run directly counter to United States policy, which aimed at making the Guardia Nicaragua's only armed force. On the day of Moncada's inauguration a new order, further advancing this policy, went into effect, giving the Guardia alone the right to arrest civilians and stating that the Marines were to take an active combat role only when the Guardia proved unable to handle the situation.[22]

Moncada's solution for creating a force loyal to himself and waging a more efficient campaign against Sandino was to send into the field a force of *voluntarios,* led by Nicaraguan officers, but operating in conjunction with Marine patrols. General Feland, the Second Brigade's Commander, strongly supported this proposal, but the American Minister and General Beadle, the Guardia's commander, opposed it.[23] Eventually a compromise was arrived at. The Guardia gained control over *voluntario* funds and conducted a short training course for them, but once in the field, *voluntarios* operated independently.[24]

Two columns of *voluntarios,* each containing about ninety men, operated in the field during 1929. The men were armed with the Krag rifle, standard weapon of the Guardia, had khaki uniforms and wore campaign hats, around which they placed their only identification, an inch-and-one-half blue and white ribbon.[25] Their most distinguishing characteristic was intense political partisanship; not being members of the Guardia, they were freed from the nonpartisan requirements of that force and most were intense supporters of General Moncada.[26] The character of the officers was debatable at best. Commander of one of the columns was General Juan Escamilla, a Mexican who had fled to Nicaragua after participating in the De la Huerta revolt and later served General Moncada in the 1926–1927 civil war. The commander of the Marine patrol that accompanied his force considered him an adventurer and the State Department openly expressed alarm at this appointment.[27]

Despite such unpromising material, hope persisted in some

quarters that this force might solve the problem of combatting Sandino. General Feland saw their chief virtue as a reputed ability to distinguish between guerrillas and peaceful civilians, thus solving the major problem of identifying the enemy.[28] Once in the field, however, the *voluntarios* proved of little worth. One column's major accomplishment was to violate the Honduran border, setting off an acrimonious international dispute.[29] The other group, led by General Escamilla, did manage to kill one Sandinista, but spent most of its time terrorizing local inhabitants, creating a major refugee problem and causing many to join Sandino in order to survive.[30] An official Marine report described the *voluntarios* as "poorly led," "undisciplined," and more expensive than the Guardia, requiring constant supervision to prevent them from committing excesses against their political enemies.[31] With the Marines no longer supporting the force and the State Department pressing for their elimination, this experiment came to an unlamented end in August 1929 with the disbanding of the entire force.[32] The project for supplementing the Guardia with some type of "National Army," modeled on traditional Nicaraguan military patterns, however, did not die with the *voluntarios.* It was to be raised, in varying forms, again and again throughout the period of American intervention.

Despite the *voluntario* fiasco, Sandino's fortunes seemed to have reached a low point. Hoping for help from abroad, he had written in January to Mexican President Emilio Portes Gil, asking permission to come to Mexico and confer with him.[33] This request placed Portes Gil, who admired Sandino, but did not want to jeopardize relations with the United States, in an awkward position. The Mexican President discussed his problem quite frankly with the American Ambassador, Dwight Morrow. Ultimately they agreed that in return for the United States' raising no objection to the visit, Portes Gil would keep the guerrilla chieftain in Merida, Yucatan, and not allow him to set up a base of operations within Mexico.[34] Secretary of State Kellogg readily approved this arrangement, noting that he "would prefer to have Sandino in Mexico, under surveillance than in Costa Rica, Guatemala or Honduras where he might otherwise go."[35] Because of various delays, Sandino did not arrive in Mexico until June 1929. Once there, he was, as promised, quickly sent to Merida where, except for a brief visit with President Portes Gil in Mexico City, he was to remain for nearly ten months.[36]

Sandino's absence did not end the fighting in Nicaragua, but it did reduce it considerably. To end even this activity the new American Minister, West Point graduate Matthew Hanna, proposed a program of road-building in areas of guerrilla activity. This would not only provide easier access for counterguerrilla forces, but would also provide employment for local residents, in the hope of causing them to transfer their loyalties from Sandino to the government.[37] In August 1929 an effort was made to put part of this program into action, but limited funds and Moncada's insistence on using it to employ personal favorites such as General Escamilla made it generally ineffective and it was ended in September 1930.[38]

The Guardia as well as the road-building program suffered from lack of funds in 1930. The onset of the Depression produced a crisis in Nicaraguan finances and, since the Guardia consumed a quarter of the government's income, President Moncada was determined to cut his expenses.[39] The State Department opposed any cut in the Guardia's strength, but, aware of the depth of the financial crisis, agreed to reexamine the possibility of supplementing it with auxiliary forces. One possibility, favored by Minister Hanna, was to reestablish municipal police (under Guardia control, but paid by the towns in which they served) throughout the nation. Hanna argued that this would not only cut Guardia expenses without reducing the force available for combat operations, but would also reduce the growing friction between the Guardia and the civil population arising from the exercise of police powers.[40]

The Marines favored an alternate plan which would supplement the Guardia with local citizens trained as an emergency auxiliary. Urban areas were encouraged to form local volunteer defense groups whose members, called *cívicos,* would be issued arms by the local Guardia commander whenever Sandinista activity in their area became threatening. In rural areas companies and landowners were encouraged to hire watchmen who would be paid by them, but enlisted as *cívicos* "to bring them under Guardia control."[41] The *cívico* plan was eventually put into effect, providing a definite, but limited aid to the Guardia's budgetary and personnel problems. They were, however, strictly a defensive organization and could contribute little to any offensive attempts to eliminate Sandino's forces.

President Moncada's proposed solution to both budgetary and military problems was a revival, with a few modifications, of his old *voluntario* scheme (now called *auxiliares*). Discussion concerning the formation of such a force began in April 1930. Moncada's proposals were presented to the Americans by his Sub-Secretary for Foreign Affairs, General Anastasio Somoza. The Americans showed little enthusiasm for this approach, so Moncada temporarily dropped the idea.[42]

While Moncada and the Americans were debating ways of cutting Guardia expenses, Sandino was planning his return to Nicaragua. In April 1930 he slipped away from his Mexican hosts and made his way back to his native land. Conditions in Nicaragua had changed during his absence. The Marines had been pulled back to the larger towns and, except for air support, active combat operations had been turned over to the Guardia.[43] This reduced the forces available for counterinsurgency campaigns, forcing the Guardia's Marine officers to seek other means of dealing with the guerrillas. Since much of the population in the thinly settled provinces of Jinotega and Nueva Segovia were, if not part-time guerrillas, at least sympathetic to Sandino, the Guardia commander at Ocotal suggested a massive forced resettlement program for the area. After the population was removed, this proposal called for the destruction of all buildings in the area and for treating as enemies any who remained.[44] President Moncada approved this idea, but efforts to put it into practice were disastrous. Thousands of refugees poured into Matagalpa and Jinotega where no preparations had been made for them. When word of this reached the American Minister, who had not been consulted, he immediately urged Moncada to end the program. Moncada promptly complied with this "request."[45] It was too late, however, to prevent the episode from hurting the Guardia's image in the area and, consequently, increasing Sandino's local support just at the time he returned to action.

Sandino announced his return by gathering nearly 400 men near Jinotega and preparing to attack that city. His plans were upset when this concentration was discovered and attacked by Marine aircraft. These attacks and a ground assault by the Jinotega garrison forced Sandino to abandon his plans and disperse his force.[46] Despite this fiasco, his return encouraged his men and from June 1930 until the end of the American intervention the Guardia Nacional would know few periods of rest or security.

Twice during 1930 the Guardia attempted to crush Sandino's forces with major, sweeping offensives and both times these efforts failed. While all available Guardia patrols tramped through the jungle, searching for the guerrillas, bands of Sandinistas slipped around their flanks and raided other areas virtually stripped of protection.[47]

A more effective means of controlling the guerrillas was adopted in the mountainous area around Jinotega. Here the Guardia's Company M, commanded by Captain Lewis B. (Chesty) Puller and Lieutenant William Lee, established a classic pattern of counterinsurgency patrolling. The basic plan of operations was simple; garrisons were maintained in key towns while Puller and Lee led thirty Guardia enlisted men on highly mobile patrols against any reported Sandinista bands.[48] Actually Company M maintained two patrols, one of which remained in Jinotega while the other operated in the field. This assured that in an emergency, the garrison could always send out a fresh patrol.[49]

Though often in combat, Company M was never defeated and became, in time, the terror of guerrilla bands throughout Central Nicaragua. The key to its success was its mobility and freedom, due to a lack of any defensive assignments, to move to any sector.[50] Puller recruited local Indians for his command, feeling that for endurance, loyalty, and combat ability they had few equals. The Indians respected Puller in turn and as his fame spread, they flocked into Jinotega, begging to join Company M.[51] Puller was not the only Marine who preferred recruiting Indians over any other citizens of Nicaragua. In camp or on garrison duty Indians presented some problems, including a tendency to get drunk, but on patrol they would "hike day after day under the most trying conditions and remain cheerful throughout," rarely complaining and often looking forward to a "good fight."[52]

Company M's activities did not go unnoticed by Sandino. He placed a price of 5,000 córdobas on Puller's head and his supporters circulated a host of atrocity stories concerning both Puller and his second-in-command, William Lee.[53] No one ever collected the 5,000 córdobas, but the atrocity stories have continued down to the present day.[54]

Unfortunately for the Guardia, Company M was rather unique and the situation in other areas remained critical. A plan was introduced to organize eight similar units, distributing them throughout the most active combat areas, but the lack of funds kept this from ever being accomplished.[55] The failure of the Guardia offensives in 1930, coupled with a guerrilla attack on

New Year's Eve which killed eight of ten Marines on a Patrol repairing telephone lines, set the stage for a very active and perilous 1931.[56]

The death of the eight Marines greatly increased pressures in the United States to withdraw Americans from combat in Nicaragua and made the State Department somewhat more receptive to President Moncada's continued pressure to create a force of *auxiliares*. The Guardia's *Jefe Director,* General McDougal, Minister Hanna, and Secretary of State Stimson now agreed to allow the formation of a 500-man force of *auxiliares,* provided that they were "subject to the exclusive administration and control of the Jefe Director of the Guardia Nacional."[57] Moncada, who objected to tight Guardia controls, now proposed reducing the force to 125 men and appointing two Nicaraguans to field-grade ranks to serve as "advisors" with the *auxiliares.* Both Hanna and McDougal rejected these proposals, fearing that the Nicaraguan "advisors" would "introduce complications, misunderstandings and possibly divided control."[58] This dispute lasted several months. During this period the Guardia's position became even more vulnerable when Secretary of State Stimson announced that 1,000 of the 1,500 Marines in Nicaragua would be withdrawn during 1931 and the remainder, except for those serving directly with the Guardia, would be confined to an instructional battalion in Managua and a single aviation squadron.[59] The Nicaraguan government did agree to furnish funds to expand the Guardia by an additional 500 men who were to be used exclusively in combat areas, but before this buildup could take place, Sandino struck again.

In April 1931 the guerrillas launched a series of major attacks against Nicaragua's isolated East Coast. With the support of the local Deputy in the Nicaraguan Congress, Adolfo Cockburn, several Sandinista columns managed to penetrate deep into the area before being detected. One force, commanded by Pedro Blandón, seized the headquarters of the American-owned Bragman's Bluff Lumber Company, massacring the American and British employees and sacking the company town. A Guardia patrol that arived later was ambushed and driven back to Puerto Cabezas. Meanwhile another guerrilla column briefly seized the northernmost settlement on Nicaragua's east coast, Cabo Gracias a Dios, and panic began to spread among Americans in Puerto Cabezas.[60] At this point the American chargé in Managua, Willard Beaulac, asked the Navy to dispatch a Special Service Squadron cruiser to Puerto Cabezas. This action received considerable criticism as both the Squadron's commander and the Guardia's *Jefe Director* questioned Beaulac's right to make such a request and Secretary of State Stimson complained that the action was taken without consulting either himself or the Secretary of the Navy.[61] A cruiser was dispatched and a force landed, but Secretary Stimson made it clear that in the future he would approve such landings "only when it was absolutely to save the lives of American and foreign people excluding property."[62] The entire situation angered the Secretary and led him to question the Guardia's organization and leadership. On April 15, he telegraphed the American Minister in Managua a report that four separate "bandit" columns were moving on the East Coast and added that such developments "without earlier warning would seem to indicate a serious lack in the leaders of the Guardia."[63]

Stimson's comments touched upon the continuing failure to develop an effective and reliable intelligence system. This was due, in large part, to the support Sandino enjoyed from the inhabitants of the areas in which he operated. This not only denied information to the Guardia, it also provided Sandino with an extremely effective intelligence service of his own, keeping him well informed of Guardia movements.[64] Captain Puller was once informed that before he could hope to catch Sandino, he would have to eliminate all the spies in Jinotega, a task which, unless one were willing to shoot or otherwise remove the majority of the population, was probably impossible.[65]

Guardia forces from other East Coast points were rushed to Puerto Cabezas to prevent that port from being overrun. For a while the situation was critical, but after a sharp exchange in which the guerrilla chief, Blandón, was killed, the Sandinistas withdrew from the area.[66] At the same time additional naval vessels were dispatched to Cabo Gracias a Dios and to Bluefields.[67] The guerrillas, however, were withdrawing and the vessels soon returned to Panama.

Severe as was the damage done on these raids, it pales into insignificance beside the catastrophe which a much more powerful force inflicted on Managua. On March 31, 1931, that city was devastated by an earthquake and subsequent fire. The Guardia compound at the Campo de Marte, including the new Military Academy, was destroyed. Two Guardia officers were killed and three others injured when the National Penitentiary also collapsed.[68]

Immediately following the quake, the Guardia was called upon to provide emergency medical aid, ensure food distribution, and fight the fires that raged throughout the city. This last task proved doubly difficult as the city's water supply had been destroyed in the quake.[69] In desperation, the Marines and Guardia used dynamite to try to halt the flames, giving rise to later rumors that they had deliberately destroyed much of the city. Even with their efforts some fires burned for five days, but most of the destruction was confined to the downtown area.[70] The Guardia was also assigned the tasks of burying the dead, preventing looting, and reestablishing communications between Managua and the outside world. For their efforts sixteen Guardia officers received Presidential Gold Medals of Merit from the Nicaraguan Government.[71] In this case, at least, the Guardia and its American officers contributed to the saving, rather than thc taking of lives in Nicaragua.

Taking advantage of the confusion following this disaster, the guerrillas now moved their attacks inland. They suffered a major loss in May when one of their most able generals, Miguel Angel Ortez, was killed, but they gained a measure of revenge for this the following month when General Pedrón Altamirano ambushed another Guardia patrol, killing both American officers and one Nicaraguan enlisted man.[72] The officers were largely responsible for their own defeat. They had stopped inside a small house to eat without taking the elementary precaution of first posting a guard outside. This allowed Pedrón to position his men before opening fire, making his victory almost inevitable.[73]

The conflict between the Guardia and Sandino continued to escalate into the summer. Action reached a peak in July when the Guardia reported fourteen contacts with the guerrillas and lost two killed and fourteen wounded.[74] By fall, fighting was again spreading into new, hitherto peaceful areas. An especially threatening development occurred in November 1931, when two guerrilla columns, under Generals Juan Pablo Umanzor and Juan Gregorio Colindres, invaded the thickly settled Department of León. They occupied the sugar production center of Chichigalpa, throwing the department into a panic. This forced the State Department to take two unpleasant steps: giving consent to Moncada's long-deferred plan to organize a force of *auxiliares* and again sending Marines outside of Managua, this time as guards on trains between the capital and Corinto.[75] These actions freed enough Guardia to drive the rebels back into the hills following several sharp engagements.

The new *auxiliares* worked out surprisingly well. Initially three hundred were raised, with the men being paid $12 a month plus uniforms and a $.20-a-day food allowance. Placed under Guardia regulations and command, they were used to supplement combat patrols as conditions seemed to warrant. The program was continued through 1932, during which 250 additional *auxiliares* were recruited.[76] Anxious to speed their own withdrawal the Americans now dropped their opposition to this force. Indeed, less than a month before the final withdrawal, the last American *Jefe Director* specifically requested permission from President Moncada to recruit an additional 100 *auxiliares.*[77]

The fighting in 1931 had clearly demonstrated that the Guardia even with Marine air support, was hard pressed to contain, let alone destroy, Sandino's forces. In November the American chargé, Willard Beaulac, glumly noted: "The bandit situation is as grave or graver than at any time since I have been in Nicaragua."[78] Nevertheless, 1932 opened on a quiet note with the Guardia reporting only five light contacts and no casualities during January. During February, however, there were fifteen clashes with four guardsmen killed and eight others including one *cívico,* wounded.[79] This pace continued for much of the rest of the year, with 104 contacts between Guardia and guerrilla forces reported from April through September.[80]

Throughout the fighting fairly accurate reports were kept of Marine and Guardia casualties, but since the guerrillas usually carried off their dead and wounded, estimates of their losses were often unreliable. During the years of fighting with Sandino, 122 combined Marine and Guardia combat deaths were reported. The Guardia alone reported 1,115 guerrillas killed in this same period, but this total is undoubtedly exaggerated.[81] An example of the problems involved in reporting Sandinista casualties occurred in March 1932, when two Guardia patrols mistakenly fired upon each other. One patrol soon realized its error and broke off the contact, but the other reported this conflict as a clash with 200 "bandits" and claimed to have killed at least two of them. In reality the force they had engaged consisted of twenty-seven Guardia and it had suffered no losses.[82]

The Nicaraguan presidential election overshadowed the fight with Sandino during the fall of 1932. The victorious candidate was Liberal Juan Bautista Sacasa, the former Vice-President. His victory raised hopes that, following American withdrawal, Sandino would reach terms with the man he had formerly fought for. The election did not influence the conflict for the rest of 1932, however, as twenty-seven contacts, costing the Guardia three killed and six wounded, were reported during November and December.[83]

The most spectacular of these engagements occurred less than a week before the Marines departed. As one of his last official acts, President Moncada planned to dedicate a new section of the National Railway. Sandino, who hated Moncada, hoped to use this occasion to strike a final blow at his former commander, but the Guardia heard of his plans and sent Captain Puller, seven lieutenants, and sixty picked men to thwart him. They surprised 250 men, under General Umanzor, who were busily engaged in looting the railroad camp's commissary. In the ensuing battle the guerrillas were badly beaten, even being forced for once to leave their dead behind. Thirty guerrillas were lost in this engagement, against Guardia casualties of only three killed and three wounded.[84] The new line was peacefully inaugurated two days later.

In more than five years of warfare the Guardia and the Marines failed to eliminate Sandino, leaving him as great a threat in January 1933 as he had been at any previous point in his career. On the other hand, the guerrillas, except for occasional daring forays, had been largely confined to isolated, thinly populated sections of Nicaragua and had never taken a major city. The campaign was a frustrating one for the Guardia, but at the end of 1932 they showed no signs of being ready to abandon the fight. How the struggle would progress without American officers and American air support remained to be seen.

NOTES

1. See the works previously cited in Chapter 3 by Macaulay, Selser, and Cummins and also John Milton Wearmouth, "The Second Marine Intervention in Nicaragua: 1927–1932" (M.A. thesis, Georgetown University, 1952).

2. *New York Times,* July 19, 1927, p. 10.

3. Eberhardt to Kellogg, July 20, 1927, *Foreign Relations,* 1927, III, pp. 441–42.

4. Eberhardt to Kellogg, July 17, 1927, *Foreign Relations,* 1927 III, p. 440.

5. Major Oliver Floyd, "Field Message Number 4, July 26, 1927," Nicaragua Microfilm, Reel 10, MCHA.

6. Gregorio Selser, *Sandino, General de los hombres libres,* Vol. I (Buenos Aires: Editorial Triángulo, 1958), pp. 288–90.

7. "Combat Operations in Nicaragua," *Marine Corps Gazette* XIV (March 1929) 25–26.

8. Kellogg to Eberhardt, July 27, 1927, NA RG 59 817.00/4953b.

9. Munro to Kellogg, October 18, 1927, *Foreign Relations,* 1927, III, pp. 448–49.

10. Neill Macaulay, *The Sandino Affair* (Chicago: Quadrangle Books, 1967), p. 96.

11. The Secretary of the Navy to the Commander, Special Service Squadron, December 9, 1927, NA RG 59, 817.1051/(no document number).

12. "Combat Operations in Nicaragua" *Marine Corps Gazette* XIV (June 1929) 84.

13. Macaulay, *Sandino Affair,* pp. 98–104.

14. Ibid., pp. 109–11.

15. Ibid., pp. 96–98.

16. Lt. Wilburt Brown to Major E. N. McClellan, November 20, 1930, Wilburt S. Brown Papers (United States Marine Corps History and Museums Division, Washington Navy Yard, Washington, D.C.).

17. Rear Admiral David F. Sellers to Sandino, January 20, 1928, in Rear Admiral David Foote Sellers, USN, Papers (Naval Historical Foundation Collection, Library of Congress, Washington, D.C.). Cited hereafter as Sellers Papers; Sandino to Sellers, February 3, 1928, *Foreign Relations,* 1928, III, p. 569.

18. Telegram to General Frank McCoy, March 3, 1928, NA RG 59, 817.00/5444a.

19. McCoy to Kellogg, March 5, 1928, NA RG 59, 817.00/5450.

20. Smith et al., *Review,* pp. 310–11.

21. Moncada's efforts to utilize the Guardia for his own political purposes are described in Chapter 5.

22. Wearmouth, "Second Marine Intervention," p. 94.

23. Eberhardt to Kellogg, January 22, 1929, NA RG 59, 817.1051/238.

24. Eberhardt to Kellogg, March 16, 1929, *Foreign Relations,* 1929, III, p. 552.

25. Major Herman H. Hanneken, "A Discussion of the Voluntario Troops in Nicaragua," *Marine Corps Gazette* XXVI (November 1942) 247.

26. Report, Headquarters, 2nd Brigade, USMC, July 18, 1929, NA RG 59, 817.1051/(no document number).

27. Hanneken, "Voluntario Troops," p. 248; Kellogg to Eberhardt, March 12, 1929, *Foreign Relations,* 1929, III, pp. 551–52.

28. *New York Times,* January 29, 1929, p. 20.

29. Macaulay, *Sandino Affair,* pp. 142–43.

30. Ibid., p. 143; Colonel Francisco Gaitán, G.N., "Historia de la Guardia Nacional de Nicaragua," Chapter VI (pages not numbered), unpublished ms., copy in possession of author.

31. Report Headquarters, 2nd Brigade, USMC, July 18, 1929, NA RG 59, 817.1051/ (no document number).

32. The American Minister to Nicaragua, Matthew Hanna, to Secretary of State Stimson, June 12, 1929, *Foreign Relations,* 1929, III, p. 575; Report, Headquarters, 2nd Brigade, USMC, July 18, 1929, NA RG 59, 817.1051/(no document number).

33. Sandino to President Emilio Portes Gil, printed in Selser, *Sandino,* II, pp. 59–60.

34. Emilio Portes Gil, *Quince años de política Mexicana,* 2nd ed. (Mexico, D.F: Ediciones Botas, 1941),pp 342–48; Ambassador Dwight Morrow to Kellogg, February 21, 1929, and Morrow to Stimson, April 30, 1929, *Foreign Relations* 1929, III, 581–82 and 585–86.

35. Kellogg to Morrow, February 25, 1925, *Foreign Relations,* 1929, III, pp. 583–84.

36. Macaulay, *Sandino Affair,* pp. 148–50 and 157–60.

37. Hanna to Stimson, June 12, 1929, and June 13, *Foreign Relations,* 1929, III, pp. 575–76 and 696.

38. Smith et al., *Review,* pp. 100–101; Lejeune Cummins, *Quijote on a Burro* (Mexico, D.F.: Impresoro Azteca, 1958), pp. 81–82; Hanna to Stimson, October 2 1930, NA RG 59, 817.1051/435.

39. Memorandum, Hanna to Dana Munro, Division of Latin American Affairs, March 18, 1930, NA RG 59, 817.1051/397.

40. Ibid.; Hanna to Stimson, November 29, 1930, NA RG 59, 817.1051/464.

41. Smith et al., *Review,* p.17.

42. Hanna to Stimson, May 15, 1930, NA RG 59, 817.1051/400.

43. Macaulay , *Sandino Affair,* p. 161.

44. Hanna to Stimson, June 6, 1930, NA RG 59, 817.00/6673.

45. Hanna to Francis White, June 7, 1930, NA RG 59, 817.00/6709; Hanna to Stimson, June 6, 1930, NA RG 59, 817.00/6673.

46. Macaulay, *Sandino Affair,* pp. 166–67.

47. Ibid., pp. 166–82; Smith et al., *Review,* pp. 29–31.

48. Evans F. Carlson, "The Guardia Nacional de Nicaragua," *Marine Corps Gazette* XXI (August 1937) 15–16.

49. Interview with Lt. Gen. Smith, Alexandria, Va., November 1965.

50. Smith et al., *Review,* p. 37.

51. Interview with Lt. Gen. Smith, Alexandria, Va., May 1964; Puller and Lee Tapes; U.S. Marine Corps Museum History Office, Navy Yard, Washington, D.C.

52. Capt. William L. Bales, "The Guardia Nacional de Nicaragua," *Leatherneck* XV (October 1932) 19.

53. Burke Davis, *Marine! The Life of Lt. Gen. Lewis B. (Chesty) Puller, USMC (ret.)* (Boston: Little, Brown, 1962), p. 76.

54. Macaulay, *Sandino Affair,* p. 229. For examples of these stories, see Frente Unitario Nicargüense, *Intervención Sangrienta: Nicaragua y su Pueblo* (Caracas: n.p., 1961); and Domingo Ibarra Grijalva, *The Last Night of General Augusto César Sandino* (New York: Vantage Press, 1973).

55. Smith et al., *Review,* p. 38.

56. Macaulay, *Sandino Affair,* p. 183.

57. Hanna to Stimson, January 8, 1931, and January 9, 1931, *Foreign Relations,* 1931, II, pp. 833–34.

58. Hanna to Stimson, January 14, 1931, *Foreign Relations,* 1931, II, p. 836.

59. Stimson to Hanna, February 14, 1931; and Secretary of the Navy Adams to Stimson, February 24, 1931, *Foreign Relations,* 1931, II, pp. 844–45.

60. Macaulay, *Sandino Affair,* pp. 186–92.

61. Stimson Diary, XV, April 12, 1931; Willard L Beaulac, *Career Ambassador* (New York: Macmillan, 1951), p. 125.

62. Stimson Diary, XV, April 4, 1931.

63. Stimson to Hanna, April 16, 1931, *Foreign Relations,* 1931, II, p. 807.

64. Smith et al., *Review,* p. 34.

65. Puller and Lee tapes.

66. Macaulay, *Sandino Affair,* pp. 194–98.

67. Stimson to the American Vice Consul at Bluefields, Rowe, April 18, 1931, and Rowe to Stimson, April 18, 1931, *Foreign Relations,* 1931, II, pp. 812–13.

68. Smith et al., *Review,* p. 126.

69. Beaulac, *Career Ambassador,* p. 132.

70. Smith et al., *Review,* p. 126.

71. Hanna to Stimson, April 5, 1931, *Foreign Relations,* 1931, II, pp. 792–93; Smith et al., *Review,* pp. 128–34.

72. 1st Lt. J. Ogden Brauer to Area Commander, May 18, 1931, NA RG 127; Major Julian C. Smith to *Jefe Director,* G.N., June 18, 1931, printed in Smith et al., *Review,* pp. 260–63.

73. Interview with Lt. Gen. Smith, Alexandria, Va., May 1964.

74. Anastasio Somoza García, *El verdadero Sandino,* (Managua: Tipografía Robelo, 1936), pp. 274–75; Beaulac to Stimson, October 19, 1931, NA RG 59, 817.1051/570; *La Noticia* (Managua), October 23, 1931, p.1.

75. Beaulac to Stimson, November 23, 1931, and Stimson to Beaulac, November 19, 1931, *Foreign Relations,* 1931, II, pp. 825–27.

76. Smith et al., *Review,* p. 16.

77. General Calvin B. Matthews to President Moncada, December 5, 1932, Nicaraguan Records, Box 12, File 32, MCHA.

78. Beaulac to Stimson, November 25, 1931, *Foreign Relations,* 1931, II, pp. 827–28.

79. Smith et al., *Review,* pp. 369–72.

80. Macaulay, *Sandino Affair,* p. 225.

81. Ibid., p. 239.

82. 2nd Lt. Wallace D. Martin to Department Commander, Matagalpa, March 17, 1932, NA RG 127.

83. Smith et al., *Review,* pp. 401–07.

84. Ibid., p. 407; Carlson, "The Guardia Nacional," p. 19.

V

POLITICS AND PERSONALITIES NICARAGUAN AND AMERICAN

A variety of political problems dogged the Guardia from its inception. In Nicaragua these included conflicts over its constitutionality, efforts to destroy its nonpartisan character, conflicts between the two major parties in which the Guardia became involved, disputes over the budget, and the involvement of the Guardia in supervising elections. On the American side there were conflicts between military and civilian officials, disputes within the military itself, and the pressure of opposition to American intervention from within the United States. On a wider scale, problems were created by the opposition throughout Latin America to American intervention in Nicaragua.

Political problems within Nicaragua greatly affected the Guardia's development. Those involving the signing of the Guardia agreement between the United States and Nicaragua and the unsuccessful efforts to ratify it during the Díaz administration have already been detailed. Not content with blocking ratification of the agreement, the opposition in the Nicaraguan Congress, led by General Chamorro, also strove to keep Guardia funds out of the regular budget and to reduce the number of American officers attached to the force.[1] Chamorro also managed to prevent Congressional passage of the American-designed electoral law, forcing President Díaz to issue it as a Presidential Decree.[2]

The State Department hoped that the results of the 1928 elections would resolve many of these political obstacles to the Guardia's development, but conducting the elections produced its own set of problems. The head of the American Electoral Commission was an Army officer, Brigadier General Frank R. McCoy. General McCoy had considerable prior experience in Latin America, having directed Cuban financial affairs under the

American military government from 1900 to 1902 and having served as Military Attaché in Mexico in 1917. He had also been Chief of Staff of the Woods-Forbes investigation mission in the Philippines and had served as Director of the Army's Bureau of Insular Affairs, the unit that administered the customs receiverships in Haiti and the Dominican Republic.[3] General McCoy also possessed important personal qualifications including an ability to speak Spanish and a reputation for carrying out his assignments in a firm, consistent, and diplomatic manner.[4]

The State Department was quite satisfied with McCoy's appointment. Had a civilian been appointed, the Department "would have had to pay his salary out of its very small emergency fund or would have had to ask for an appropriation," a course which the controversy over the American presence in Nicaragua made highly undesirable. In addition, the Department felt that the military situation made it necessary to appoint, as Chairman of the Electoral Commission, someone with military experience who could "control the Marines."[5] Under such conditions General McCoy, who had the firm support of Stimson, seemed the logical choice. The State Department, however, overlooked the problems of interservice rivalry which were created by placing an Army officer in a position where he would exercise some control over Marine operations.

The Guardia Nacional occupied an important position in American plans for supervising the elections. In October 1927, the American chargé had noted that unless the Guardia was expanded sufficiently to exercise control over all the important departments in Nicaragua, it would be "impossible to hold a satisfactory election next year."[6] On March 21, 1928, the State Department asked President Díaz to turn over control of the Guardia to General McCoy. At the same time the Secretary of State expressed the hope that McCoy would conduct Guardia operations through the appropriate Marine officers.[7] President Díaz, as usual, complied with the State Department's wish. His decree establishing the electoral law included an article giving General McCoy "authority to command the services of the National Constabulary (Guardia Nacional), to give that force such orders as he may deem necessary and appropriate to insure a free and impartial election."[8]

The Navy was upset by this action and by what they felt was McCoy's tendency to interfere in military matters, especially his effort to investigate the overall military situation for the State Department. Within a few weeks Admiral Sellers, Commander of the Special Service Squadron and ranking Naval officer in the area, was complaining that the General was "in everybody's mess, but nobody's wash."[9]

While voicing complaints privately, the Admiral worked openly to minimize possible conflicts of authority. He sent McCoy a copy of the Secretary of the Navy's letter of December 9, 1927, governing relations among military units in Nicaragua, and pointed out that some features of this order were in direct conflict with President Díaz' decree. Sellers added that he would ask the Secretary of the Navy to modify his orders to eliminate this conflict and pledged that he and those under his command would "render all possible assistance to the personal representative of the President of the United States in carrying out the important work in Nicaragua upon which he is now engaged."[10]

The amiable tone of this communication proved somewhat ephemeral. On April 18, during a meeting at the American Legation, General McCoy criticized the Marines' campaign against Sandino, declaring "unless you get Sandino by a month from now you will have failed and I will so report to the State Department."[11] Admiral Sellers complained to the Navy Department that the General's statement "would seem to indicate that he is under the impression that he too has certain responsibilities relative to the conduct of operations over and above the obligation simply to make recommendations to the President and the Secretary of State."[12] Sellers was further upset because General McCoy, bypassing the normal chain of command, was issuing orders directly to the Guardia's commander, Lieutenant Colonel (Brigadier General in the Guardia) Elias Beadle. The Admiral felt that McCoy should go through regular channels and only make recommendations, not issue direct orders.[13] Early in May a direct conference between Sellers and McCoy temporarily resolved their disputes, with the General disclaiming any illusions "as to his responsibility for the conduct of military operations in Nicaragua."[14]

The conflict revived in July when, without consulting either Sellers or General Feland, the Marine Brigade Commander, General McCoy ordered Beadle to distribute Guardia personnel only at departmental capitals. Sellers complained that such actions resulted in the Guardia, whose mission he saw as "almost identical" with that of the Marine Brigade, "being completely divorced officially from the military operations of this Brigade, the organization immediately responsible to our Government for military activities in Nicaragua."[15] The Navy Department may well have sympathized with Sellers' complaints, but McCoy had the confidence of the State Department, and nothing was done to change the situation.

General McCoy's next dispute involved the Guardia's commander, General Beadle, who opposed the Board of Election's plan to have members of the Guardia seated directly at the tables where Nicaraguans cast their ballots. Beadle feared this plan would leave the Guardia open to charges of partisanship and argued that their duties should be confined to efforts to maintain order.[16] McCoy, however, opposed having Marines exercise such civil police functions and expressed his desire that at least two members of the Guardia help supervise each polling place.[17] This proposal was endorsed by General Feland, who argued that the Guardia's closer contacts with Nicaraguan citizens would make them more efficient in dealing with complaints.[18]

While unwilling to use Marines to investigate electoral complaints, the Brigade's Commander evidently had no such compunctions when it came to arresting opponents of the intervention. Toribio Tijerino, the leader of the small, pro-Sandino Nationalist Party, had incurred the wrath of the Marines and, despite McCoy's protests, Feland had him arrested shortly before the election. Pressure from both Eberhardt and McCoy, however, soon forced his release.[19]

Despite such incidents American supervision of both registration and voting in 1928 proved remarkably successful. To curb the traditional Nicaraguan practice of voting at as many precincts as one could reach in a day, each voter's finger was dipped in mercurochrome dye. The Sandinistas denounced the election and circulated a rumor that the dye was poison, but despite such efforts 133,000 Nicaraguans, nearly 90 percent of those eligible, voted, giving General Moncada and the Liberals a decisive 19,000-vote victory.[20] Even the opposition Conservatives, the first party in power in Nicaragua's history to lose an election, acknowledged that the results were valid.[21]

The Marines were greatly relieved to see McCoy's mission conclude and the Army General return to the United States. His presence in Nicaragua had generated fears that the State Department might be considering replacing the Marines attached to the Guardia with Army officers. In October 1928, in an apparent effort to forestall any such action, Colonel L. McCarty Little, Director of Marine Corps Operations and Training, drafted a lengthy memorandum justifying the Corps' involvement in developing armed forces throughout Latin America. The Colonel wrote:

> Questions dealing with Central America have been handled for many years by the State Department whose representatives have been sustained when necessary by our naval forces, the nature of whose duties serves to keep them in close touch with the varying situations which exist there. In other words the support of our diplomatic agents has become and is recognized at home and abroad as a function of the Navy. This is especially true of our relations with Central America. This assignment of functions to the Navy has been endorsed by decision of the joint Army and Navy Board and is more or less recognized by foreign powers. . . .
>
> To take from the Navy a problem it has successfully handled for a century and to assign such duty to the Army of whose functions it is not properly a part would be uneconomic to say the least.
>
> An Army officer assigned in charge of the problems of Nicaragua would under the present system depend mainly upon naval sustenance or rather upon the support of a service with whose technical limitations he is not wholly familiar. Why introduce this possibly jarring note? There certainly appear to be in the Naval service officers of proven ability who would fill the bill and be at all times in understanding relations to our naval forces.
>
> To assign Army officers to the Guardia Nacional is to introduce an additional system of training. Unless the work of those officers who have so far been charged with its development shows an amount of deficiency which warrants a change, an additional system would but cause obstruction. Army officers detailed for duty under Marines would require instruction in our special type of training. Army training placed over a Marine system would to a large degree undo the results of last year's work. Marines have so far proved their ability, why then not allow them to carry on?[22]

Admiral Sellers supported the Marines' stand, observing that:

> from my experience during the past year with Army officers in Nicaragua I am very decidedly of the opinion that the best results will not be obtained by mixing the Army with the Navy and Marine Corps in matters like the present operation. . . . To import a lot of Army officers whose standards, traditions and methods differ from ours does not tend to promote harmony, efficiency or develop esprit de corps.[23]

The adamant stand of the Navy and Marines upon this point prevailed. No Army officers were attached to the Guardia and, in both 1930 and 1932, a Naval officer served as Chairman of the Electoral Commision, thereby preventing any additional interservice rivalries during the intervention.

While General McCoy's departure, following the 1928 elections, resolved one set of problems facing the Marines and the Guardia, the inauguration of the victorious General Moncada as President created numerous new difficulties. Ambitious and somewhat Machiavellian, Moncada, unlike his predecessor, Adolfo Díaz, was determined not to be an American puppet.

Realizing that he would have little success in confrontations with a unified American position in Nicaragua, the new President sought ways to divide the military and diplomatic representatives of the United States. He began by cultivating the Brigade's Commander, General Feland. Even before his inauguration, Moncada had written Admiral Sellers to suggest that Feland be given the authority to coordinate the "work of such officials as I may be able to secure from your Government," adding that he believed the General "better equipped to undertake this work than any other person."[24] Feland was attracted by this proposal, which would have made him virtually an American High Commissioner in Nicaragua. He wrote the Marine Corps Commandant, urging him to seek State Department approval, adding that his appointment would "be the best consolidation of our position that the Navy Department, with the Marine Corps as its active agent, is the one most concerned with the carving out of American policies in Latin America, particularly in Central America."[25]

Despite endorsements by both Feland and Sellers, the American Minister had no sympathy for Moncada's proposal. Highly suspicious of possible military encroachments on State Department prerogatives, Eberhardt had already clashed with Sellers and Feland over a Nicaraguan proposal to give them the rank of "ministers plenipotentiary and envoys extraordinary of the United States."[26] The Minister was generally supported in his opposition to Moncada's proposals by Lieutenant Colonel Elias Beadle, the Guardia's *Jefe Director,* who had earlier offended the Nicaraguan President by refusing to charge, without evidence, soldiers whom Moncada had accused of being criminals.[27] Beadle and Eberhardt had also unsuccessfully opposed Moncada's effort to enlist his political supporters as *voluntarios* and use them in the campaign against Sandino.

By late January 1929, Eberhardt had become convinced that General Feland and President Moncada were conspiring to convert the Guardia into a partisan force with the Marine General virtually functioning as Moncada's Minister of War.[28] A Nicaraguan proposal to place Guardia operations directly under Feland's control was taken as further evidence of such a conspiracy and, with Colonel Beadle's support, Eberhardt urged State Department action to block this effort.[29] This pressure ultimately proved successful as the Chief of Naval Operations, after consultation with the State Department, announced that it would be unwise and illegal to place the Guardia under the Commander of the Marine Brigade since that would make that officer subject to the orders of Nicaragua's President.[30]

After some hesitation, Eberhardt informed the State Department that the continued disputes among American leaders in Nicaragua made it necessary to replace both Beadle and Feland. While defending Beadle's actions, the American Minister recognized that it would be extremely awkward to remove Feland alone. In addition the Nicaraguan President had expressed a lack of confidence in the *Jefe Director,* a situation Eberhardt blamed on Feland's influence.[31]

The day Eberhardt sent his message calling for these replacements, the Navy Department announced that Beadle would be replaced as Guardia commander by Colonel Douglas C. McDougal, a former commander of the American-led Garde d'Haiti.[32] When, however, Feland's transfer was delayed, Eberhardt complained bitterly to the State Department, charging that the General's actions had "seriously damaged the prestige of the Legation, the Guardia and the Marine Corps," adding that his retention would "jeopardize our whole Nicaraguan program."[33]

Admiral Sellers opposed Feland's removal, leading the American Minister to accuse both officers of obstructing United States policy and encouraging Moncada's efforts to convert the Guardia into a partisan political force.[34] Both officers heatedly denied the accusations, which Feland declared were based upon "a single piece of underhand gossip" which the Minister had heard in a Nicaraguan night club. Sellers added that Eberhardt was aware that the charges were false, but persisted in "furnishing the Department of State with . . . gross misinformation which places the Squadron Commander in a false position.[35] With the Special Service Squadron Commander and the American Minister not speaking to each other, it now became necessary to replace them as well as Beadle and Feland and by later 1929 all four had been removed from the Nicaraguan scene.

This entire dispute served to emphasize the primacy of the State Department in determining Nicaraguan policy. Acting under State Department instructions, the Navy Department informed Sellers', Feland's and Beadle's successors that:

> the American Minister in Nicaragua and, in his absence, the Chargé d'Affaires, is the only personal representative of the President of the United States in Nicaragua and that the officers of the American armed forces in Nicaragua should not advise the President of Nicaragua or other Nicaraguan officials independently. Whenever the officers of the American armed forces desire to discuss matters with the President or a Minister of the Cabinet, the Navy Department will arrange that they should request the American Minister or the Chargé d'Affaires to request the interview and take them to it, and that matters in which they may disagree with the Chief of Mission shall not be taken up with the Government of Nicaragua without first being submitted to the Government of the United States for its decision.[36]

Under these guidelines President Moncada could no longer seek American military support for his disputes with the legation. At the same time Marine criticism of State Department policy became more muted. Since officers who continued to oppose established policies could expect no support from their superiors in Washington, most Marines simply followed State Department policy even when it seemed to them to be erroneous. They also avoided close contacts with President Moncada, feeling they had little to gain and much to lose from such relationships. Moncada, in turn, became more difficult to get along with, even forcing one prominent Marine officer, Colonel Clayton B. Vogel, to be removed as the Guardia's Chief of Staff because of his refusal to purge Conservatives from the force.[37] The Guardia's *Jefe Director* complained that "Moncada is a difficult man to do business with. He is a hard drinker and is despotic and erratic to a degree when he is in his cups. He dislikes Americans."[38]

Under these circumstances the Marines found it desirable to carry on, whenever possible, all contacts with the President through a Nicaraguan intermediary. This vital position came to be filled by a personable young Nicaraguan with a fluent command of English, Anastasio Somoza García. Increasingly, American officers tended to take their problems with the Nicaraguan government first to Somoza. In return he transmitted and even explained and gave suggestions as to possible responses for Moncada's messages to the officers. The Marines felt, in the words of the Guardia's last American Chief of Staff, that Somoza "always played the game fairly with us," and they came to develop considerable respect for him.[39] This attitude would prove of inestimable value to General Somoza when it came time to select a Nicaraguan *Jefe Director* for the Guardia Nacional.

President Moncada's maneuvers to gain control over the Guardia were not confined to efforts to influence American officers. The Munro-Cuadra Pasos Agreement had still not been ratified when he took office, so President Moncada tried to have the agreement amended in such a way as to make the force more subject to his control. He claimed that his proposals simply "clarified" the text's meaning, but Minister Eberhardt was convinced that his proposals would "change the agreement so radically as virtually to destroy the purpose for which it was intended."[40] Eberhardt felt that most Nicaraguans wanted a nonpartisan Guardia, but that leaders of both parties were opposed to such a force and would defeat it if they could place the blame for this action upon their opponents. The cure for this situation, the Minister argued, was to have the State Department authorize him, accompanied by the Brigade and Special Service Squadron Commanders, to issue a demand that Moncada push the agreement through Congress without amendments.[41]

In order to justify his efforts to gain control over the Guardia, Moncada began to accuse that force of inefficiency and of squandering its budget on lavish receptions. Eberhardt dismissed this accusation as absurd, noting that during the past year the Guardia had held only five receptions, every one of which was organized at the specific order of Nicaragua's President.[42] At this point Moncada openly stated that he did not believe a nonpartisan military was possible in Nicaragua and, despite State Department objections, proceeded to support major amendments to the Guardia agreement which Congress obediently added before finally ratifying it on February 19, 1929.[43]

The State Department had major objections to virtually every amendment made by the Nicaraguan government. One seemed to limit the Guardia's strength to that originally authorized in the Munro-Cuadra Pasos Agreement, a force entirely too small to deal with Sandino's rebellion. Other changes apparently empowered local Nicaraguan officials to issue orders to the Guardia, made officers subject to local courts for actions taken in the line of duty, and required all American officers attached to the force to have a working knowledge of Spanish, a regulation that would have drastically reduced the number of Marines available for such duty.[44] Moncada had begun to take advantage of the apparent subordination of the Guardia to local political officials, notably the *Jefes Políticos* in each department, who were presidential appointees, even before the amended agreement cleared Congress. On February 12, 1929, his private secretary informed General Beadle that "the Jefe of the Guardia in every Department must obey the Jefe Político in all attributions conferred upon them by law," adding that "the President has the intention of exercising control over the Guardia through his Secretaries of State and his Jefes Políticos."[45]

In May, in an effort to resolve these disputes, the State Department drafted a note for the Nicaraguan government to present to the United States agreeing to interpret the amendments in a manner that would meet American objections.[46] Under Díaz it had been possible for the State Department to draft statements which the Nicaraguan President would later issue as an official statement of his government's policy, but Moncada would have nothing to do with such tactics. A similar effort by the State Department in 1930 proved equally unsuccessful.[47] By the end of that year efforts to secure a Guardia agreement satisfactory to all concerned were overshadowed by disputes over budget allocations, but as late as November 1931 State Department officials were still drafting long memoranda examining the constitutionality of the Munro-Pasos Agreement and the implications of the Nicaraguan amendments to it.[48]

Throughout this period, Moncada continued his efforts to use the force to advance his own political interests. In April 1929, he ordered the Guardia to imprison sixteen of his political opponents, including the editor of *La Nueva Prensa.*[49] This upset the State Department, which urged the Guardia not to make the arrests until the reasons for such actions were known.[50] The Guardia's position was doubly complicated because, having assumed the nation's police duties, it could hardly avoid arresting Nicaraguan citizens upon orders issued by that nation's courts. With the courts under presidential control, Guardia involvement in political arrests became virtually inevitable.

Seeking to avoid the involvement of the Guardia in political arrests, Secretary of State Stimson wrote Moncada that Nicaragua's future depended greatly upon "the establishment of an absolutely non-partisan, non-political Guardia which will devote its entire attention to the preservation of peace, law and order."[51] This appeal made little, if any impression on the Nicaraguan President, who continued ordering political arrests. Justifying his actions with the patently absurd allegation that the Conservatives were plotting with Sandino to murder him and overthrow the government, he had the Guardia arrest more than forty of his enemies and eventually deport eight of them, including Adolfo Ortega Díaz, editor of *La Prensa,* Managua's leading Conservative newspaper.[52]

Opposition attacks on these actions were directed against the Guardia as well as the Moncada administration, alleging that the force had no respect for civil officials, but only for military officers.[53] The State Department also protested the actions, but again without visible result. Moncada continued his efforts to place the Guardia under closer political control. Local Liberal Party leaders were now used to pressure the Guardia to transfer or discharge Conservative officers and men stationed in their areas.[54] This effort apparently met with little success.

In December 1930, President Moncada, again claiming that his life was threatened, arrested additional opposition leaders. This time State Department protests were somewhat muted, perhaps because several of those arrested were accused of involvement in a Communist plot, making them considerably less likely subjects of the Department's sympathies than were the Conservative leaders jailed along with them.[55] Despite constant State Department rebuffs, Moncada also continued efforts to make the Guardia subject to control by local *Jefes Políticos.* In October 1931, he again brought up the subject, writing Secretary of State Stimson to demand that the Guardia be altered to "conform to the laws of this country." In reply Stimson simply pointed out that under Nicaraguan law such proposals would have to pass two sessions of Congress and, since the United States would have withdrawn by that time, such measures were now outside of American concern.[56]

The continuing conflicts with the Moncada administration produced a growing pessimism in the State Department concerning the Guardia's future. A memorandum by Willard Beaulac, then in charge of the Department's Central American desk, clearly expressed these feelings. Beaulac wrote:

> . . . . further direct interference by the President in the internal administrations of the Guardia may be expected. . . . I believe that a continuance of the policy of direct interference, particularly from now on when political passions may be expected to exercise a great influence in the affairs of Nicaragua and when the Guardia Nacional, if it is to be effective, must be more than ever impartial and independent of such political passion, will tend to render the Guardia impotent and will convert it into a tool of partisan politics.[57]

Perhaps the most important of all the conflicts between the State Department and President Moncada involving the Guardia Nacional was that concerned with budget appropriations. In the summer of 1929 Moncada suddenly demanded a complete study of Guardia costs and announced plans to reduce its enlisted strength.[58] This drew sharp protests from the Guardia's American Commander and from the American Legation, but produced a surprisingly mild response from Secretary Stimson, who reminded the Legation that, in making up the budget, the limited resources available to Nicaragua must be kept in mind and the size of the Guardia based upon that nation's minimum needs.[59]

The budget controversy intensified the following year when Nicaragua began to suffer the effects of the world depression. In February, Moncada announced that he wanted Guardia expenses cut to no more than $800,000 annually.[60] Colonel McDougal, the Guardia's *Jefe Director,* wanted an increase in his budget, but receiving no State Department support for this proposal announced that he was prepared to operate, if necessary, on an appropriation of $900,000, although this would require reducing enlisted personnel to 1,800. That in turn would necessitate abandoning many posts in the North. McDougal claimed that a budget of $800,000 would support only 1,500 men, a force too small to carry out the Guardia's assigned missions.[61]

In an effort to resolve this dispute, Matthew Hanna, who was in Washington preparatory to being appointed Minister to Nicaragua, suggested that the proposed budget cuts be approved providing that Guardia duties be confined to "seriously disturbed" areas and that forces of municipal police, paid by the communities they served, handle routine police duties.[62] This plan would also have reduced the involvement of American officers in the arrest of Nicaraguan civilians, but it was turned down by the State Department, which continued to insist that the Guardia remain the only military and police force in Nicaragua. With no plan of its own to offer, the Department attempted to temporize, expressing a desire to "be guided by the wishes of the Nicaraguan Government," but adding that "it would not be disposed to concur in the reduction of the existing force to the point where its efficiency and ability to maintain order was seriously impaired."[63]

The financial crisis eased somewhat during the spring of 1930, but by summer it was again a problem. In addition to pressing for overall reduction in the Guardia's budget, Moncada now called for cuts of up to 20 percent in the salaries paid to American officers.[64] This proposal upset the Marines more than anything since the Beadle-Feland feud. Marine Corps Headquarters argued that the proposed pay cut was "only one cog in the policy to destroy the Guardia. Without asking that the U.S. withdraw the Marines attached to the Guardia he kills it by non-support and thus lays the blame for the death on the United States and attains his end: that of substituting Nicaraguans of his own personal choice for United States Marines."[65]

Colonel McDougal also attacked the proposals, claiming that the United States would either have to greatly reinforce the Marines in Nicaragua in order to make up for cuts in the Guardia or else should withdraw all Marines as rapidly as possible "to avoid becoming involved in the inevitable disorders following the reduction of the Guardia."[66]

Unwilling to accept either of McDougal's proposals, Secretary Stimson held an urgent meeting with Secretary of the Navy Adams, Admiral Pratt, and Marine Generals Fuller and Williams to discuss the problem, but they were unable to formulate any solution.[67] A discussion with President Hoover the following day proved of even less help as the President, bedeviled by the economic crisis, considered the Nicaraguan situation "just one more trouble."[68] The problem was referred back to the American Legation where the Commanders of the Special Service Squadron, the Marine Brigade, and the Guardia met with the American Minister to discuss the situation. This meeting was held November 1, only two weeks before an order of Moncada's reducing the Guardia to 1,500 men was to take effect. The participants agreed that such a reduction would make it impossible to maintain order, but that if local police, trained by and enlisted in the Guardia, but paid by the towns they served, were created and the Guardia maintained at its present strength of 2,000 men until these police could replace 500 of them, the proposed reductions would ultimately be acceptable.[69]

On the results of this and other conferences a letter from Stimson to Moncada was drawn up in which the Secretary of State grudgingly agreed to reducing Guardia strength to under 2,000 enlisted men *after* the creation of an auxiliary force of local police. Stimson warned of the danger of mutiny if the force was not paid on time, adding that the United States would not expose its officers to such a threat. He demanded that the Nicaraguan President give the American Collector General of Customs "explicit and irrevocable instructions" to pay the Guardia's commander on the first of each month enough to maintain a force of 2,000 men until such time as the two governments arrived at a mutual agreement to reduce the force. Stimson made such provision a *sine qua non* for continued American support, bluntly stating that "this government would hesitate to continue to cooperate with the Guardia unless its expenses are met."[70]

Moncada accepted the idea of replacing some Guardia with municipal police, but again asked that American officers' salaries be cut 20 percent and declared that the requirements of foreign bondholders prevented his obtaining the needed funds from the Collector General.[71] In response Stimson did make several concessions. These included reducing the pay of Americans to be detailed to the Guardia, although this was not to apply to those already on duty, cutting the ration allowance from $.25 to $.20 per day and, ultimately, reducing the Guardia to a strength of 160 officers and 1,650 men at an annual cost of $799,652.[72]

These concessions seemingly pleased Moncada, who passed them on to McDougal, taking special care to emphasize that reductions should take place "as conditions permit."[73] Conditions never did permit these cuts. In 1931, an increase in Sandino's activities meant that a larger, not a smaller, force was needed. The formation of a Guardia Municipal, as the urban police were known, continued, but this produced no corresponding cuts in regular Guardia strength.

Early in 1931 Nicaragua's financial situation was eased by a $1,000,000 loan from the International Acceptance Bank. Only $75,000 of this could be spent each month, $15,000 of which was to be spent on the Segovias, which meant in the fight against Sandino. In February, the National Bank of Nicaragua agreed to loan the government an equal amount, permitting expansion of the Guardia to a strength of 2,150 men.[74] Slow expansion continued for most of the rest of the intervention with the force reaching 303 officers, 2,274 enlisted men, and 33 prisoners on September 30, 1932.[75] Thanks, in part, to Sandino, the Guardia emerged from the budget crisis stronger than ever.

American intervention in Nicaragua encountered political difficulties not only in that nation, but at home and throughout the Western Hemisphere as well. While few of these problems directly involved the Guardia, they did affect American policy and therefore helped shape the Guardia's development.

Within the United States, a long-time leader of opposition to American intervention was Senator William E. Borah of Idaho. As early as 1922, Senator Borah had charged that "the people of Nicaragua are being exploited in shameless fashion by American corporations protected by United States Marines."[76] Following the 1926 intervention, Borah, along with Senators Shipstead and Wheeler, introduced resolutions condemning the action.

In 1928 a rash of books and articles, attacking the intervention and demanding immediate withdrawal from Nicaragua, began to appear with contents that ranged from intelligent criticism to wild accounts of alleged atrocities.[77] The Communist-supported All American Anti-Imperialist League held rallies to denounce the Marines and gather funds for medicines for Sandino's troops.[78] In Congress, Americans in Nicaragua were denounced as "ambassadors of death" and Senator Wheeler sarcastically suggested that if Marines were going to fight bandits, they should be sent to Chicago instead of Nicaragua.[79]

As it became obvious that the campaign against Sandino would take years, not weeks, opposition in the United States increased. In 1928 the Senate held detailed hearings on American Naval forces in Nicaragua, hearings that gave opponents of the intervention a major forum for denouncing American policy.[80] In 1929, Congressional opponents made a determined, but unsuccessful, effort to attach a rider to the Naval appropriations bill cutting off all funds for the Marines in Nicaragua.

The growing opposition in Congress strengthened Stimson's determination to end the intervention after Nicaragua's 1932 elections. To demonstrate his determination on this point, the Secretary, in February 1931, had it announced that the Marines would withdraw from combat duty in Nicaragua by June 1 and that the Marine Brigade would be reduced to a training battalion of approximately 500 men, stationed in Managua, plus a small aviation force.[81] The Marines did not fully approve of this policy. The Marine Corps Commandant, Major General B.H. Fuller, testified before a House committee that "it would not do to take the Marines away or the brigade away from Nicaragua, leaving American officers in charge of those Indians because they would be very likely to mutiny and chase our officers out. They will not do that so long as there are 1,000 Marines close by in the country as a reserve and a backing for the officers in the National Guard."[82] Fuller's objections were apparently ignored by both Congress and the State Department and the reduction of the Marine force took place as planned.

Such efforts muted criticism for a time, but by 1932 Stimson could no longer restrain the anti-intervention forces in Congress. When the Navy refused to incur a deficiency expense for the costs of supervising the 1932 elections, Secretary Stimson held long conferences with members of both the House and Senate in an effort to obtain a Congressional appropriation of the needed funds. These efforts, however, proved unavailing as the Senate refused to appropriate any funds for the election and even passed a rider to the Appropriations Bill forbidding the Navy to use funds for that purpose, thereby placing the Senate clearly on record as favoring a prompt end to the intervention. Despite this setback, President Hoover instructed Stimson to get the needed funds from "other sources" and not to interpret the Senate's action as a prohibition against supervising the elections.[83]

Some Americans, of course, favored the intervention, but only those individuals or companies directly involved in Nicaragua were active in making their opinions public. Their continued pleas for expanded American interference in Nicaraguan internal affairs probably did Stimson's cause more harm than good, leading him ultimately to issue his statement that Marines would no longer be sent inland to protect American property in Nicaragua.[84] The opinion of most Americans on Nicaragua was probably best summed up by Will Rogers, who once asked, "Why are we in Nicaragua and what the Hell are we doing there?"[85] By 1932 Stimson may well have been asking himself the same question.

Criticism of American actions in Nicaragua was widespread throughout Latin America. Sandino's efforts received the enthusiastic support of such notable figures as the Mexican educator José Vasconcelos, the Chilean poetess Gabriela Mistral, and the Peruvian politician Victor Raúl Haya de la Torre. Numerous accounts appeared in Spanish, glorifying Sandino and condemning Americans as savages and oppressors of a free people.[86] Sandino's fame even reached China, where one of the Kuomintang's divisions was named after him.[87]

Of much greater concern to the United States was the effect of the intervention on relations with other hemispheric nations. Despite American efforts to keep it off the agenda, the intervention emerged as a major issue during the Sixth International Conference of American States, held in Havana from January 16 to February 20, 1928. Both El Salvador and Argentina urged the Conference to adopt a statement condemning intervention, with the Argentinian delegation declaring that intervention constituted "an attempt against the independence of nations" which no plea of protection for the intervening power's citizens could justify.[88] Secretary of State Hughes defended American policy as designed to secure the peace and independence of Nicaragua and attempted to redefine United States actions as being not intervention, but "interposition of a temporary character."[89]

Despite support from Mexico, Colombia, Honduras, and Argentina, the delegate from El Salvador ultimately withdrew his motion condemning intervention, but the issue was hardly resolved by this action.[90] Latin American opponents of intervention continued to oppose American policy throughout the Hoover administration. They hampered Guardia efforts to close the border with Honduras, kept Mexico from recognizing the Moncada regime, and also provided supplies to Sandino. Their continued attacks on the intervention proved increasingly embarrassing to Stimson in his efforts to mobilize support against Japanese actions in Manchuria, giving him one more reason for wanting to withdraw the Marines from Nicaragua as rapidly as possible.

The net effect of all these conflicts upon the Guardia Nacional is difficult to assess. Within Nicaragua, political problems certainly had adverse effects, diverting the Guardia's attention into political instead of military areas and hampering the recruitment and training of the organization. Most significantly, Moncada's actions left a dangerous heritage of direct involvement of the supposedly nonpartisan Guardia in internal Nicaraguan politics.

Problems encountered in the United States and in that nation's Latin American policy also limited the Guardia's effectiveness. They helped sustain Sandino and, at the same time, had a frustrating effect upon the morale of the Marines stationed with the Guardia.[91] Probably their most important influence was in greatly increasing pressure for American withdrawal, thus forcing the Guardia into combat before it was fully ready to assume this duty. This cut short the period of American leadership of the force, and ultimately contributed to the withdrawal of all Americans before the Marines had trained enough officers to fully replace them. It is, perhaps, ironic that opposition to American imperialism in Nicaragua failed to alter the State Department's determination to create a new, better equipped, and more powerful Nicaraguan armed force, but may well have made it even easier for Somoza later to convert this force into an instrument of his own political ambitions.

NOTES

1. *La Noticia* (Managua), January 27, 1928, p. 1, and March 9, 1928, p. 1.

2. Eberhardt to Kellogg, March 12, 1928 (11 A.M.), March 13, 1928 (10 P.M.), and March 24, 1928; Acting Secretary of State Olds to Eberhardt, March 15, 1928, *Foreign Relations,* 1928, III, pp. 475–76, 478–79, and 482–85.

3. For details of General McCoy's career, see Niles B. Norton, "Frank McCoy and American Diplomacy, 1928–1932," (Ph.D. dissertation, University of Denver, 1966).

4. Interview with General Matthew B. Ridgway, USA (ret.), Pittsburgh, October, 1965.

5. Letter to author from Dr. Dana G. Munro, December 30, 1965.

6. Munro to Kellogg, October 15, 1927, NA RG 59, 817.1051/167.

7. Kellogg to Eberhardt, March 21, 1928, *Foreign Relations,* 1928, III, pp. 481–82.

8. Kellogg to Eberhardt, March 24, 1928, *Foreign Relations,* 1928, III, p. 485.

9. Sellers to unidentified Admiral, April 6, 1928, Sellers Papers.

10. Sellers to McCoy, March 29, 1928, Sellers Papers.

11. Feland to Sellers, April 19, 1928, Sellers Papers.

12. Sellers to Navy Department, April 29, 1928, Sellers Papers.

13. Sellers to Feland, April 29, 1928, Sellers Papers.

14. Sellers to Chief of Naval Operations (CNO), May 4, 1928, Sellers Papers.

15. Sellers to CNO, July 21, 1928, NA RG 59, 817.00/5890.

16. Beadle to McCoy, August 22, 1928, Nicaraguan Papers, Box 6, File 1, MCHA.

17. McCoy to Beadle, August 30, 1928, Nicaraguan Papers, Box 6, File 1, MCHA.

18. Feland to Col. F. Parker, Acting Chairman, National Board of Elections, June 6, 1928, Nicaraguan Records, Box 6, File 3, MCHA.

19. Thomas J. Dodd, Jr., "The United States in Nicaraguan Politics, Supervised Elections, 1927–1932," (Ph.D. dissertation, George Washington University, 1966), pp. 158–60.

20. Major Edwin North McClellan, "Supervising Nicaraguan Elections, 1928," *United States Naval Institute Proceedings* LIX (January 1933) 38.

21. Dodd, Jr., "U.S. in Nicaraguan Politics," pp. 158–60.

22. Sellers to Admiral Hughes, n.d., Sellers Papers, Box 3.

23. Sellers to Admiral Hughes, December 30, 1928, Sellers Papers.

24. Moncada to Sellers, December 29, 1928, Papers of Major General John A. Lejeune, Box 4, Library of Congress, Washington, D.C. Hereafter cited as Lejeune Papers.

25. Feland to Lejeune, January 3, 1929, Lejeune Papers, Box 4.

26. Eberhardt to Kellogg, January 7, 1929, *Foreign Relations,* 1929, III, p. 642.

27. Sellers to CNO, February 19, 1929, Sellers Papers.

28. Eberhardt to Kellogg, January 22, 1929, NA RG 59, 817.1051/238.

29. Sellers to CNO, January 30, 1929, and February 14, 1929, Sellers Papers; Memorandum by E. C. Dodds, November 13, 1928, Major General Frank R. McCoy Papers, Library of Congress, Washington, D.C.; Eberhardt to Kellogg, January 22, 1929, NA RG 59, 817.1051/238.

30. CNO to Sellers, March 9, 1929, Adjutant and Inspector General's Correspondence, NA RG 127.

31. Eberhardt to Kellogg, January 31, 1929, NA RG 59, 817.1051/244; Eberhardt to Kellogg, February 16, 1929, *Foreign Relations,* 1929, III, p. 619.

32. Secretary of the Navy Curtis Wilbur to Kellogg, January 31, 1929, NA RG 59, 817.1051/248.

33. Eberhardt to Kellogg, February 28, 1929, NA RG 59, 817.00/6222.

34. Eberhardt to Kellogg, February 9, 1929, NA RG 59, 817.1051/256.

35. Feland to Sellers, February 26, 1929, and Sellers to CNO, February 25, 1929, Sellers Papers.

36. Kellogg to Eberhardt, February 2, 1929, *Foreign Relations,* 1929, III, p. 644.

37. Letter from Major General Douglas C. McDougal, Jefe Director, Guardia Nacional de Nicaragua, to Major General Lejeune, no date, Papers of Lieutenant General Clayton B. Vogel, USMC (United States Marine Corps History and Museums Division, Washington Navy Yard, Washington, D.C.), hereafter cited as Vogel Papers.

38. McDougal to Major General Fuller, Commandant, USMC, October 7, 1930, NA RG 59, 817.1051/470a (enclosure).

39. Interview with Lt. Gen. Julian C. Smith, Alexandria, Va., October 1965; interview with Major Ward Scott, USMC, former military aide to President Moncada, Tampa, Fla., January 1966.

40. Eberhardt to Kellogg, January 26, 1929, *Foreign Relations,* 1929, III, pp. 607–609.

41. Eberhardt to Kellogg, January 31, 1929 *Foreign Relations,* 1929, III, p. 613.

42. Kellogg to Eberhardt, February 4, 1929, NA RG 59, 817.1051/252; Eberhardt to Kellogg, February 8, 1929, NA RG 59, 817.1051/254.

43. Eberhardt to Kellogg, February 14, 1929, and February 20, 1929, and Kellogg to Eberhardt, February 16, 1929, *Foreign Relations,* 1929, III, pp. 614–15 and 617–19.

44. Stimson to the American Minister to Nicaragua, Matthew Hanna, May 29, 1939, *Foreign Relations,* 1929, III, pp. 629–33.

45. Carlos Braco, President Moncada's Private Secretary, to General Beadle, January 12, 1929, NA RG 127, Entry 197, Box 2.

46. Stimson to Hanna, May 29, 1929, *Foreign Relations,* 1929, III, pp. 633–35.

47. Hanna to Stimson, May 23, 1930, and June 26, 1930, *Foreign Relations,* 1930, III, pp. 659–61 and 669–71.

48. Memorandum from the State Department Solicitor to Mr. Baker, NA RG 59, FW817.00/7270.

49. Eberhardt to Stimson, April 8, 1929, and April 10, 1929, *Foreign Relations,* 1929, III, pp. 590–91.

50. Stimson to Eberhardt, April 11, 1929, *Foreign Relations,* 1929, III, p. 592.

51. Stimson to Moncada, April 24, 1929, NA RG 59, 111.11 Stimson/1.

52. Hanna to Stimson, September 9, 19, 25, and 29, 1929, October 1, 3, and 4, 1929, *Foreign Relations,* 1929, III, pp. 596–601.

53. *La Prensa* (Managua), October 19, 1929, p. 8.

54. Memorandum, Headquarters, Guardia Nacional de Nicaragua, December 3, 1929, Box 10, File 14, MCHA.

55. Hanna to Stimson, Decmber 16, 1930, and Stimson to Hanna, January 3, 1931, *Foreign Relations,* 1930, III, pp. 703–704 and 708.

56. Moncada to Stimson, October 14, 1931, and Stimson to Moncada, December 9, 1931, NA RG 59, 817.00/7271.

57. Memorandum from Willard Beaulac to Stimson, October 3, 1931, NA RG 59, 817.1051/565.

58. Hanna to Stimson, July 2, 1929, NA RG 59, 817.1051/304.

59. Memorandum by Hanna and Gen. McDougal, July 1, 1929, NA RG 59, 817.1051/304; Stimson to Hanna, July 22, 1929, NA RG 59, 817.1051/308.

60. Beaulac to Stimson, February 1, 1930, NA RG 59, 817.1051/361.

61. Beaulac to Stimson, February 5, 1930, NA RG 59, 817.1051/376.

62. Memorandum by Hanna, March 17, 1930, NA RG 59, 817.00/6601.

63. Acting Secretary of State Francis White to Hanna, April 19, 1930, *Foreign Relations,* 1930, III, pp. 657–58.

64. Acting Secretary of State Carr to Hanna, July 30, 1930, *Foreign Relations,* 1930, III, p. 672.

65. Unsigned, undated Memorandum from Headquarters, USMC, Adjutant and Inspector General's Correspondence, NA RG 127.

66. Gen. McDougal to Gen., Fuller, October 17, 1930, NA RG 59, 817.1051/571 (enclosure).

67. Stimson Diary, X, October 21, 1930.

68. Ibid., October 22, 1930.

69. Hanna to Stimson, November 1, 1930, NA RG 59, 817.1051/442.

70. Stimson to Moncada, November 7, 1930, *Foreign Relations,* 1930, III, pp. 675–78.

71. Moncada to Stimson, November 7, 1930, *Foreign Relations,* 1930, III, pp. 679–83.

72. Stimson to Moncada, November 24, 1930, *Foreign Relations,* 1930, III, pp. 683–91.

73. Hanna to Stimson, December 13, 1930, and December 16, 1930, *Foreign Relations,* 1930, III, pp. 691–93.

74. Hanna to Stimson, January 21, 1931, and Memorandum by Stimson, March 12, 1931, *Foreign Relations,* 1931, II, pp. 839 and 841–42.

75. "Annual Report of the Guardia Nacional de Nicaragua for the Period from 10/1/31 to 9/30/32," Nicaraguan Records, Box 10, Folder 14, MCHA.

76. Claudius O. Johnson, *Borah of Idaho* (New York: Longmans, 1936), p. 343.

77. Carlton Beals, *Banana Gold* (Philadelphia: Lippincott, 1932), is a good example of the former, and Rafael de Nogales, *The Looting of Nicaragua* (New York: Robert M. McBride & Co., 1928), a good example of the latter category.

78. State Department records contain numerous letters from angry citizens who received literature from this organization, with the envelope bearing a gruesome anti-Marine illustration, and who wanted the Department to have such material barred from the mails.

79. Neill Macaulay, *The Sandino Affair* (Chicago: Quadrangle Books, 1967), p. 84.

80. U.S. Congress, Senate, *Hearings, Use of the United States Navy in Nicaragua,* 70th Congress, 1st Session, 1928.

81. Dana G. Munro, *The United States and the Caribbean Republics, 1921–1933* (Princeton, N.J: Princeton University Press, 1974), pp. 266–67.

82. Gen. Fuller to the Secretary of the Navy, March 4, 1931, NA RG 59, 817.1051/470a (enclosure).

83. Stimson Diary, XII, May 24, 1932, May 27, 1932, and June 18, 1932.

84. Henry W. Stimson and McGeorge Bundy, *On Active Service in Peace and War* (New York: Harper, 1948), pp. 181–82.

85. Lejeune Cummins, *Quijote on a Burro* (Mexico, D.F.: Impresora Azteca, 1958), p. 111.

86. Maximo Soto Hall, *Nicaragua y el imperialismo Norteamericano* (Buenos Aires: Artes y Letras Editorial, 1928), is an example of this writing.

87. Macaulay, *Sandino Affair,* p. 114.

88. David Bryn-Jones, *Frank B. Kellogg: A Biography* (New York: Putnam, 1937), p. 198.

89. *Report of the Delegates of the United States of America to the Sixth International Conference of American States* (Washington: Government Printing Office, 1928), p. 13.

90. Ibid., pp. 13 and 16.

91. This is still apparent in interviews with Marines who served with the Guardia.

VI

CHANGING COMMAND

As early as 1927, when a Nicaraguan proposal to detail American officers to the Guardia for a period of twelve years was rejected, the State Department had made it clear that American control over the Guardia Nacional was to be only temporary.[1] Before withdrawing, the Marines were supposed to create an efficient, well-armed, and disciplined fighting force which would function both as an army and as a national police force. This effort has already been discussed as has the less successful effort to restore peace and maintain internal security throughout Nicaragua. Finally, the Marines were expected to develop a native officer corps endowed with a spirit of loyalty to the nation and nonpartisanship in domestic politics. Unfortunately, serious efforts to train Nicaraguan officers were not begun until several years after the Guardia's creation, but efforts to promote nonpartisanship among enlisted men began almost immediately.

In an effort to eliminate partisan politics from the Guardia's ranks, every recruit was forced to take an oath "renouncing all political affiliation." Prompt punishment was promised for any who subsequently gave "overt expression of preference for one party."[2] In at least one case an enlisted man was discharged for shouting "Vivas" for a particular party.[3] This effort was contrary to Nicaraguan political tradition, but it seems to have been surprisingly successful. One reason for this may have been the Nicaraguan's traditional loyalty to his commanding officer, his *Jefe.* As long as this officer was nonpartisan, the average private found it much easier to avoid political involvement. Any system that depended upon loyalty to an individual was, of course, open to wide abuse should the officers develop their own political ambitions. Repeated efforts were made to transfer the enlisted man's loyalty from the individual officer to the institution that officer represented, but such efforts enjoyed little success.[4]

While the development of a corps of Nicaraguan officers to

assume command of the Guardia Nacional was obviously vital for the ultimate success of that organization, it was not until April 1930 that any formal effort was made in this area. That month a Nicaraguan Military Academy was opened with a staff of three Marine officers and a student body of nine Nicaraguan cadets who were supposed to receive eight to nine months of classroom instruction, plus from one to two months' field work. The cadets actually received only a little over two months of instruction before increased Sandinista activity forced their premature graduation on June 22, 1930. The lowest ranking member of this class was a former enlisted man, Francisco Gaitán.[5] Despite this unpromising beginning, he would play a greater role in the Guardia's future than any of his fellow cadets.

By September 30, 1930, the Guardia still had only 15 Nicaraguan officers out of a total officers' corps of 220 and the task of replacing the American officers before the final withdrawal was becoming increasingly imposing.[6] The *Academia Militar* was expanded with a Nicaraguan graduate of the first class being added to the staff, additional texts translated into Spanish, and larger quarters obtained in the *Campo de Marte.* Ninety-seven Nicaraguans applied for admission to the next class, which began in November 1930, but only thirty-seven were accepted, including four who were already serving as Guardia officers.[7] Efforts of the *Academia's* staff to inculcate political nonpartisanship in the cadets were hampered from the start. The *Jefe Director* had ordered the rejection of all applicants who had been involved in recent politics or whose families were notably active in politics. President Moncada, however, had to approve all admissions and he showed a definite interest in party affiliations, rejecting Conservatives and favoring Liberals.[8] The studies of this *Academia* class were plagued by constant interruptions. The class spent over a month in the field chasing Sandinistas, then lost their building in the March 1931 earthquake. Despite such setbacks twenty-seven of the original thirty-eight cadets graduated on June 1.[9] This graduation still left the great majority of Guardia officer posts filled by Marines. As late as March 1932 the force had only thirty-nine Nicaraguan officers, all of them lieutenants.[10]

The *Academia's* third class, which entered July 15, 1931, had 187 applicants for 75 places. Successful applicants had to pass a battery of academic tests, a physical examination, a security check, and a personal interview. In addition they had to be between 20 and 35 years old, stand at least 5'4", weigh a minimum of 135 pounds, and submit recommendations from two well-known citizens.[11] Because of these requirements the majority of the *Academia's* cadets probably came from the small middle-class and artisan sectors of Nicaragua's population. Educational requirements eliminated the mass of the population and sons of the upper class found little attraction in the life or salary of a second lieutenant. Furthermore, the Liberal Party, whose applicants the President favored, drew its strongest support from urban artisans and business men, while wealthy rural families were more likely to support the Conservatives.

The *Academia's* third class devoted more time to classroom instruction than had its predecessors. The curriculum covered everything from basic military training through law, engineering, and administration to such academic subjects as Nicaraguan history and geography and composition.[12] In addition, in what must have been one of the first operations of its kind, they were airlifted into the Department of Estelí, where they had four contacts with Sandino's forces and also trained eighty *auxiliares*. On April 7, 1932, fifty-nine of the cadets received commissions as Guardia second lieutenants.[13]

With the United States committed to ending the intervention and turning over control of the Guardia to Nicaraguans by January 1933, the officer training program was still producing far from adequate results. The size of the *Academia's* final class was expanded to eighty, but, despite a decrease in the Guardia's officer requirements by using contract physicians, this barely filled the force's company grade officer positions, leaving the problem of field grade officers unsettled.[14] The State Department and the Marine Corps had already devoted considerable effort to finding some solution to this problem. Their final decision would be crucial as the Guardia's future would be determined by the men who replaced the Marines in the higher ranks.

This problem had first appeared in March 1931 when General Calvin B. Matthews, the Guardia's *Jefe Director,* informed the State Department that he believed the *Academia* could graduate enough officers to fill "all except the higher ranks of the Guardia by January 1, 1933."[15] While the lack of any provision for filling higher positions was clearly implied in this message, it was not until the following February that State Department officials expressed concern over this situation. Laurence Duggan of the Division of Latin American Affairs discovered that the Guardia had no regular promotion procedures and there was nothing to "prevent the President from appointing to all the high commands his own henchmen, pledged to carry out his personal or party wishes."[16] Duggan urged the rapid creation of a plan for filling these posts and suggested that a phased withdrawal of Marine officers from the Guardia might aid in the transition.[17]

At last aware of the problem, the State Department in March 1932 asked the American Legation for a report on the steps being taken to prepare for Nicaraguan control of the Guardia. The Legation's reply stated that present plans called for turning over the higher commands to the Nicaraguans on January 2, 1933, the day after final American withdrawal, in order to allow the incoming Nicaraguan President to commission these officers.[18] The Legation also enclosed a proposal by General Matthews that the Nicaraguans adopt a new basic law for their armed forces. Such a law, which would free the Guardia of local political control and prohibit any political participation, including voting, by its officers and men, was seen by Matthews as an absolute prerequisite for the retention of an "efficient, well-disciplined force" in Nicaragua. Matthews felt that his military position prevented his bringing this matter to President Moncada's attention, but that the State Department could, indeed must, do so.[19] This message was sent to the Legation in November 1931, but for some reason was not passed on to the Department until April 1932. By then chances of action on any such law by the Nicaraguan Congress before the Marines withdrew were virtually nil.

In a later memorandum, General Matthews pointedly declared that the *Academia* graduates had neither the requisite age nor experience for the Guardia's higher commands; therefore the post of *Jefe Director* and those of the other field grade officers would have to be filled by "Nicaraguans of mature age and with previous military experience," chosen by the victor in the 1932 elections. The obvious implication in this recommendation was that such Nicaraguans would have acquired their military experience outside of the Guardia Nacional and that they would be political supporters of the incoming President. Matthews did suggest that such appointments be made two months before withdrawal so that the Marines could give their successors some orientation.[20]

The reaction of some State Department officials to this problem seems to have been to engage in wishful thinking rather than to grapple with the realities of Nicaraguan politics. A striking example of this attitude was provided by Acting Secretary of State Francis White in a May 17, 1932, letter to the American Minister in Nicaragua. White wrote:

> It is going to be difficult to maintain the theory of the Guardia as a nonpartisan organization if outsiders are to be appointed to high commands. However, in view of the fact that no Nicaraguans have so far been trained to hold grades higher than that of lieutenant, I suppose it may be necessary to go outside of the Guardia for some of the appointments to higher grades. It would of course, be advisable if such appointments could be given to Nicaraguans who do not have a record of strong political partisanship and that the appointments be made by General Matthews in order that the present officers and men of the Guardia have confidence in these appointments.[21]

Sentiments such as these flew in the face of political realities. As General Matthews had pointed out, those appointed to the higher grades would have to have some military experience. The only way anyone outside of the Guardia had obtained such experience had been in violently partisan political struggles, making it impossible to fill the positions with Nicaraguans who did not "have a record of strong political partisanship." Furthermore, it was extremely unlikely that any Nicaraguan President would willingly give General Matthews or anyone else the power to appoint men, who might well be his political enemies, to high positions in the armed forces.

On June 15, 1932, General Matthews revised his plan for filling the command positions. He pointed out that it would probably be necessary to have the incoming President make these appointments, a logical suggestion since, if his predecessor's appointments were unsatisfactory, he would undoubtedly try to change them, precipitating a major conflict within hours after the Marine's final withdrawal. As it would take at least two months to appoint these men and prepare them for their positions, Matthews urged the State Department to allow fifty Marine officers to serve with the Guardia for two months following the January 1, 1933, inauguration.[22] Stimson would have nothing to do with this suggestion, declaring that "it would not be advisable to leave any Marines in Nicaragua after the date already announced for their withdrawal."[23] While the reasons for this adamant stand are not completely clear, it is probable that Stimson feared that adoption of any such proposal would convince the intervention's critics that the United States was trying to prolong its direct controls over

Nicaragua and would lead to increased attacks upon and unfavorable publicity for the Department's policies.

As an alternative, General Matthews now suggested that the two major presidential candidates should each draw up a list, divided equally among Conservatives and Liberals, of candidates for the Guardia's higher posts. As soon as the election was decided, President Moncada should appoint the officers on the winning candidate's list, thereby giving the Marines almost two months to indoctrinate their replacements before the final withdrawal.[24]

These suggestions gained rapid State Department approval. Acting Secretary of State Castle declared that besides meeting Department objections to retention of Americans in the Guardia after January 1, Matthews' latest plan also provided for "continuance of the non-partisan basis of the Guardia since its officers will be drawn equally from the two historic political parties."[25] This claim was wrong. Instead of continuing the policy of nonpartisanship, the plan signaled the final abandonment of that effort. The agreement later signed by both parties to put this plan into effect, while theoretically providing for a nonpartisan Guardia, first specifically exempted the post of *Jefe Director* from these provisions, a key omission, then agreed to select the other officers on a bipartisan basis.[26] Bipartisan, however, was not the same as nonpartisan! Under this plan officers were selected because of their political ties, not because of their lack of them. This ensured that the Guardia's top ranks would be filled by men of definite political loyalties and that the *Jefe Director* would be a picked representative of the ruling party. This once again placed control of Nicaragua's armed forces in partisan, political hands. By 1934, Arthur Bliss Lane, who succeeded Hanna as Minister to Nicaragua, saw clearly that the agreement on bipartisan officer selection had represented a major shift in United States policy, adding that "persons who should be in a position to know tell me that the very provision that the number of officers should be equally divided between the two historical political parties is, in itself, an emphasis upon the political construction of the Guardia."[27]

As the time for withdrawal approached, many Nicaraguan political leaders sought some way of prolonging the Marines' presence in their nation. These included the Conservative's presidential candidate, Adolfo Díaz, and surprisingly, the

The 1928 Thanksgiving meal hosted by General José María Moncada in honor of Brigadier General Logan Feland was attended by Anastasio Somoza García** (front right)* ***and two prominent Marine officers. This was the incubation period of the Somoza dynasty.

Liberal's candidate, Juan Bautista Sacasa, against whom the original intervention had been aimed. Most were alarmed at the prospect of leaving the Guardia, in the hands of untried leaders, facing a threat from Sandino which was, in Minister Hanna's words, "fully as strong as, if not stronger than any time since its inception."[28] While Hanna probably sympathized with the requests for a continued Marine presence, Stimson did not. All the American Minister could do in response to repeated pleas was to hold out the hope that American withdrawal would make possible negotiations with Sandino.

With the United States determined to pull out on schedule, it only remained to put Matthews' plan into action, President Moncada suggested this be done by having both parties' candidates sign a document, pledging to observe the arrangement for appointing higher officers and to continue the Guardia on a nonpartisan basis after January 1. In addition, Moncada urged that the signing take place in the presence of a State Department representative, explaining that Nicaraguans attached "great respect to a simple promise made before the Government of the United States."[29] This last suggestion probably represented an effort to commit the United States to enforcement of the agreement, an assumption that Nicaraguans later made repeatedly.

The State Department approved these suggestions and General Matthews sent letters to the leaders of both parties, explaining the proposals for drawing up lists of nominees for the Guardia's higher officers and for keeping the Guardia nonpartisan after January 1. On November 5, 1932, the day before the election, both candidates, plus General Somoza, acting Foreign Minister and representative of the Moncada administration, signed the agreement in Hanna's presence. This pledged them to maintain the Guardia as the nation's only armed force, to keep the organization on a nonpartisan basis (a provision which, by the interpretation placed upon it, requiring bipartisanship in selecting and replacing higher officers and exempting the *Jefe Director* from these restrictions, was already negated), and to give the President, in agreement with the *Jefe Director,* the right to select officers for posts on the General Staff.[30]

The last apparent obstacle to American withdrawal was the successful holding of the 1932 elections. The State Department was determined to see this done and had earlier firmly rebuffed proposals by Moncada which would have postponed the elections two years, extending his term in office. To direct the Board of Elections the Department chose Rear Admiral Clark H. Woodward, a veteran of Caribbean service. The selection of a naval officer avoided the possibility of a recurrence of the interservice rivalries which had plagued the 1928 election supervision, but numerous problems still remained. Admiral Woodward was soon calling for an additional 1,800 Marines to help supervise the elections, a request the State Department found completely impossible to fulfill. After considerable debate a plan was worked out providing for a mission of 643 American officers and men, with no accompanying support forces, at a cost of $200,000.[31]

Both major parties were plagued with preelection problems. A bitter dispute within the Liberal Party between President Moncada and former Vice-President Sacasa was only resolved under tremendous pressure from Admiral Woodward.[32] The Liberals' nominations ultimately went to Sacasa for President and Rodolfo Espinosa for Vice-President, but the animosity between Moncada and Sacasa remained unresolved and was destined to have grave consequences in the future.

The Conservatives were plagued by apathy and lack of funds. They had nominated Adolfo Díaz for President and Emiliano Chamorro for Vice-President, but later considered joining in coalition with Moncada to back one of his supporters against Sacasa, in return for which Moncada offered the Conservatives the Vice-Presidential nomination and half the cabinet posts. When this proposal fell through, they even considered withdrawing entirely from the campaign.[33] Under strong American pressure, they ultimately decided to remain in the contest and the campaign continued. The Liberals won by a wide margin, placing Sacasa in the position he had fought so hard to gain in 1926–1927. Considering their lack of funds and enthusiasm, the Conservatives did surprisingly well in the Congressional races, holding their own in the Chamber of Deputies and actually gaining a seat in the Senate.[34]

The Guardia performed well during the elections, drawing praise from Admiral Woodward for their "very active and efficient" service.[35] Even the defeated Conservatives acknowledged that the Guardia and the urban police had remained totally neutral.[36] Perhaps the happiest person to see the elections end was the Admiral who, in his final report, suggested that "the Government of the United States seek, by every means possible to avoid again becoming involved in a commitment of the nature of the three recent Supervisions of Elections in Nicaragua."[37]

Since Sacasa had won the 1932 elections, it was supposedly his selections who would be appointed to the Guardia's higher posts, but these appointments were to be made by President Moncada, who was no friend of Sacasa's. Moncada undoubtedly insisted on a voice in Sacasa's choices, especially for the post of *Jefe Director.*[38] This influence became obvious when the name of the Guardia's first Nicaraguan *Jefe Director* was announced. This man, appointed from a list revised from that originally proposed by Sacasa, and approved by both Moncada and Matthew Hanna, was Moncada's long-time protégé, Anastasio Somoza García.[39]

The American Minister also exercised an important influence in Somoza's selection. For years many Nicaraguans have claimed that Somoza was handpicked by Hanna, a view at least partly confirmed by both Willard Beaulac, Hanna's First Secretary in Managua, and Arthur Bliss Lane, his successor as Minister to Nicaragua.[40] As early as October 28, 1932, Hanna had informed the State Department of his preference for Somoza, declaring, "I look on him as the best man in the country for the position" and adding that "no one will labor as intelligently or conscientiously to maintain the non-partisan character of the Guardia or will be as efficient in all matters connected with the administration and command of the Force."[41] General Matthews and most of the other Marines holding Guardia command positions also favored Somoza and supported efforts to have him appointed *Jefe Director.*[42] When the appointment was announced, both Hanna and Matthews were clearly pleased, with Hanna claiming that Somoza had previously played a successful part in the 1926–1927 revolutionary movement, a claim certainly open to dispute, and adding that while some criticized the new *Jefe Director* for being too close to Moncada, the appointment was "generally applauded here."[43]

The pressure from both Moncada and Hanna obviously left Sacasa far from free in his choice of a *Jefe Director.* A letter from General Matthews to Moncada, written November 12, 1932, gives final confirmation of this. Matthews wrote that Sacasa had been given three names, Somoza, General Gustavo Abaunza, and General José María Zelaya, all supporters of Moncada, from which to choose the "higher officials."[44] Since Abaunza was later appointed to Chief of the General Staff *(Estado Mayor),* and since Matthews referred to choosing officials, not an official, it appears that some unspecified person or persons virtually forced upon Sacasa the individuals who would fill the higher posts, leaving him only a very limited choice.[45] Somoza and Sacasa were related by marriage, as Somoza's wife was Sacasa's niece, so Sacasa probably picked Somoza hoping that this tie would give him more influence than he could otherwise have over either of the other candidates. There is no evidence in official files as to who drew up this list or how it was presented to Sacasa. Recent statements, however, by General Somoza's widow, Doña Salvadora Debayle de Somoza, help fill this gap. According to her the final choices were agreed upon in a meeting between Moncada and Sacasa. Sacasa had originally wanted to appoint General Carlos Castro Wassmer, but ultimately gave in and agreed to appoint Somoza.[46] Her account, however, still leaves unanswered the question of who drew up the list of possible candidates, Moncada, Hanna, General Matthews, or some combination of these three. It is not likely that General Matthews would take such action without first gaining the approval of the American Minister, but aside from this condition, it remains impossible to fix final responsibility. What is clear is that Somoza was certainly not Sacasa's first choice, creating a situation that favored the rapid development of a breach between the new Nicaraguan President and the commander of his armed forces.

Under the terms of the November 5, 1932, agreement, Guardia field grade positions, below the rank of *Jefe Director,* were to be equally divided between Liberals and Conservatives. However, in addition to Somoza, three out of five colonels and six of the eight majors appointed by Sacasa were Liberals, creating a Liberal Party domination over the Guardia from the start of Sacasa's administration.[47]

A few minor problems remained before the final turnover to Nicaraguan control on January 1, 1933. Both Dr. Sacasa and General Somoza made a final plea for retention of an American military mission after that date. Word of their efforts leaked to the press, which attacked the project as an American plot to avoid complete withdrawal. Hanna reiterated the State Department's determination to end all direct involvement with the Guardia on schedule, noting that any suggestion to the contrary was "political dynamite" in Nicaragua.[48] The press also criticized the American role in endorsing the November 5 biparty agreement on the Guardia, saying this represented continued United States control over the Guardia. Pressure was brought to bear upon both Díaz and Sacasa to abrogate the agreement, with some Conservatives going so far as to claim that their party should have nothing to do with the success or failure of the Guardia under a Liberal administration.[49] Nothing came of these efforts and plans for American withdrawal continued on schedule.

The Marines gave the new officers a rush, two-week course that was strictly military, concentrating upon such practical matters as organization, techniques of command, and principles of combat. After this, the new officers picked up their uniforms and equipment and left for their duty stations throughout Nicaragua.[50] Concentration of the Marine officers in a few key cities took place from December 13 to December 15 and, as the Americans evacuated their posts, the command was given over to the Nicaraguans.[51] General Matthews and his staff busied themselves preparing a large body of proposed laws governing the Guardia Nacional which they turned over to President Moncada in December. By then it was too late for his administration to act upon them and no subsequent administration ever tried to secure their adoption.[52]

On January 1, 1933, the history of Marine leadership of the Guardia Nacional came to an end. General Matthews attended Sacasa's inauguration, then immediately turned over command of the Guardia to Somoza and departed, leaving in such a rush that his Chief of Staff doubts that he had time to finish packing.[53] The following day the last Marines boarded transports at Corinto, leaving the future of the Guardia Nacional in Nicaraguan hands.

From a strictly military standpoint, the more than five years of American leadership had given Nicaragua a better trained, disciplined, and equipped army than it had ever known. The Guardia possessed 259 machine guns, 54 Thompson submachine guns, 23 Browning automatic rifles, and 4,474 of the standard Krag rifles.[54] Despite the limited time available, the *Academia Militar* graduates were better trained than any previous group of Nicaraguan officers. For the first time a Nicaraguan army had organized, separate medical, communications, and quartermaster's departments.

There were, however, weaknesses as well as strengths. Sandino was still unbeaten and capable of waging a determined battle for control of the nation. The Guardia was now left without air support, a loss many Nicaraguans felt quite keenly. The withdrawal also meant the closing of the *Academia Militar,* leaving the nation with no regular procedure for training new officers. Finally, the appointment of outsiders to the higher ranks produced considerable discontent among the *Academia* graduates who had hoped to obtain at least some of these posts themselves.[55] This rift in the officer corps would have serious consequences within a few weeks.

From a political standpoint, the net result of American training of the Guardia was quite unsatisfactory. In a statement marking the American withdrawal from Nicaragua, Secretary Stimson claimed that the United States had successfully developed an efficient, nonpartisan Guardia Nacional. He declared that the force was well disciplined and "grounded upon the fundamental precept of service to the country as a whole," but this statement was far from accurate.[56] Already many people in the State Department and in the Marine Corps were aware that the Guardia was rapidly destined to become a partisan political instrument.

As early as December 1929, Walter Thurston, former chargé in Nicaragua, warned the State Department that if Moncada insisted upon introducing large numbers of Liberals into the Guardia and if the Liberal Party press continued to attack the force, there would be "very little hope for it."[57] Laurence Duggan was even more pessimistic two years later, observing that the animosity between Nicaragua's traditional parties made it impossible to establish a nonpartisan constabulary and asking what had ever prompted American officials to think it might be possible to create such a force.[58]

By March 1932, Duggan's pessimism regarding the future of the Guardia Nacional had increased even further. In a memorandum for Edward Wilson, Chief of the Latin American Division, Duggan made a remarkably accurate prediction when he wrote:

> Upon the withdrawal of the Marine officers in the Guardia next fall, the forces of disintegration will be set into action which will eventually impair the present organization and esprit de corps of that body. It is a foregone conclusion that Nicaragua will not maintain the Guardia along present Marine Corps lines. The loss of the spirit of impartial service, so laboriously instilled, involves a return to a partisan, political constabulary. Judging from the historical position of the Army in Central America and more particularly in Nicaragua,

> a strictly non-partisan military organization is not, at the present time, a possibility.[59]

While Duggan's pessimism may not have been shared by everyone in the State Department, even Francis White was forced to admit that it would "be difficult to maintain the theory of the Guardia as a non-partisan organization if outsiders are appointed to high commands."[60]

The Marines also had evidence that it would be impossible to keep the Guardia nonpartisan after they withdrew. A group of Conservative politicians openly told the Marines that there were Conservatives in the Guardia, posing as Liberals, who would deliver arms and ammunition to the Conservatives after the Marines left.[61] The fact that Conservatives had to pose as Liberals demonstrated that the Guardia already had a pro-Liberal bias, while the willingness of some officers to turn over arms to political compatriots outside of the force demonstrated that, in at least some cases, efforts to replace party with national loyalty had failed. Further confirmation of these conditions came with an October 1932 intelligence report. This noted a general consensus that some sort of revolutionary upheaval after the Marines' departure was inevitable and that the present composition and organization of the Guardia Nacional would not long survive the American withdrawal.[62]

Similar conclusions were expressed independently by at least one prominent former Guardia officer, Lieutenant Colonel Robert Denig, who had served as Guardia Chief of Staff in 1931. In the November 1932 issue of the *Marine Corps Gazette,* he criticized the plan for appointing Guardia officers after the 1932 elections, then went on to observe: "At best there is sure to be a shakeup in the Guardia; it will soon become a partisan force, used to further the party in power."[63] Political considerations, as well as memories of the fate of officers, such as General Feland, who had previously criticised State Department policy, evidently kept Marines on active duty with the Guardia from making too blunt statements about their views on the Guardia's future or pressing these views on the American Legation. The critical statements concerning the Guardia made by the Marine Corps Commandant, General B. H. Fuller, before a House committee in 1931 unleashed a storm of criticism and led Fuller to write that he would not have spoken so freely if he had known his statements would be made public. In private correspondence, however, Fuller defended his views, adding, "It takes a good while to make a good soldier out of anybody and it takes much longer to make one out of a Nicaraguan. The National Guard would be very inefficient under present circumstances if it were officered by anybody but Americans."[64]

Even General Matthews, the Guardia's last American commander, gave a measure of support to the gloomy forecasts concerning the Guardia's future, admitting that the best that could be hoped for in the newly appointed officers was a minimum, not a lack, of political bias. He even acknowledged that such bias was already present in the Guardia, since Moncada had rejected many qualified *Academia* candidates solely on the ground of political or family ties and had even made Matthews investigate the enlistments of Conservatives as privates. The *Jefe Director* added that "everyone" was familiar with these conditions.[65]

In the face of this evidence, the State Department continued to work for agreements supposedly designed to maintain a nonpartisan Guardia after the Marines withdrew. Such efforts were doomed to failure. This failure was underlined by the acquiescence, and even support, which the Department gave to the proposal exempting the *Jefe Director* from the nonpartisan status specified for the Guardia Nacional. It is ironic that, in the agreement designed to ensure the continuance of the Guardia on a bipartisan basis after the withdrawal, the clause exempting the *Jefe Director* from this requirement was drafted not by the Nicaraguans, but by the American Legation.[66]

The United States had given Nicaragua the best trained and equipped army it had ever known, but it had also given that nation an instrument potentially capable of crushing political opposition with greater efficiency than ever before in that nation. The Guardia had been envisioned as an instrument for ending the tradition of using the military for partisan political purposes, yet before the Marines left, partisanship had already entered its ranks with the acquiescense of the State Department. In addition, the danger of a break between the new *Jefe Director* and the Nicaraguan President existed before either of them had even taken office. This represented the real heritage left by the United States when the Marines turned over command of the Guardia. Under these conditions, the violent upheavals that occurred in Nicaragua during the ensuing four years came as no surprise to many American veterans of the intervention.

NOTES

1. Kellogg to Munro, December 8, 1927, NA RG 59, 817.1051/178.

2. Eberhardt to Kellogg, May 18, 1928, NA RG 59, 817.1051/20.

3. John Milton Wearmouth, "The Second Marine Intervention in Nicaragua, 1927–1932" (M.A. Thesis, Georgetown University, 1952), p. 39.

4. H. C. Reisinger, "La Palabra del Gringo, Leadership in the Nicaraguan National Guard," *United States Naval Institute Proceedings* LXI (February 1935) 215–21, contains many examples of the importance of the Marines' use of the "Jefe" image in developing the Guardia Nacional.

5. "Annual Report of the Guardia Nacional de Nicaragua from 10/1/29 to 9/30/30," Nicaraguan Records, Box 10, File 14, MCHA.

6. Ibid.

7. Smith et al., *Review,* p. 103.

8. Hanna to Stimson, December 11, 1930, NA RG 59, 817.223/2.

9. Smith et al., *Review,* p. 104.

10. Memorandum, Laurence Duggan to Ed Wilson, March 7, 1932, NA RG 59, 817.1051/612½.

11. Captain Edward L. Trumble, "The National Military Academy of Nicaragua," *Leatherneck* XV (October 1932) 17; Smith et al., *Review,* p. 105.

12. Trumble, "National Military Academy," pp. 17 and 60.

13. "Annual Report of the Nicaraguan Military Academy, 10/1/31 to 9/30/32," Nicaraguan Records, Box 10, Folder 14, MCHA.

14. Beaulac to Stimson, April 2, 1932, and Gen. Matthews to Beaulac, April 4, 1932, *Foreign Relations,* 1932, V, pp. 853 and 857–59.

15. Hanna to Stimson, March 12, 1931, *Foreign Relations,* 1931, II, p. 846.

16. Memorandum from Duggan to Wilson, February 25, 1932, NA RG 59, 817.1051/611.

17. Memorandum from Duggan to Wilson, March 7, 1932, NA RG 59, 817.1051/612½.

18. Stimson to Beaulac, March 11, 1932, and Beaulac to Stimson, April 2, 1932, *Foreign Relations,* 1932, V, pp. 852–53.

19. Gen. Matthews to Beaulac, November 16, 1931, *Foreign Relations,* 1932, V, pp. 855–57.

20. Gen. Matthews to Beaulac, April 4, 1932, *Foreign Relations,* 1932, V, p. 858.

21. Francis White to Hanna, April 17, 1932, NA RG 59, 817.1051/643.

22. Gen. Matthews to Hanna, June 15, 1932, printed in Smith et al., *Review,* p. 149.

23. Stimson to Hanna, July 19, 1932, *Foreign Relations,* 1932, V, p. 866.

24. Gen. Matthews to Hanna, August 8, 1932, *Foreign Relations,* 1932, V, pp. 868–70.

25. Acting Secretary of State Castle to Hanna, August 30, 1932, *Foreign Relations,* 1932, V, pp. 871–72.

26. "Agreement Signed on November 5, 1932, Providing for the Maintenance of the Non-Partisan Character of the Guardia Nacional de Nicaragua," and White to Hanna, December 1, 1932, *Foreign Relations,* 1932, V, pp. 887 and 900–901.

27. The American Minister to Nicaragua, Arthur Bliss Lane, to Edwin Wilson, February 3, 1934, in Arthur Bliss Lane Papers, Yale University Library, New Haven, Connecticut. Cited hereafter as Lane Papers.

28. Hanna to Stimson, November 4, 1932, *Foreign Relations,* 1932, V, p. 876.

29. Moncada to Hanna, contained in a dispatch from Hanna to Stimson, September 16, 1932, *Foreign Relations,* 1932, V, p. 873.

30. "Agreement Signed on November 5, 1932, Providing for the Maintenance of the Non-Partisan Character of the Guardia Nacional de Nicaragua," *Foreign Relations,* 1932, V, p. 887.

31. White to Beaulac, March 30, 1932, Beaulac to White, April 12, 1932, Admiral Woodward to Stimson, May 25, 1932, and Castle to Hanna, May 28, 1932, *Foreign Relations,* 1932, V, pp. 794–98, and 803–805.

32. Numerous relevant documents are printed in *Foreign Relations,* 1932, V, pp. 810–22.

33. Emiliano Chamorro, "Autobiografía," *Revista Conservadora* II (October 1961) 167; Hanna to Stimson, November 19, 1932, NA RG 59, 817.00/7637.

34. Hanna to Stimson, November 13, 1932, *Foreign Relations,* 1932, V, p. 829.

35. Hanna to Stimson, November 7, 1932, *Foreign Relations,* 1932, V, p. 829.

36. *La Prensa* (Managua), November 8, 1932, p. 1, and November 9, 1932, p. 1.

37. Duggan to Wilson, January 27, 1933, *Foreign Relations,* 1932, V, p. 832.

38. Interview with Ildefonso Solórzano, Managua, October 1963.

39. Gen. Matthews to President Moncada, November 17, 1932, printed in Smith et al., *Review,* p. 160.

40. Bryce Wood, *The Making of the Good Neighbor Policy* (New York: W. W. Norton, 1944), p. 138; interview with Willard Beaulac, Fairfax, Va., April 1964; Typeset of "Autobiography of Arthur Bliss Lane," Lane Papers. Many Nicaraguans claim that Hanna strongly supported Somoza's nomination because Somoza had charmed Mrs. Hanna with his dancing ability, excellent English, and other masculine charms. This

influence is reported in William Krehn, *Democracia y Tirania en el Caribe* (Mexico, D. F.: Unión Democrática Centroamericana, 1949), and repeated in William Kammen, *A Search for Stability: United States Diplomacy Toward Nicaragua, 1925–1933* (Notre Dame, Ind.: University of Notre Dame Press, 1968), p. 210.

41. Hanna to White, October 28, 1932, NA RG 59, 817.1051/701½.

42. Interview with Lt. Gen. Smith, Alexandria, Va., October 1965.

43. Hanna to Stimson, November 21, 1932, *Foreign Relations,* 1932, V, pp. 899–900.

44. Gen. Matthews to Moncada, November 21, 1932, Nicaraguan Records, Box 11, MCHA.

45. *La Prensa* (Managua), November 19, 1932, p. 1; *La Noticia* (Managua), November 17, 1932, p. 1. Both record Abaunza's appointment and also the appointment of José María Zelaya as one of the two Liberal colonels.

46. Interview with Doña Salvadora Debayle de Somoza, August 14, 1972, cited in Ternot MacRenato, "Anastasio Somoza: a Nicaraguan Caudillo" (M.A. thesis, University of San Francisco, 1974), p. 89.

47. *La Prensa* (Managua), November 19, 1932, pp. 1 and 6; "Personality Reports on Guardia Nacional Officers," undated memorandum signed F. A. S., NA RG 59, 817.1051/764.

48. Hanna to Wilson, December 3, 1932, Matthew B. Hanna Papers, NA RG 59. Cited hereafter as Hanna Papers.

49. Hanna to Francis White, December 5, 1932, Hanna Papers, NA RG 59.

50. Smith et al., *Review,* p. 161.

51. "Jefe Director to All Area and Department Commanders, December 3, 1932," printed in Smith et al., *Review,* p. 464; Hanna to Stimson, December 7, 1932, *Foreign Relations,* 1932, V, pp. 907–908.

52. Hanna to Stimson, December 24, 1932, *Foreign Relations,* 1932, V, p. 922. The proposed legislation is printed in Smith et al., *Review,* pp. 165–202.

53. Interview with Lt. Gen. Smith, Alexandria, Va., May, 1964. For a more complete discussion of the withdrawal, see John J. Tierney, Jr., "The United States and Nicaragua, 1927–1932: Decisions for De-Escalation and Withdrawal," (Ph.D. dissertation, University of Pennsylvania, 1969).

54. Memorandum by Major L. E. Rea, November 10, 1932, Nicaraguan Records, Box 11, MCHA.

55. *La Prensa* (Managua), December 10, 1932, p. 1. This attitude had reportedly been encouraged by some of the Marines. See MacRenato, "A Nicaraguan Caudillo," pp. 90–91.

56. Department of State Press Release, *Foreign Relations,* 1932, V, pp. 923–24.

57. Memorandum by Walter Thurston, December 14, 1929, NA RG 59, 817.1051/343.

58. Memorandum by Duggan, November 16, 1931, NA RG 59, 711.17/253.

59. Memorandum from Duggan to Wilson, March 23, 1932, NA RG 59, 817.1051/613½.

60. White to Hanna, May 17, 1932, NA RG 59, 817.1051/643.

61. "Interview with Conservative Politicians," October 14, 1932, Records of the Guardia Nacional, NA RG 127.

62. Captain Evans F. Carlson to the *Jefe Director,* October 14, 1932, Records of the Guardia Nacional, NA RG 127.

63. Lt. Col. Robert L. Denig, "Native Officer Corps, Guardia Nacional de Nicaragua." *Marine Corps Gazette* XVII (November 1932) 77.

64. Gen. Fuller to the Secretary of the Navy, March 4, 1931, NA RG 59, 817.1051/470a (enclosure).

65. Matthews to Hanna, June 15, 1932, and August 8, 1932, printed in Smith et al., *Review,* pp. 149 and 151–52.

66. Hanna to Gen. Chamorro, November 3, 1932, *Foreign Relations,* 1932, V, pp. 885–86.

VII

SOMOZA TAKES CHARGE

The Marines were gone from Nicaragua in January 1933, but Augusto César Sandino remained and, according to the American Minister, was as strong as, if not stronger than, any time in the past.[1] The continued struggle against him was exhausting the nation and draining government revenues, already reduced by the effects of the depression. Ending this conflict was obviously the most important task facing the new Sacasa administration.

The appointment of Sofonías Salvatierra, an educator who was related to Sandino and had reportedly once been his choice for President of Nicaragua, as Sacasa's Minister of Agriculture and Labor, proved the key to opening negotiations with the rebel leader.[2] Salvatierra had written Sandino, asking for his proposals for a peace settlement. Sandino replied on December 24, 1932, indicating a willingness to enter into formal peace negotiations with a commission authorized by the Sacasa administration.[3]

Acting on Sacasa's instruction, Salvatierra proceeded to organize a party of prominent Nicaraguans, including Sandino's father, and set off for the Segovias to initiate peace negotiations. As he was preparing to leave, the government's need to end the fighting became even more urgent. Within a week after the departure of the Marines a major plot had been discovered among the officers of the Guardia Nacional.

The fight against Sandino had continued unabated during the first weeks of January, with at least one pitched battle taking place between a Guardia unit and a guerrilla force estimated at 300 men which had tried to seize the town of San Isidro.[4] The problem was so severe that Somoza was forced to bring back Juan Escamilla, the Mexican adventurer who had commanded a *voluntario* force in 1929, and send him back in the field with a force of 100 *auxiliares*.[5]

The Guardia's combat effectiveness was severely limited by the anger of many *Academia Militar* graduates over having the Guardia's higher positions awarded to political appointees. The graduates had received some promotions during the turnover to Nicaraguan command, with several being made captains and all the officers who had graduated prior to 1932 being at least promoted to the rank of first lieutenant.[6] These promotions had not satisfied many of the officers and they had organized a plot to force Sacasa to dismiss all the political appointees except Somoza and appoint *Academia* graduates to replace them. The plot was discovered at the last minute, narrowly averting a confrontation that might well have created chaos in the Guardia and perhaps even have thrown open the path to power for Sandino.[7]

Once discovered, the plot was defused by arresting the two suspected ringleaders and offering concessions to the other *Academia* graduates. The American Minister was greatly impressed with the "speed, wisdom and tact" exhibited by Somoza in dealing with the situation, but feared that the danger might simply be dormant, rather than actually resolved.[8] Since almost all the lower-ranking officers were *Academia* graduates, this meant that they controlled most of the combat units and arms of the Guardia, making any move against them extremely dangerous.

In this critical situation, Sacasa did what Nicaraguan presidents had done for decades. He sent for the American Minister and, accompanied by Somoza, asked for the Legation's solution. Much to their suprise, Hanna refused to do more than listen sympathetically and make a few simple suggestions.[9] The United States had determined to return the major responsibility for solving Nicaraguan problems, even those created by U.S. intervention, to the Nicaraguan government. It would take the Nicaraguans several years to get accustomed to this change.

Not daring to use force against the disaffected officers, Somoza and Sacasa finally decided simply to transfer the suspected ringleaders. One of them was shipped off to León where he would be closely watched by General Abaunza, the Guardia's Chief of Staff. Another suspect, Captain Gaitán, was sent to Puerto Cabezas, effectively isolating him from contact with the great majority of the officers. Somoza then sought to obtain loyalty pledges from the graduates in the field and President Sacasa appointed emergency officers to remain on duty in the Campo de Marte in case of an uprising.[10]

The threatened revolt was probably ultimately averted as much by dramatic developments in the negotiations with Sandino as by any of the government's actions. On January 23, Salvatierra returned to Managua bearing Sandino's peace proposals and Sacasa declared a fifteen-day truce to facilitate further negotiations.[11] The threat of a peace treaty with their common enemy, Sandino, may well have restored at least a measure of internal unity among the Guardia's officers.

Sandino's original peace terms included demands for an end to "foreign intervention" in the Guardia Nacional, the creation of a huge new department in the North, stretching from the Segovias to the Atlantic, where his men would retain their arms and appoint all officials, the destruction of all government records referring to himself or his men as bandits, and the calling of a Pan-American conference to revise the Bryan-Chamorro Treaty.[12] Sacasa could not accept such terms, but feared that Sandino might launch an offensive which the internally divided Guardia, low on arms and ammunition, could not handle. He sought credits from the American War Department to purchase additional war materials, but was refused because Nicaragua was badly in default on previous credits. He finally managed to obtain some supplies from Salvador and, at a cost of $11 each, 2,000 used Krag Jorgenson rifles from a private New York firm.[13] By the time this transaction was completed, Sandino had agreed to terms.

Salvatierra had returned to Sandino's headquarters in the hills above San Rafael del Norte, covering the last few miles on a mule furnished by the Guardia. Upon his arrival, Sandino informed him that he had decided to go to Managua to negotiate directly with President Sacasa. This news was promptly wired to Managua and a plane was dispatched to take the guerrilla leader to the capital.[14] Sandino reached Managua on February 2, proclaiming that all Nicaraguans, including his troops and members of the Guardia, were brothers, an attitude he emphasized by riding to the Presidential Palace in General Somoza's automobile.[15] Once there, his delegates and the government's began intensive work on peace terms, reaching an agreement shortly before midnight. The terms called for (1) an immediate cessation of all hostilities; (2) a complete amnesty for all of the guerrillas; and (3) a partial disarmament of Sandino's men with Salvatierra collecting the arms. Sandino was to retain enough arms for a force of 100 men who were to preserve order in an area along the Rio Coco where his supporters could settle and farm on public lands. The government agreed to pay the expenses of this force for one year. At the end of that time the status of the force was to be reviewed. The government agreed to undertake a public works program in the northern area, giving special job preferences to Sandino's followers. Sandino and his supporters agreed to obey the government and preserve peace and order in their section of Nicaragua.[16]

The signing of the treaty set off a period of public rejoicing. The leading newspapers of both parties hailed the event, Somoza and Sandino embraced, Sacasa issued a proclamation praising the treaty, and Sandino even declared that he had never believed that United States actions in Nicaragua represented the actual sentiments of most Americans and that he had no hostility toward Americans who came to Nicaragua to work, providing they did not come as bosses.[17] On February 3, Sandino flew back to tell his followers about the treaty, leaving behind a nation apparently united in acceptance of the peace terms.

Somoza may have embraced Sandino in public, but in private the *Jefe Director* and many of his subordinates were unhappy with the terms. The Guardia had been busily engaged in recruiting 1,250 *auxiliares* and many officers felt that this force could and should have been used to destroy Sandino. Somoza shared this view and was even more upset by Sandino's being allowed to surrender his arms to his friend, Sofonías Salvatierra, instead of to the Guardia.[18] These attitudes within the Guardia boded ill for Nicaragua's future. Some of Sandino's men were also unhappy with the treaty, but the rebel leader promptly crushed this by shooting the two men he felt were most responsible.[19]

Sacasa kept his part of the terms, pushing an appropriation for $120,000 for the promised public works projects through the Congress and sending Salvatierra to San Rafael del Norte to collect Sandino's arms.[20] Somoza and the Guardia's objections to Salvatierra's role in this procedure increased as the task progressed. By the disarmament's conclusion in early March, only 338 to 489 rifles, 18 to 21 machine guns, and 3,129 rounds of ammunition had been collected. The government returned to Sandino all the machine guns, all the ammunition, and nearly 100 rifles for the use of his own "emergency" force. The small amount of weapons collected led Somoza to suspect that the guerrillas had hidden most of their arms for future use.[21] Since between 1,800 and 3,000 men were involved in the disarmament, it does appear that considerably fewer arms than might reasonably have been expected were turned in.

Shortly after the peace treaty was signed, the Guardia began to experience renewed budget problems. *La Noticia,* the Liberal Party's organ in Managua, began a campaign to separate the Guardia and the police and to cut the Guardia's budget, which had reached the astonishing total, for Nicaragua, of $116,185 per month.[22] General Somoza responded that the large force of *auxiliares* was responsible for most of the increase in Guardia costs and proceeded to dismiss all but 100 of the 1,409 men in this category. Far from being satisfied, *La Noticia* broadened its attacks to include denunciations of Guardia *fueros,* which gave its members immunity from civil prosecution.[23] The attacks increased in April when Congress began debating the 1934 budget. *La Noticia* now argued that one way to cut the budget was to reduce officers' salaries, cutting the *Jefe Director* from C$300 to C$200 a month and reducing the pay of all other officers down to a minimum of C$45 each month for second lieutenants.[24]

Conservatives seemed more concerned about the Guardia's composition than about its costs. Their fears in this area were increased when Sacasa, shortly after his inauguration, brought 300 handpicked Liberals into the Guardia, using them to double the Managua garrison.[25] General Chamorro went to the President to request information about the political affiliation of Guardia troops and to complain about alleged abuses that soldiers were committing against Conservatives. Sacasa refused to give him any information and only the intervention of the American Minister won for the Conservative leader the right to confer with General Somoza about matters concerning the Guardia.[26]

With leaders in both parties unhappy, it was not surprising that the budget debate in the Nicaraguan Congress produced sharp attacks on the Guardia. One Deputy proposed cutting the force to 1,500 men, another wanted it cut to 300 and replaced in most areas by Hacienda Guards, while a third urged that it be abolished and replaced by the traditional, pre-1927 Nicaraguan army. A budget providing C$9,000 a month for the Guardia was finally passed in June.[27] At almost the same time trouble with Sandino began once again.

Conflict between Sandino and the Guardia had been threatening for months. In May, Sandino objected to the establishment of a Guardia post only twenty-five miles from his territory. When the President refused to move it, he offered to leave the country, but Sacasa discouraged him from doing this.[28] Sandino then began attacking the Guardia Nacional as an institution, charging that the organization was unconstitutional, an enemy of the government and of his men, then demanding that it be reformed and brought in line with the Constitution or that the President arm the civilian population to protect their liberties.[29] For the Guardia, such charges represented a basic threat to their existence. The seeds of conflict were being nurtured by both sides and would soon produce an open clash.

Meanwhile, the continued dismissal of the *auxiliares* from government service had reduced, by July 1, the number of men under Guardia control to 2,891.[30] While this represented a considerable decrease from the peak strength of over 4,000, which had been reached in February, it was still larger than at any time during the American intervention. Expenses were also being trimmed. Because of the continued decline in the nation's economy, General Somoza, in July, reduced the salaries of all officers. The *Jefe Director* himself took the largest cut, dropping from C$300 to C$260 a month. Colonels were cut from C$175 to C$150 and second lieutenants from C$75 to C$70.[31] Despite such actions, widespread criticism of Guardia costs continued.

Increasing tension was suddenly revealed in August 1933, when, in a series of violent explosions, the main arsenal in Managua was destroyed. The explosions rattled windows all over the city and gave an equal shaking to government nerves. Congress immediately declared a state of war in Managua and a state of seige throughout the rest of the nation and Sacasa gave government arms to 700 Liberals in León and ordered the arrest of 300 leading Conservatives. Protestations of innocence and attacks on these actions led to the imposition of press censorship.[32] One of the most significant responses came from Sandino, who wired an offer to come to the government's aid with 600 armed men, explaining that he had obtained arms for the extra 500 from recently defeated Honduran rebels.[33] The offer was refused, as no help was needed, but it must have been extremely upsetting to Somoza and the Guardia to discover that Sandino could raise a force of 600 armed men almost overnight.

It was soon obvious that the Conservatives had nothing to do with the explosion, but Sacasa did not release the last of the political prisoners until August 18 and did not lift the censorship until September 13.[34] Both Matthew Hanna and General Somoza were upset with the President's response to the incident, which they felt only led to increased attacks upon the Guardia.[35] Hanna reported that Sacasa's fear of internal disorder had "steadily increased until it had become an unreasonable fear amounting to an obsession." At the same time, the American Minister had only praise for Somoza's actions, which he felt had "kept the Guardia loyal and at its posts in spite of serious difficulties," one of which was the government's failure to pay Guardia salaries for June or July.[36] Somoza had good reason to keep the Guardia at its assigned duties. With the officer corps still divided and Sandino free in the mountains with a potential force of at least 600 armed men, the *Jefe Director* could hardly afford an open break with the President. Somoza was ambitious, but not foolhardy, and he would maintain at least a semblance of loyalty to Sacasa until he felt that the time was right for a complete takeover.

Somoza still did not dare to move against the *Academia* graduates, but there was one other element within the officer corps that he did not trust and wanted to remove. These were the Conservative officers appointed under the bipartisan agreements. In October 1933, two of these, Colonel José Andrés Urtecho and Major Gustavo R. Lacayo, chief and *auxiliar* of the Guardia's Law Department, were tried on a charge of infidelity in confidential military correspondence. The charges revolved around a letter written by Somoza, which contained some very caustic criticisms of Vice-President Espinosa. Somoza gave this letter to Urtecho and Lacayo for safekeeping, and a few days later it showed up in Espinosa's hands. Major Lacayo agreed to resign and charges against him were dropped, but Colonel Urtecho insisted that he was being framed as part of a plot to drive Conservatives out of the Guardia.[37] In making his defense, Urtecho pointed out that, since the arsenal explosion, he had been without a safe which only he could open, and added that if he had wanted to embarrass Somoza, he could have used much more incriminating documents. Despite his pleas he was found guilty by the court-martial and sentenced to a bad conduct discharge. Somoza changed this to a simple "discharge for the convenience of the government."[38]

Managua's leading Liberal newspaper used this case as an excuse for an editorial attack on the idea of trying to create a nonpartisan army, an effort which the editor described as "a bad experience."[39] Efforts to destroy the last shreds of nonpartisanship within the Guardia also received support from the Sacasa administration. In December, the Minister for Foreign Affairs, Dr. Leonardo Argüello, denounced the agreements to keep the Guardia bipartisan, declaring that "Communists" might use them, in some unspecified manner, to "provoke disturbances." Argüello's remedy for this was a complete reorganization of the Guardia, a proposal for which he sought, but failed to obtain, American approval.[40]

In November, President Sacasa contracted malaria and went to his coffee plantation, El Encanto, to recover. His illness raised rumors of an impending clash between the President and the military. These rumors gained strength when Gabry Rivas, editor of *La Nueva Prensa,* suggested that the Guardia take over all the powers of state and assume in its budget the duties of the cabinet ministries. Rivas quoted the Guardia's Chief of Staff as saying that Franklin Roosevelt's new Latin American policy allowed the Guardia to abrogate the bipartisan agreement.[41] All this alarmed Sandino who, in mid-November, flew to Managua to see Sacasa.

Tension between the Sandinistas and the Guardia had been steadily increasing in recent months. In August five of Sandino's followers were killed by a Guardia patrol, an incident the Guardia blamed on the failure of Sandino men to inform them that they would be in the arca.[42] Somoza had reportedly been protesting continued government payments for, and ammunition shipments to, Sandino's troops in the North. At one point he had even told President Sacasa, "I will not permit this to go on and you will be guilty of what happens."[43] The conversations held by Sandino, first with Sacasa at his coffee plantation, and later with Somoza in Managua, eased the tension. Declarations from Sandino, pledging to respect the legal authorities of the government, and from Somoza, ordering the Guardia not to molest Sandino's men, were published on December 5.[44] These declarations, however, produced only a brief lull before the final confrontation in 1934.

At this critical time, a new American Minister, Arthur Bliss Lane, replaced Matthew Hanna as American Minister to Nicaragua. This removed from Managua a man who was probably too close to Somoza, but who might have been able to exercise some control over the General during the coming crisis with Sandino. This was Lane's first post as Minister and he would find it a hectic, at times dangerous, and often frustrating experience.

Sandino left Managua on December 9. That same day Lane heard from Somoza of yet another clash between the Guardia and the Sandinistas. Lane described the General's tone, when discussing Sandino, as "very hostile."[45] A few days later General Estrada, commander of Sandino's troops, arrived in Managua to request additional arms and ammunition. To grant the request would infuriate the Guardia and strengthen Sandino, but refusal might lead the guerrillas to resume the war. Caught between two unpleasant prospects, President Sacasa did nothing. While he procrastinated, the situation rapidly got worse. Sandino's representative in Managua, Dr. Zepeda, told Lane that Sandino might have to "protect" the President from the Guardia, while Somoza announced that Sandino would have to give up his remaining arms in February, as one year would have elapsed since the signing of the peace treaty. Somoza added that he expected the President to give in if Sandino refused to disarm and complained that "the Guardia had not been permitted to finish Sandino."[46]

The key to the dispute was the demand that Sandino give up his arms. Both Somoza and Sacasa claimed that he was obliged to do this on the anniversary of the peace treaty. Actually the treaty only gave the government the right to reduce the number of men under Sandino and to change their officers after one year, a right which could be used to disarm them if the administration so chose.[47] Somoza's demand for the surrender of the arms was originally published in the journal, *Guardia Nacional,* and reprinted in the February 4, 1934, issue of *La Noticia.* According to the *Jefe Director,* if Sandino failed to "keep his promise" and give up his arms, this would create an intolerable situation of a state existing within a state, but if he did disarm, he was promised protection of his rights and safety. Somoza even offered to incorporate some of Sandino's men into local military units.[48] No action was specified if he failed to disarm, but it was clear that the Guardia would take some action

This situation created numerous problems for the new American Minister, Arthur Bliss Lane. Nicaraguans of all factions constantly approached him, seeking advice or approval for their own plans. Since any official expression of American views was regarded in Nicaragua as "an important factor," Lane found it "virtually impossible for us to give advice, even in a discreet manner, without assuming responsibility for the advice given."[49] This problem became even more acute when, on February 9, Somoza told Lane that "if I would only give my word he would 'lock Sandino up.' " The American Minister expressed strong disapproval of any such action and secured Somoza's promise "not to do anything without first having your [Lane's] approval."[50]

While the Guardia's attitude was growing progressively more belligerent, Sandino was continuing his attacks on that organization, denouncing it as illegal and unconstitutional and demanding its immediate reform. On January 26, he wrote President Sacasa, refusing to give up any of his arms and declaring that he would protect the President from the "unconstitutional" Guardia Nacional.[51] This letter's threatening tone at last forced Sacasa to take some action. He finally refused Sandino's request for more arms and ammunition, but instead of again demanding that the guerrillas disarm, he simply requested that Sandino come to Managua to discuss the situation. To Lane, this indicated that the President was more afraid of the Guardia than he was of Sandino.[52] This invitation was accepted, although Sandino commented that the trip was unnecessary "as everything had already been settled."[53] This decision to return to the center of Somoza's power would cost him his life.

On January 31, 1934, *La Noticia* reported that a highly secret meeting of Guardia officers from all over the nation was going on in Managua. Commanders had arrived from as far away as Bluefields, but the newspaper was unable to discover the reason for the meeting.[54] Given the approaching deadline that Somoza had set for Sandino's disarmament, it seems obvious that the meeting concerned plans for future actions against the guerrilla leader. According to two of the officers present, Somoza opposed killing Sandino, but was overruled by a junta of other officers, led by General Abaunza and Colonel Santos.[55] Sandino's decision to come to Managua gave the Guardia a golden opportunity to carry out this decision.

When Sandino arrived in the capital, on February 16, he found the city in a state of extreme tension. A few days before, Somoza had again promised that the Guardia would be loyal and would take no action that might embarrass the President, but Lane doubted the degree of control that the *Jefe Director* had over his fellow officers.[56] The situation in the North was also very tense and Lane was informed that Guardia troops in that area seemed to be seeking a "pretext" to attack the Sandinistas.[57] It was clear that the situation would have to be resolved before Sandino could ever leave Managua.

Despite the obvious danger, Sandino was in a far from conciliatory mood. He again characterized the Guardia as an unconstitutional agency, declared he would never turn over his arms to it, and demanded its immediate reform. Finally, he accused it of killing seventeen of his men in the past year and arresting many more, but added that he did not want war and would consider going abroad and issuing a manifesto if the conflict could not be resolved.[58]

These statements infuriated Somoza and during lunch with Arthur Bliss Lane, he asked the American envoy to "wink my eye" so he could "lock up Sandino." He got a decidedly negative response from the Minister, who had him repeat his promise not to move against Sandino. Somoza issued Sandino a safe-conduct pass, then joined Lane at a baseball game, an event later cited by those who accused them of conspiring together.[59]

On February 19, Sandino's position apparently hardened still further. In a letter to the President he attacked the Guardia as a "military institution with regulations foreign to our fundamental charter," while at the same time, he claimed his own force was completely constitutional and belonged to President Sacasa. He demanded that the government guarantee the "constitutionalization of the Guardia" and the lives and interests of his supporters.[60]

Somehow, in the hours between the dispatch of this letter and Sacasa's reply the following day, a compromise was achieved. Sacasa announced his determination to bring the Guardia into line with the Constitution during the first six months of 1934. He also agreed to appoint a Presidential Delegate for the northern areas who would protect the interests of Sandino and his followers while the Guardia was being reformed and would also collect "all the arms which may be found outside of the control of the government."[61] In the crucial matter of selecting the Delegate, the President gave in completely to Sandino, appointing one of his advisors, General Horacio Portocarrero.

This satisfied Sandino, but not Somoza, who made no effort to disguise his anger. He wrote the President that he had "done everything humanly possible in complying with my duty for the purpose of preventing the disturbances which this type of appointment would bring," adding that if Portocarrero were appointed, he would not be responsible for the consequences.[62] The *Jefe Director* complained to Bliss Lane that the appointment was "an insult to the Guardia," and that it would make his troops in the North subject to Sandino's control. He then asked the American Minister to do something about the situation, adding that the Guardia had almost gotten out of control over the incident, but if Lane would just let him "lock up Sandino," everything would be settled. Lane refused to do this, but agreed to investigate the situation.[63]

Lane was informed that Portocarrero had become quite disillusioned with Sandino and would be totally loyal to the Sacasa administration. The Minister carried this report to Somoza, who again promised to personally do nothing, but added that his force would still "be furious at the insult and that things had reached a point where he could not longer control the Guardia." [64] The President was greatly upset over the Guardia's attitude, which he characterized as "nothing short of revolt," but since, as Lane observed, he had little control over Somoza and Somoza's own control over the military was rather dubious, Sacasa could do nothing about the situation except complain.[65]

The conflict between Sandino and the Guardia reached its climax on the night of February 21. That evening, two different meetings were held in Managua. At the Presidential Palace, Sacasa and Sofonías Salvatierra were having a farewell dinner for Sandino and his supporters, including Generals Umanzor and Estrada. At about ten o'clock, Salvatierra, Sandino, Umanzor, and Estrada left in Salvatierra's auto. The other meeting had broken up shortly before this. It had been held in the Campo de Marte and most of the Guardia's higher-ranking officers, including Generals Somoza and Abaunza, had been present. All available sources agree that those present decided to move immediately against Sandino, and no one denies that Somoza was the one who eventually gave the order to shoot Sandino. There is, however, no agreement as to *how* they arrived at this decision. Somoza, in a ghostwritten account, claims that the meeting only decided to arrest Sandino and that the decision to kill him was made only after he had been seized.[66] Other accounts dispute this. According to one account the decision to kill Sandino was taken at this meeting and it was Somoza who urged it. The *Jefe Director* reportedly claimed that he had gained American approval for the elimination of Sandino, an action which the other officers present confirmed and set about to accomplish.[67]

Two high-ranking officers directly involved in the meeting contradict this account. They claimed that the officer corps had to

General Augusto C. Sandino (center) and other victims of Somoza's ambition, murdered in 1934.

Five Sandinista guerrillas, captured and tied by U. S. Marines, being led to confinement.

force a frightened Somoza to agree to Sandino's death. Somoza did not want to spare Sandino because of any fondness for the guerrilla leader, but because of fear over the consequences that his murder might entail.[68] A more recent account, written by a former Guardia officer, does claim that Lane and Somoza met several times on February 21, then adds the interesting detail that Somoza and General Abaunza managed to lock up all uninvolved Guardia officers in Managua at a poetry recital, assuring them that there would be no military oppostition to their actions. This account pictures Abaunza as, at the least, considerably more determined than Somoza to proceed with the murder.[69]

However the decision was made, its results were obvious. A strong Guardia patrol blocked the road from the Presidential Palace to downtown Managua at the point where it passed the Campo de Marte and the national penitentiary. As Salvatierra's car approached this point, it was ordered to halt and was immediately surrounded by armed troops, who ordered the occupants to leave the car. Surprised and confused by these events, Sandino managed to persuade the patrol's commander, Major Delgadillo, to carry a message to Somoza asking for a chance to talk with him.[70] Delgadillo phoned the request to Somoza, who almost weakened at this last moment, especially since Sandino appealed to the fact that they both were Masons, and Abaunza had to take the phone away from the *Jefe Director* and order the Major to proceed with the "execution."[71] Sandino's father and Salvatierra were then locked up and Sandino, Umanzor, and Estrada were loaded onto a truck and driven to the airfield. There they were lined up and shot, then buried in great secrecy under the airport runway.[72]

These three were not the only ones to die that night. Sócrates Sandino, Augusto's brother, along with General Santos López, had stayed with Salvatierra's son-in-law, Roland Murillo, in Salvatierra's house. A Guardia patrol was sent to capture them, but they resisted. In the ensuing fight, Sócrates was killed and Murillo mortally wounded, but General López managed to escape.[73]

Somoza may possibly have claimed to have had Lane's support for these actions, but it is clear that Lane did not approve. He heard the shots from Salvatierra's house and tried to phone Somoza, but discovered that his phone had been cut, an action that convinced him that something very serious was happening.

On his way to use the Legation's phone, he passed Salvatierra's home and saw a wounded man on the pavement and a large group of Guardia, armed with machine guns and rifles. A captain told him that the occupants of the house had fired at the Guardia and that the fire had been returned. Lane continued on to the Legation and phoned the President, who urgently requested him to come up to the Palace. On his way there, Lane passed Somoza's quarters which he noticed were heavily protected with sandbags and machine gun emplacements.[74]

The Sacasa family was extremely upset. The President's daughter had witnessed part of the arrest and informed her father, who then discovered that all his communications with the Guardia had been cut. He asked Lane to go to Somoza's headquarters and bring the General to him, a request that the Minister promptly granted.[75]

The Guardia's erstwhile leader was anything but the picture of a swaggering, satisfied general who engineered a major coup. Somoza was afraid to go to the Presidential Palace for fear "somebody would take vengeance," and it was only by offering to personally accompany him that Lane was able to persuade him to go. There Somoza professed ignorance of Sandino's fate, but acknowledged that Salvatierra and Sandino's father were imprisoned. The *Jefe Director* claimed that he "could not guarantee their lives as far as the Guardia was concerned" and both he and Sacasa asked Lane to take the prisoners to the American Legation. Lane did this and later, under the protection of the Legation's car, delivered them to the Presidential Palace.[76]

Orders had also been issued for the Guardia to concentrate around Sandino's camp at Wiwili and forcibly disarm his troops, and to arrest several leading Conservatives. The President blocked the latter action, but could only postpone the former, which specified that if Sandino's men did not give up their arms, they were to be exterminated.[77] This order was carried out ruthlessly. The Guardia claimed that only twenty-two men were killed in the attack on Wiwili, but other accounts place the total at over 300 and accuse the Guardia of slaughtering women and children.[78] The Guardia even tried to secure the services of an American aviator to bomb the Sandinistas, a move the State Department managed to block.[79] Some of Sandino's followers, notably Pedrón Altamirano, escaped and resumed guerrilla warfare. Without Sandino, however, the illiterate Pedrón could do little more than annoy the Guardia. For the moment at least, Sandinismo had been eliminated as a major political force in Nicaragua.

The murder of Sandino has traditionally been viewed as a deliberate act of Somoza's designed to clear his path to power.[80] An analysis of Somoza's actions, both before and after the killings, however, supports the thesis that Somoza was pressured by his own subordinates into taking the action.[81] Somoza had repeatedly warned Bliss Lane about the Guardia's attitude, had declared he could not control the force, and had begged to be allowed to imprison Sandino. Two days after the assassination, he apologized to Lane, stating that he could not keep his promise because "feeling among the Guardia officers was too strong against Sandino," though he admitted that those who seized and shot Sandino acted under orders.[82]

These statements are not necessarily contradictory. Somoza did issue the orders to kill Sandino, but he did so in response to growing pressure from other officers. While he remained alive, Sandino was a threat to the position of virtually every officer in the Guardia. Sandino had openly denounced the Guardia, had fought it in the Segovias for years and declared his independence of it, and even offered to protect the President against it. Sandino saw in the Guardia of his time an embryonic monster that could one day betray Nicaragua. He had been prepared to retain his arms in defiance of Guardia orders and, finally, one of his advisors had been appointed Presidential Delegate, with possible command over Guardia units, in the northern area of Nicaragua, an act Somoza described as an "intolerable insult." The continued presence of such a man in Nicaragua threatened the position and degraded the status of every officer. The officers who acted against Sandino did so for their own interest, not Somoza's, and they might well have done so even if the General had not concurred. Somoza would probably have preferred to arrest and perhaps exile Sandino, but opposition from Sacasa and Bliss Lane made this virtually impossible. Left with the alternative of either killing Sandino or allowing him to leave Managua with his position greatly enhanced by Sacasa's concessions, Somoza ordered his death. He did so with considerable trepidation, fearing that the action might well lead to his own downfall, and Sandino's ghost has haunted the Somozas ever since. Somoza did covet the presidency, and two years later would oust Sacasa, but in the days following the murder, when rumors of such action were rampant, he almost crawled before the President to prove his loyalty. The fear that Lane observed in Somoza after Sandino's death is a natural reaction from a man who had been pressured into ordering a course of action he would rather have postponed or settled in some other manner.

Shortly after the killings, General Somoza under great pressure from Sacasa to punish those responsible, called in several officers and told them that "while he realized the whole Guardia was responsible, somebody must assume the guilt."[83] Such a statement makes little sense if Somoza alone initiated the plot, but it is quite natural if the other officers had urged and supported this action.

The days following Sandino's death produced a host of rumors that Somoza, supported by the United States would shortly attempt to replace Sacasa. The American Minister strove to halt such reports and to get State Department authorization to issue a statement that the United States would not recognize any regime that took power by revolutionary means, but the Department would only permit him to make such statements orally to Somoza.[84] Lane's fight to issue a public statement culminated in a February 24 telephone conversation with Ed Wilson of the Department's Latin American Division. Wilson repeated the Department's opinion that talking privately to Somoza "might serve to stabilize things and prevent a revolutionary movement." Lane was sure that this was inadequate, telling Wilson he had already spoken to Somoza and could see no value in repeating himself, adding that "the opinion seems to prevail that the United States is supporting Somoza in an attempt to bring about a coup." According to Lane, the situation in Nicaragua bordered on anarchy, with two armed governments coexisting in Managua. One was on La Loma where the President had turned his residence into an armed camp with trenches and machine guns, the other consisted of Somoza and his men, only a few hundred yards away. Unless something was done, Lane felt a clash was inevitable, stating flatly that American inaction was "inviting a military dictatorship" and if the Department still refused to act, he would "absolutely assume no responsibility for what may happen."[85]

In the short run, Lane's fears proved exaggerated, for the expected coup simply failed to materialize. Somoza, at first, went to almost every length to appease Sacasa, even offering up Captain Policarpo Gutiérrez, the one-armed officer Lane had seen at Salvatierra's house, as a scapegoat for the entire affair.[86]

As it turned out, no Guardia officer was ever punished for participating in Sandino's murder, but this was not known in February. The murders of Estrada and Umanzor and of Murillo and the *campesinos* at Wiwili likewise went unpunished.

On February 25, both the President and the *Jefe Director* issued statements on Sandino's death. Sacasa stated that the killings were done by a group of officers, acting in direct violation of his orders. He denounced their actions as "an unjustifiable crime," due to the defective functioning of Guardia, and promised to expose and punish those responsible.[87] Somoza seemed to accept these attacks upon the Guardia without complaint. In his announcement, he described the killings as "deplorable events, promised to discover those responsible, and publicly pledged his loyalty and that of the Guardia Nacional to President Sacasa."[88]

Still fearing a military coup, the President continued to protect La Loma with troops drawn from outside the Guardia and to demand copies of the Guardia codes so that his staff could decode all messages. He even called General Somoza and several of his officers up to the Presidential Palace, where he made them repeat their oaths of loyalty in the presence of the diplomatic corps. This angered Lane who, along with the other diplomats had not been informed of what was to transpire. Such action, he felt, was designed to humiliate Somoza and he resented being made a party to it.[89]

Early in March, the crisis began to ease. Somoza grudgingly agreed to the President's plan to issue decrees establishing a basic law for the Guardia and reforming it to make it conform to the Constitution. In an executive decree, Sacasa provided for presidential control over the Guardia, giving him the right to issue orders directly to any officer, to control the stationing and movement of troops, to nominate, promote, or demote officers, to approve all "extraordinary" expenses of the Guardia, to place Guardia police under the Minister of Gobernación, and to receive a daily report on Guardia activities from the *Jefe Director*.[90]

Following the issuance of this decree, Sacasa replaced several officers involved in the killings. Among these were General Abaunza, the Chief of Staff, and Major Alfonso González Cervantes, the Guardia's paymaster. Abaunza had originally been put into the Guardia to spy on Somoza, but had evidently switched loyalties. He and Somoza had even gotten drunk together, then staggered up to La Loma and called upon Sacasa to protest the continued presence of General Castro Wassmer,

Somoza's personal enemy, as commander of the forces guarding the President. Sacasa sent Castro Wassmer back to León, but also decided to dump Abaunza.[91] Major González Cervantes was ordered out at the same time, allegedly for mishandling funds and spending too much money on fiestas.[92] Somoza tried to block Abaunza's removal, though he felt he "talked too much" and was of little use to the Guardia, but Sacasa insisted. He would not even allow Somoza to assign him to other duties.[93]

In picking replacements for these officers and making new appointments, the President demonstrated a clear preference for his own relatives. Antioco Sacasa, the President's brother, became Chief of Staff of the Guardia, and Ramón Sacasa, the chief executive's cousin, was given command of the newly created western area, with headquarters in León.[94] These actions seemed to indicate that Sacasa had gained control over Somoza and the Guardia, ending the possibility of their moving against him. Such indications were soon to prove totally illusory.

NOTES

1. Hanna to Stimson, November 3, 1932, *Foeign Relations,* 1932, V. p. 876.

2. Memorandum on Sandino by J.B. Pate, Nicaraguan Records, Box 10, File 3, MCHA; Neill Macaulay, *The Sandino Affair* (Chicago: Quadrangle, 1967), p. 243.

3. Salvatierra to Sandino, November 23, 1932, and Sandino to Salvatierra, printed in Gregorio Selser, *Sandino, General de los hombres libres,* Vol. III (Buenes Aires: Editorial Tríangulo, 1958), pp. 190–91 and 196–97.

4. *La Noticia* (Managua), January 8, 12, and 22, 1933, p. 1; Anastasio Somoza García, *El verdadero Sandino: o el Calvario de las Segovias* (Managua: Tipografía Robelo, 1936), pp. 402–409.

5. *La Noticia* (Managua), January 15, 1933, p. 1; Hanna to Stimson, January 17, 1933, NA RG 59, 817.1051/738.

6. Special Order 38–1932, Headquarters, Guardia Nacional de Nicaragua, October 21, 1932, printed in Smith et al., *Review,* p.159.

7. Hanna to Stimson, January 8, 13, and 23, 1933, NA RG 59, 817.1051/738, 817.1051/747, 817.1051/758.

8. Hanna to Wilson, January 16, 1933, Hanna Papers, NA RG 59.

9. Ibid.; Hanna to Stimson, January 8 and 23, 1933, NA RG 59, 817.1051/738, 817.1051/758.

10. *La Noticia* (Managua), January 11, 1933, p. 1; Hanna to Stimson, January 22 and 23, 1933, NA RG 59, 817.1051/756, 817.1051/758.

11. Hanna to Stimson, January 24, 1933, NA RG 59, 817.00/7717; *La Noticia* (Managua), January 24, 1933, p. 1.

12. Selser, *Sandino,* II, pp. 206–207; Hanna to Stimson, January 24, 1933, NA RG 59, 817.00/7717.

13. Hanna to Stimson, January 17 and 20 and February 2, 1933, Stimson to Hanna, January 26, 1933, NA RG 59, 817.00/7698, 817.00/7719, 817.00/7737, 817.00/7698.

14. Interview with Sofonías Salvatierra, Managua, November 9, 1963; Selser, *Sandino,* II, p. 222.

15. Somoza, *El verdadero Sandino,* pp. 446–48; Selser, *Sandino,* II, p. 222.

16. Hanna to Stimson, February 3, 1933, NA RG 59, 817.00/7742; Somoza, *El verdadero Sandino,* pp. 451–54; Selser, *Sandino* II, pp. 222–24.

17, Somoza, *El verdadero Sandino,* p. 457; *La Noticia* (Managua), February 4, 1933, p.1; *La Prensa* (Managua), February 4, 1933, p. 1; Selser, *Sandino,* II, pp. 222–25.

18. Hanna to Stimson, February 6, 1933, NA RG 59, 817.00/7758.

19. *La Noticia* (Managua), February 10, 1933, p. 1; Hanna to Stimson, February 20, 1933, NA RG 59, 817.00/7772.

20. Somoza, *El verdadero Sandino,* p. 461; Hanna to Stimson, February 20, 1933, NA RG 59, 817.00/7772. The córdoba was then roughly equal to the dollar, but would soon decline in value.

21. Somoza, *El verdadero Sandino,* pp. 471–74; Hanna to Stimson, March 8, 1933, NA RG 59, 817.00/7782; Selser, *Sandino,* II, pp. 236–37; Augusto César Sandino, *Manifesto a los pueblos de la tierra y en particular al de Nicaragua* (Managua: La Prensa, 1933), p. 24; Domingo Ibarra Grijalva, *The Last Night of General Augusto César Sandino* (New York: Vantage Press, 1973), p. 181

22. *La Noticia* (Managua), February 8, 1933, p. 1, and February 11, 1933, p. 6.

23. Ibid., February 11, 1933, p. 1, February 21, 1933, p. 1, and February 22, 1933, p. 2.

24. Ibid., April 26, 1933, p. 1, and April 29, 1933, p.1.

25. Hanna to Secretary of State Cordell Hull, March 23, 1933, and April 21, 1933, NA RG 59, 817.1051/778, 817.1051/781.

26. Hanna to Hull, February 3, 1933, and March 24, 1933, NA RG 59, 817.1051/773, 817.1051/777.

27. *La Noticia* (Managua), May 16, 1933, p. 1, May 19, 1933, p. 1, and June 4, 1933, p.1.

28. Hanna to Hull, May 15, 1933, NA RG 59, 817.00/7821; Somoza, *El verdadero Sandino,* p. 494.

29. Somoza, *El verdadero Sandino,* pp. 495–96 and 506–509; Selser, *Sandino,* II, pp. 250–53; *La Noticia* (Managua), June 21, 1933, p. 1.

30. Hanna to Hull, July 7, 1933, NA RG 59, 817.1051/789.

31. Hanna to Hull, July 10, 1933, NA RG 59, 817.1051/792; *La Prensa* (Managua), July 8, 1933, p. 1.

32. *La Noticia* (Managua), August 3, 1933, pp. 1 and 6; *La Prensa* (Managua) July 8, 1933, p. 1, August 5, 1933, p. 1, and August 6, 1933, p. 1.

33. Hanna to Hull, August 16, 1933, NA RG 59, 817.00/7867; Sandino to President Sacasa, August 7, 1933, printed in Selser, *Sandino,* II, p. 258.

34. *La Prensa* (Managua), August 18, 1933, p. 1, August 20, 1933, p. 1, and September 14, 1933, p. 1; *La Noticia* (Managua), August 18, 1933, p. 1.

35. Hanna to Hull, August 15, 1933, Hanna Papers, NA RG 59.

36. Hanna to Hull, August 18, 1933, NA RG 59, 817.1051/796.

37. Ildefonso Solórzano [Ildo Sol], *La Guardia Nacional de Nicaragua: Su trajectoria y incógnito, 1927–1944* (Granada, Nicaragua: El Centro-Americano, 1944), p. 82; Paul C. Daniels, chargé in Nicaragua, to Hull, October 25, 1933, NA RG 59, 817.1051/805.

38. Solórzano, *La Guardia Nacional,* p. 83; *La Noticia* (Managua), October 21, 1933, p. 1.

39. *La Noticia* (Managua), October 25, 1933, p. 1.

40. Memorandum of a conversation between Hull and Dr. Leonardo Argüello, December 9, 1933, NA RG 59, 817.1051/806½.

41. Daniels to Hull, November 4, 1933, NA RG 59, 817.00/7904.

42. Sacasa to Sandino, August 21, 1933, printed in Selser, *Sandino,* II, pp. 261–62; Daniels to Hull, November 25, 1933, NA RG 59, 817.00/7910; *La Noticia* (Managua), November 23, 1933, p. 1.

43. Ibarra Grijalva, *Last Night of Sandino,* p. 189.

44. *La Noticia* (Managua), December 5, 1933, p. 1.

45. Lane to Hull, December 12, 1933, NA RG 59, 817.00/7916.

46. Lane to Hull, January 3, 1934, NA RG 59, 817.00/7922.

47. Ibid.

48. General Anastasio Somoza García, "Editorial," *Guardia Nacional,* January 1933, p. 1. Reprinted in *La Noticia* (Managua), February 4, 1934, pp. 1 and 6.

49. Lane to Wilson, February 3, 1934, Lane Papers.

50. Lane to Josephus Daniels, March 4, 1934, Lane Papers.

51. Lane to Hull, February 5, 1934, NA RG 59, 817.00/7932.

52. Lane to Hull, February 5, 1934, NA RG 59, 817.00/7932 and 817.00/7933.

53. Selser, *Sandino,* II, p. 276; Lane to Hull, February 9, 1934, *Foreign Relations,* 1934, V, p. 527.

54. *La Noticia* (Managua), January 31, 1934, p. 1.

55. Interviews with Major Alfonso González Cervantes and Brigadier General Camilo González, Managua. November and December 1963.

56. Lane to Hull, February 14, 1934, *Foreign Relations,* 1934, V, pp. 527–28.

57. Lane to Hull, February 14, 1934, and February 22, 1934, *Foreign Relations,* 1934, V, pp. 527–29.

58. *La Noticia* (Managua), February 17, 1934, p. 1; *La Prensa* (Managua), February 18, 1934, pp. 1 and 6; Lane to Hull, February 20, 1934, *Foreign Relations,* 1934, V, p. 528; Adolfo Reyes Huete, *ETAPAS del Ejercito* (Managua: Talleres Nacionales, n.d.), p. 63.

59. Lane to Josephus Daniels, March 4, 1934, Lane Papers; Lane to Hull, February 20, 1934, *Foreign Relations,* 1934, V, p. 528; Macaulay, *Sandino Affair,* p. 249.

60. Translation of letter from Sandino to Sacasa, February 19, 1934, Lane Papers.

61. Translation of letter from Sacasa to Sandino, February 20, 1934, Lane Papers.

62. Somoza to Sacasa, printed in Anastasio Somoza García, *El verdadero Sandino* (Managua: Tipografía Robelo, 1936), pp. 562–63.

63. Lane to Hull, February 22, 1934, *Foreign Relations,* 1934, V. pp. 530–31; Lane to Josephus Daniels, March 4, 1934, Lane Papers.

64. Ibid.

65. Ibid.

66. Somoza, *El veradero Sandino,* pp. 564–65.

67. Lt. Abelardo Cuadra, G.N. quoted in Selser, *Sandino,* II, p. 295. Cuadra was later imprisoned and then exiled for plotting against Somoza.

68. Interviews with Major Alfonso González Cervantes and Brigadier General Camilo González, Managua, November and December 1963.

69. Ibarra Grijalva, *Last Night of Sandino,* pp. 229–38.

70. Interview with Sofonías Salvatierra, Managua, October 1963: interviews with Major Alfonso González Cervantes and Brigadier General Camilo González, Managua, November and December 1963; Selser *Sandino,* II, pp. 296; Ibarra Grijalva, *Last Night of Sandino,* pp. 237–38.

71. Interviews with Major Alfonso González Cervantes and Brigadier General Camilo González, Managua, November and December 1963; Macaulay, *Sandino Affair,* p. 255; Ibarra Grijalva, *Last Night of Sandino,* p. 238.

72. Selser, *Sandino,* II, pp. 297–99; interview with Major Julio d'Arbelles, Corinto, Nicaragua, December 1963.

73. Interviews with Major Alfonso González Cervantes and Brigadier General Camilo González, Managua, November and December 1963; Selser, *Sandino,* II, p. 229; Ibarra Grijalva, *Last Night of Sandino,* p. 246.

74. Lane to Hull, February 22, 1934, *Foreign Relations,* 1934, V, p. 530; Lane to Josephus Daniels, March 4, 1934, Lane Papers.

75. Ibid.; Selser, *Sandino,* II, p. 296.

76. Ibid.; interview with Sofonías Salvatierra, Managua, November 1963.

77. Lane to Hull, February 22, 1934 (two messages), *Foreign Relations,* 1934, V, pp. 530–32.

78. *La Noticia* (Managua), March 3, 1934, p. 1; Selser, *Sandino,* II, p. 301; William Krehm, *Democracia y tiranía en el Caribe,* (Mexico, D.F.: Unión Democrática Centro-Americana, 1949), p. 162; interview with Sofonías Salvatierra, Managua, October 1963; interview with Ildefonso Solórzano, Managua, October 1963.

79. Lane to Hull, February 25, 1934, *Foreign Relations,* 1934, V, p. 538.

80. Lejeune Cummins, *Quijote on a Burro* (Mexico, D.F.: Impresora Azteca, 1958), p. 109; Marvin Goldwert, *The Constabulary in the Dominican Republic and Nicaragua,* Latin American Monographs No.17 (Gainesville: University of Florida Press, 1961), p. 44.

81. Interviews with Major Alfonso Gonzáles Cervantes, Managua, November 1963; Krehm, *Democracia y tiranía,* p. 162. Krehm quotes Somoza as saying, in response to Sandino's request to talk with him, that he was "terribly confused" by Sandino's pleas, but that he couldn't change the orders of his "subordinates."

82. Lane to Hull, February 23, 1934, *Foreign Relations,* 1934, V, pp. 534–35.

83. Ibid.

84. Lane to Hull, February 22, 23, and 24, 1934, and Hull to Lane, February 23 and 26, 1934, *Foreign Relations,* 1934, V, pp. 533, 535–36, and 539.

85. Transcript of telephone conversation between Lane and Wilson, February 4, 1934, Lane Papers. The transcript is printed in Vladimir Petrov, *A Study in Diplomacy: The Story of Arthur Bliss Lane* (Chicago: Regnery, 1971), pp. 45–48.

86. Lane to Hull, February 23, 1934, *Foreign Relations,* 1934, V, p. 534.

87. *La Prensa* (Managua), February 25, 1934, p. 1.

88. Ibid.

89. Lane to Hull, February 23, 1934 and March 1, 1934, *Foreign Relations,* 1934, V, pp. 535 and 546–47; Lane to Josephus Daniels, March 4, 1934, Lane Papers.

90. *La Noticia* (Managua), March 3, 1934, p. 1; Lane to Hull, February 28, 1934, March 1, 1934 (3 P.M.), March 1, 1934 (11 P.M.), *Foreign Relations,* 1934, V, pp. 542–46.

91. Lane to Hull, April 5, 1934, NA RG 59, 817.1051/840.

92. Lane to Hull, April 6, 1934, NA RG 59, 817.1051/837; memorandum of conversation between Paul Daniels and President Sacasa, April 27, 1934, NA RG 59, 817.1051/848.

93. Lane to Hull, April 12, 1934, 817.1051/844.

94. Lane to Hull, March 5, 1934, *Foreign Relations,* 1934, V, p. 548; Lane to Hull, April 9, 1934, NA RG 59, 817.1051/839.

VIII

THE FALL OF SACASA

Reports of renewed political activities by Somoza soon increased tensions between the *Jefe Director* and the President. The General was reportedly subsidizing an anti-administration newspaper, *La Nueva Prensa,* and involved in the defeat of several government measures in Congress. Under these circumstances, Minister Lane recommended against lifting the embargo on arms shipments to Nicaragua, arguing that such action would only inflame tensions. He feared that machine gun cartridges ordered by the government might be used against the Guardia, noting that new concrete machine-gun emplacements facing the Campo de Marte had just been built on La Loma.[1]

In the weeks following Sandino's death, Somoza had carefully avoided any open break with the President, but in May the introduction in Congress of a bill providing amnesty for those involved in the murders signaled the end of this. Somoza predicted that the bill would be passed, vetoed, and then repassed, and this was exactly what happened.[2] While the bill was being debated, the *Jefe Director* openly praised the killing of Sandino and admitted that he had issued orders for it.[3] He also implied that the American Minister was implicated in the murder and that he supported Somoza's political ambitions. This angered Lane and the General promised to stop making such statements, but, as Lane noted, he continued making them, especially when drunk.[4] Under these circumstances, the State Department finally authorized the issuance of a public statement, disclaiming any part by the Legation in Sandino's death or in the promotion of any Nicaraguan's political ambitions.[5]

In July, Somoza's ambitions were set back by the discovery of a plot, within the Guardia, to murder him. Captain Gabriel Castillo, supposedly with the support of some *Academia* graduates, planned to lure Somoza and Colonel Antioco Sacasa to Estelí and then kill them. Word of the plot leaked to Colonel Rigoberto

Reyes, Guardia commander in Jinotega, and he sent word to Somoza to get Castillo to Managua "on any pretext" and arrest him. Castillo, two other captains, and nine lieutenants suspected of involvement in the plot were arrested and tried before a secret courtmartial, held inside the Campo de Marte.[6] Throughout the trial, Somoza acted with considerable caution and political skill. The eleven-man court-martial board was made up of *Academia* graduates to demonstrate that the General held no prejudice against this type of officer. Castillo denied none of the charges and was sentenced to twenty years' imprisonment and a dishonorable discharge. He was the only officer actually tried, but twenty others resigned following the investigation.[7]

The President attributed the plot to internal Guardia opposition to Somoza's political ambitions. Others expressed the belief that it represented continued dissatisfaction by *Academia* graduates over the appointment of nongraduates to higher ranks. Some even claimed that General Moncada was behind the plot to dispose of his erstwhile protégé, while the Mexican Minister felt that the whole thing might have been engineered by the President's relatives to get rid of Somoza.[8] Somoza apparently shared this view, as he later expressed the belief that the President's relatives had indeed been in on the plot.[9]

The General now began speculating on ways he might succeed Sacasa without violating the Constitution, Article 105, title 13 of which prohibited anyone related to the incumbent President from succeeding to that office within six months. Somoza was affected by this since his wife was Sacasa's niece. To get around this obstacle he considered forcing Sacasa to resign six months before the end of his term, amending the Constitution, or, if need be, even divorcing his wife.[10]

Disciplinary problems within the Guardia provided another barrier to Somoza's ambitions. On September 12, 1934, the arsenal at the Campo de Marte again exploded. Damage was largely confined to one building used to store old ammunition, but the explosion sent the President into what the American chargé described as a "blue funk."[11] The incident actually had nothing to do with Nicaraguan politics. The Chief of Police in Managua had hired two enlisted men to destroy the building in order to gain revenge in a quarrel with the Guardia's supply officer.[12] This additional evidence of the Guardia's lack of discipline alarmed Somoza. He began to take a large party of armed troops with him whenever he went out and would eat out only at the Officers Club or the American Legation.[13]

Many of those around Sacasa, including his wife and all of the cabinet except the Minister of Education, put pressure on the President to remove Somoza before he gained full control over the Guardia. They accused the *Jefe Director* of misuse of Guardia funds, illegal campaign activities, and using the Guardia for illegal arrests and murders. They even approached the American Minister in an effort to gain his support for the removal, but were turned down. Lane was no partisan of either side, feeling that neither the administration nor the Guardia were popular in Nicaragua, but he was convinced that any effort to remove Somoza would lead to "civil war and ruin."[14] While Lane's opposition stopped the plotting for a while, it did not ease the tension. Rumors of a possible Guardia coup circulated constantly and Sacasa, too, began to take armed guards with him on all his travels. When he visited León in November, he used a special six-car train. Two cars were loaded with presidential guards armed with rifles, another with guards with machine guns, and a fourth was a flat car with several three-inch mountain guns mounted on it. At every stop soldiers cleared the public from the station before Sacasa left the train.[15]

While the President was in León, Somoza held a "spontaneous demonstration," in honor of himself and paid for by Guardia funds. Free liquor and even free money failed to attract a large crowd, as only 2,000 people showed up to listen to speakers compare Somoza to Hitler and Mussolini and proclaim him the hope of the nation's youth.[16]

The relative failure of this demonstration put something of a damper on Somoza's ambitions and there was a lull in his conflict with the administration from December 1934 until March 1935. During this period, the General concentrated on building up his support in Congress and within the Liberal Party, efforts that enjoyed considerable success. The political truce came to an end in March when pro-administration and Conservative Deputies joined in a Congressional effort to grant amnesty to Lieutenant López, the officer convicted of causing September's explosion in the Campo de Marte. López had originally been sentenced to death, but Somoza, at Sacasa's request, had commuted his sentence to life imprisonment. The *Jefe Director* was furious over the Deputies' effort to release López and vowed he would never be released alive. He held a parade of troops to demonstrate Guardia support for his position and a thoroughly cowed Chamber of Deputies hurriedly rescinded the amnesty decree.[17]

Victory in this dispute restored Somoza's self-confidence and revived his presidential ambitions. He now felt more confident of the Guardia's loyalty, having reorganized his staff by bringing in trusted men from outlying areas. Two constitutional provisions, however, still barred his path to the *Casa Presidencial.* One was the previously mentioned provision barring any relative of "the person holding the office of president during the last six months prior to the election" from succeeding him. The other obstacle was Article 141, which barred soldiers on active duty from obtaining "office by popular election."[18] Somoza now advocated calling a constituent assembly to remove these obstacles, a course Sacasa professed to support.

Plans for the constituent assembly were upset in late April when the Guardia experienced yet another internal uprising. This one was led by a young *Academia* graduate previously suspected of involvement in the Castillo plot, Lieutenant Abelardo Cuadra. This plot, however, bore much closer resemblance to Batista's recent revolution in Cuba than it did to earlier Guardia revolts. This similarity was picked up by the Managua press, which labeled the uprising "La Batistada."[19]

Cuadra had played upon enlisted discontent over recent pay cuts. He had come to Managua to ask the *Jefe Director* to restore the former pay scale and, while there, had managed to persuade most of the enlisted men in the Second Battalion to demonstrate in favor of his demands. Somoza then ordered Cuadra confined to quarters, but the Lieutenant managed to leave the Campo de Marte and spent the rest of the day plotting with enlisted men in the Managua garrison and Police Company to revolt on the following day (April 18). According to one account Cuadra promised the men that they could assume the rank of any officer they killed. Cuadra's return to the Campo on April 18 was to be the signal for the revolt, but as usual somebody talked. Somoza hurriedly placed machine guns, manned by officers, at strategic points and arrested Cuadra when he walked into the Campo. Twenty enlisted men were also arrested and others evidently discharged since, within a few days, sixty-five replacements arrived for the Second Battalion.[20]

Cuadra's court-martial almost precipitated an open conflict between Sacasa and Somoza. The court-martial board wasted little time condemning the Lieutenant to death, a sentence Somoza approved. The President, however, refused to approve the sentence, noting that the Constitution prohibited the death penalty. For a time, Somoza seemed determined to carry out the execution, but was persuaded by Lane to avoid open rebellion and to compromise on prison sentences for Cuadra and the enlisted men involved in the plot.[21]

Only Lane's intervention had prevented an open clash and Somoza's increasing willingness to defy orders and precipitate such a clash alarmed Sacasa. An indecisive, frightened man, dominated by his family, he seemed unable to decide on any firm course of action. In conversations with Somoza, he appeared to favor the plan to have a constituent assembly amend the Constitution and possibly select Somoza as President without bothering with popular elections. Yet in private he would lose his temper and denounce the plan whenever it was mentioned. The American Minister urged Sacasa to make his position clear, but had no confidence in the effect of his advice. As for the *Jefe Director,* Lane had come to realize that Somoza "intends to be President, no matter what. If he cannot reach the Presidency constitutionally . . .he will use force to attain his ends."[22]

In an effort to produce a counterweight to the Cuardia, the President sought to create a several-hundred-man civilian police force under the control of the Minister of Gobernación, but this proposal encountered determined Guardia opposition and was abandoned, as was a project for bringing in Chilean instructors for the Guardia Nacional.[23] Frustrated in this area, the President's supporters embarked on a campaign to have the United States assume responsibility for the post-1933 actions of the Guardia. In the fall of 1935 repeated efforts in this regard were made in both Managua and in Washington, but in every case such efforts encountered the blunt retort that the United States "had no responsibility for what the Guardia did."[24] Such a stand was consistent with the principles of the "Good Neighbor Policy," but to many Nicaraguans it seemed that the United States had created a monster, then gone off, and left them to try to tame it.

As 1935 progressed, Somoza's presidential drive intensified. Despite a presidential decree forbidding any campaigning until eight months before the election, his candidacy was formally proclaimed on September 14, 1935. At this point Mrs. Sacasa, who, as Josephus Daniels had once observed, was the one who "really wore the pants in the family," and who, according to Lane, harbored "a deep-seated animosity towards Somoza and wished to humiliate him at all costs," decided to take direct action.[25]

She had been secretly obtaining munitions from abroad, brought in in packages marked "medicine," and had gained promises from the Salvadorean and Honduran governments to cooperate in any clash with Somoza. She now proposed demanding Somoza's resignation. If he resigned, he was to be offered a post abroad, but if he resisted, planes from Honduras would bomb his headquarters, while units loyal to Sacasa would attack his supporters on the ground.

These plans, which seemed to promise at the least a bloody civil war and possibly a general Central American conflict, appalled Lane. He not only refused to support Mrs. Sacasa, but obtained permission from the State Department to advise against such action. American opposition contributed to the collapse of this plan, which may have offered the last real opportunity to prevent Somoza from becoming president.[26] The *Jefe Director,* by his own admission, had gone so far in his presidential campaign that he could no longer turn back.[27] As 1936 began, the prospects for a peaceful completion of Sacasa's term of office seemed increasingly remote.

At the end of 1935, Arthur Bliss Lane had learned that he would soon be transferred to the post of Minister to Estonia, Latvia, and Lithuania. Despite his increasing frustration with the situation, the American Minister wanted to make a final effort to prevent open conflict between the President and the Guardia. Both Guardia headquarters and the Presidential Palace were being fortified in preparation for possible hostilities and Lane was discouraged by Somoza's "quite dangerous attitude," but nevertheless he requested and obtained an extension of his tour in Nicaragua until March 1, 1936, in order to make a final effort to restrain the *Jefe Director.*[28]

On January 30, Sacasa asked Lane to arrange an immediate conference for him with Somoza. Lane drove the General to the *Casa Presidencial,* but the resulting conference produced little but mutual recriminations. The Minister felt that Sacasa's "hatred and distrust" of Somoza poisoned the atmosphere, so he postponed the remainder of their conversations until the following day.[29] Before the talks were resumed, Lane met privately with Somoza and persuaded him to offer to withdraw his candidacy. In the meeting with the President, however, he offered to quit as *Jefe Director,* not as a presidential candidate, and in making the offer he pointedly refused to guarantee the results. The President protested that he did not want his resignation from the Guardia, then offered him an equal voice with the directorates of the two historic parties in the choice of a compromise candidate. Somoza declined this responsibility, a position Lane supported, noting that it was inconsistent to ask the General to withdraw from politics and then expect him to assume responsibility for the political situation. At this point, Somoza suddenly promised "to withdraw his candidacy, to support the present Government, to guarantee the impartiality of the Guardia Nacional in the forthcoming elections and to support the candidate agreed upon by the two parties." This led Lane to praise the General for his "patriotism and unselfishness."[30] The President then promised that the two parties would agree on a candidate acceptable to the Guardia and that this candidate would guarantee Somoza's position as *Jefe Director*.[31] Having apparently reached an agreement, the meeting broke up.

The agreement broke down within a week. The Conservatives announced that no Liberal other than Somoza would be an acceptable candidate and most Liberals refused to support the candidacy of any Conservative.[32] At the same time striking chauffeurs, protesting a gasoline shortage, began rioting in Managua. Sacasa, who believed Somoza had fomented the strikes to further discredit his administration, ordered the Guardia to disperse the crowds and "open fire if they refused to obey." Instead, Somoza managed to resolve the crisis by making a speech to the rioters, promising that the Guardia would take charge of gasoline distribution and declaring his personal determination to secure economic justice for them.[33] His action gave him considerable popular acclaim, with some strikers now demanding that he take over the government and even *La Noticia,* previously opposed to his candidacy, devoting not one, but two separate editorials to lauding his actions.[34] At the same time, reports that Sacasa had ordered the Guardia to fire on the strikers spread rapidly throughout the capital, greatly increasing the unpopularity of the administration.[35]

Both Sacasa and Somoza now embarked upon campaigns of mutual recriminations. Sacasa accused the General of encouraging "further meetings and rallies," and of failing to keep his promise to withdraw his candidacy, while Somoza, in turn, accused the government of failing to try to harmonize the situation and declared that he would keep his promise when the administration kept its promise to him.[36] At this point, Arthur Bliss Lane took his final departure from Managua, being replaced as United States Minister by Boaz Long.

The departure of Lane removed the last possibility of open American opposition to Somoza's seizing the presidency. The new Minister, Boaz Long, was instructed to avoid "taking any part in Nicaragua's domestic affairs, and was not even to engage in the efforts at mediation which had occupied so much of his predecessor's attention.[37] On April 30, 1936, having found it advisable to recognize President Martínez of Salvador and believing that applying different standards of recognition to Central American nations than those applied to the rest of Latin America, was incompatible with the Good Neighbor Policy, the United States announced the official abandonment of their policy of refusing recognition to Central American governments that came to power by revolution or other extralegal means.[38] (This meant that Somoza could now hope for eventual recognition no matter what means he used to gain power.) Within one month after the removal of this last American obstacle to his drive for power, Somoza resorted to violence against the incumbent administration.

In March, in order to strengthen his control over the Guardia, Somoza began to replace pro-Sacasa officers with men loyal to himself. When he moved to replace the commander at Bluefields, he encountered determined presidential opposition. Somoza had charged the commanding officer there, Major Balladeres Torres, with corruption, and replaced him with one of his own supporters, Major Baca. Sacasa ordered the *Jefe Director* to reinstate Balladeres Torres and to explain his actions in this case. Somoza promptly telegraphed to the President a large amount of alleged evidence of Torres' malfeasance in office, but refused to reinstate him, despite repeated presidential demands.[39] This open defiance of presidential authority and Sacasa's inability to do anything about it clearly illustrated the relative power of the two men in the spring of 1936.

In an effort to prevent a civil conflict, leaders of the Liberal and Conservative parties resumed efforts to agree on a candidate acceptable to both parties and to General Somoza. While these negotiations dragged on, Somoza continued to promote his own candidacy, announcing, toward the end of April, that he was a candidate for both parties' nominations.[40] By early May, he had dropped the last pretense of withdrawing, openly informing the

Nicaraguan chargé to Washington that he would not accept any agreement on another candidate. He also began to move cattle into the Campo de Marte, in Nicaragua a sure sign of impending conflict.[41]

While the Guardia provided Somoza with a potent force for the advancement of his ambitions, it did have certain limitations. For demonstrations, street brawls, and similar activities, it was less than an ideal force. To supplement the Guardia, Somoza began to support a native fascist organization, the Camisas Azules. This rather ragged group was made up of about 100 young reactionaries who hoped to set up a fascist government in Nicaragua. The Guardia provided them with guns and money and allowed them to drill openly in the streets of Managua. Late in May, they were used to burn an opposition newspaper, an operation probably planned by the Guardia.[42]

That same month, the traditional parties finally worked out an agreement to unite on a single candidate, although they had not yet decided who that candidate would be. This agreement had the effect of excluding Somoza from the presidency in 1936, although it did include a pledge to amend the constitution to make him eligible in 1940. Moncada urged him to reject the agreement and seize power, while Chamorro urged him to accept the biparty plan, promising, if he did so, to work for the calling of a constituent assembly which could make him president in two years. Somoza finally replied that he would accept the agreement if three conditions were met. He must have total control of the Guardia, he must gain control of the fort (Fortín de Acosasco) in León, and he must name the new President.[43] To put pressure on the government to accept his conditions, he now began using military force to replace local officials throughout the nation with his own supporters. He also announced his choice for President, a fellow officer and close friend, Colonel Rigoberto Reyes.[44]

The President balked at either accepting a Guardia officer as the presidential candidate or at turning over control of the fort in León. He asked the American Minister to issue a statement supporting him, but was once more turned down.[45] Sacasa finally decided to meet directly with Chamorro and Somoza in an effort to agree on a presidential candidate. They met on May 21 and Somoza again proposed Reyes. When this suggestion was rejected, the *Jefe Director* offered José Benito Ramírez, father-in-law of Colonel Camilo González, and, according to the American Minister, a criminal. Somoza's third choice was Dr. Carlos Brenes

Jarquín, physician and Congressman, who was rumored to be somewhat radical. Chamorro approved this choice, but Sacasa did not and the meeting broke up without achieving anything.[46]

The Guardia now proceeded to extend its control throughout the nation. By May 29, local officials favorable to Somoza were in power in every major town except Managua, Rivas, and Corinto.[47] The usual pattern was to foment a local disturbance, then have the Guardia take over and replace local officials on the pretext of maintaining order. Sacasa made numerous efforts to block such takeovers, but all to no avail. He even sent an order to all Department Commanders of the Guardia Nacional, stating that he had heard that they were preparing a seditious movement to remove civilian authorities and ordering them to cease any and all such actions.[48] It was, however, too late for any such appeals to have effect.

There were only two bodies of armed men whose loyalty the President could count upon. One was the Presidential Guard, made up of political supporters from León, stationed at La Loma. The other was the Fortín de Acosasco, near León, led by his cousin Major Ramón Sacasa.[49] Determined to eliminate this latter force, Somoza loaded a train with picked troops and left for León, ostensibly to confer with Major Sacasa and to have one of his men placed in command in the Fortín. For once, the President responded to a threat with some measure of speed and decision. He and leaders of the Conservatives hurriedly agreed to run Dr. Leonardo Argüello for President and Rodolfo Espinosa for reelection as Vice-President.[50] Sacasa also sent notes to the United States, Mexico, and the four other Central American nations, requesting joint action to resolve the situation produced by Somoza's actions.[51] This appeal for foreign support, like all previous attempts, failed to produce any concrete results.

In preparation for an attack on the Fortín, Somoza had gathered a force of nearly 2,000 men in León, giving him overwhelming military superiority. On May 30, both he and Major Sacasa sent messages to the President. Major Sacasa simply reported the situation, stating that Somoza had demanded his surrender and asking for instructions. The President ordered his cousin to resist, declaring that national honor depended on his actions.[52] Somoza, in a message sent by way of the American Minister, told the President that he had ordered Major Sacasa to disarm the civilians he had allowed into the Fortín and replace them with 100 Guardia regulars. The Major's refusal to obey this order was characterized as "rebellion," and Somoza expressed his determination to "use whatever means may be necessary" to force his compliance. President Sacasa was asked to order his cousin to surrender to "avoid bloodshed"; then the message concluded with a rather incongruous pledge to "maintain you in power during your entire presidential term."[53] In his reply, the President demanded that Somoza cease all efforts to alter the command at the Fortín, characterizing this as a "question of honor for the Commanding General." The power-hungry *Jefe Director* and his troops were ordered to return immediately to their quarters in Managua.[54] Somoza ignored the message and attacked the Fortín. At the same time, firing also broke out in Managua.

On the morning of May 31, firing began between Guardia machine-gun positions around La Loma and the Presidential Guard, dug in around the *Casa Presidencial* and also armed with machine guns. The fighting ceased briefly when Fletcher Warren, consul at the American Legation, went, under the American flag, to both positions. For a moment it appeared that the United States had abandoned its policy of not interfering in internal Nicaraguan politics. All Warren did, however, was to deliver to both sides a memorandum asking for protection of American lives and property.[55]

Thoroughly alarmed by the outbreak of violence the representatives of Mexico, Honduras, El Salvador, Great Britain, and France all signed an appeal to General Somoza, asking him to avoid bloodshed and use peaceful means to resolve his dispute with the President. At this point, American insistence on nonintervention began to border on the absurd as Minister Long was instructed not to endorse the appeal in order to avoid interference in Nicaraguan affairs.[56] The Legations of the United States and of the pro-Somoza government of Guatemala were the only ones that took no part in peacemaking efforts.

By the late afternoon of May 31, the President and Colonel Reyes, whom Somoza had left in command in Managua, had agreed upon an informal armistice in the capital. Fighting continued in León until June 2, when Somoza announced that if resistance continued he would end the armistice in Managua and attack both La Loma and the Fortín simultaneously. The President then agreed to the Fortín's surrender if its defenders were allowed to leave "honorably."[57] Somoza had won and the most important remaining issue was what he would do with the President.

Following this victory, Somoza made a speech, pledging his loyalty to the government and announcing that Sacasa would be allowed to finish his term under the General's "tutelage," but would not be permitted to "thwart the will of most Nicaraguans," namely, Somoza's victory in the 1936 elections.[58] It soon became clear that Sacasa had no desire to remain in office under such conditions. On June 3, the American Minister noted: "The President is so nervous that he can't talk coherently. He insists on only one thing, getting out of the country alive." He even asked the United States to send a special plane for him.[59]

Sacasa's supporters were also disillusioned and fearful for their own safety. Morale had collapsed among the armed men remaining on La Loma and the President was beginning to pay them off and send them home. General Chamorro had fled to the Mexican Legation, voicing the opinion that the President was more interested in protecting his relatives than fighting Somoza.[60] Vice-President Rodolfo Espinosa had no desire to oppose Somoza and let it be known that he would quit in return for $10,000 in cash and diplomatic appointments abroad for himself and his son. After some negotiations on the exact amount, he settled for $20,000 but no diplomatic positions in return for his resignation and "voluntary exile."[61]

President Sacasa finally sent his formal resignation to the Congress on June 6. In this document he attacked the Guardia for rebelling against his authority, then announced he was submitting an irrevocable resignation and depositing the executive power with the victor of the November 1932 elections. Since the office could not remain vacant until November, the presidency was assumed by the Minister of Gobernación, Julian Irías, and Sacasa sailed for exile in El Salvador.[62] He was destined never to return to Nicaragua.

Julian Irías' term as President was very brief. Somoza made one attempt to see him, but Irías was drunk and nothing was accomplished.[63] Steps were rapidly initiated in the Nicaraguan Congress, now completely under Somoza's control, to appoint a Presidential Designate to complete Sacasa's term. On June 9, 1936, the Congress proceeded obediently to select the General's personal choice, Dr. Carlos Brenes Jarquín, as interim President. Since the new administration had effective control over the entire nation, the United States decided to continue relations with it.[64]

The *Jefe Director* spent the next few weeks taking care of various details related to his forthcoming election to the presidency. Although Somoza was not concerned with the spirit of the law, he often tried to give at least an appearance of legality, a scruple that his son Tachito was rarely to manifest. Somoza had Congress postpone the elections until December in order that the required six-month gap between the election and the presence of one of his relatives in the presidency would exist. The leader of the proto-fascist Camisas Azules was appointed Inspector General of Education and the organization was disbanded since it was no longer of any real use to Somoza and showed signs of becoming troublesome.[65] The "Grand Convention of the Liberal Party," soon to be renamed the Liberal Nationalist Party, was now summoned to meet in León. There the Party obediently nominated Anastasio Somoza G. for President and Francisco Navarro for Vice-President.[66]

One minor obstacle, the previously nominated coalition ticket of Leonardo Argüello and Rodolfo Espinosa, which had obtained enough signatures to gain a place on the ballot, remained in Somoza's path to the presidency. Demonstrations in favor of these candidates were actually held in Managua and other cities, under close Guardia supervision, but apparently without direct interference.[67] The Guardia's control of the election machinery seemed to assure their defeat in November. This led the leaders of the opposition, ex-Presidents Chamorro, Díaz, and Sacasa, to make a last, desperate effort to get the United States to stop Somoza. They all showed up in Washington and called on Sumner Welles in the State Department to argue that the United States had a responsibility for the actions of the Guardia and to plead for American supervision of the upcoming elections.[68] Since the American refusal to respond to this plea virtually ensured their defeat, the leaders of the opposition decided to abstain from the elections.[69]

The actual election was rather peaceful. With the opposition boycotting the contest, although still on the ballot, and the Guardia counting the votes, chances for an upset were nonexistent. In order to remove the last constitutional barrier to his election, Somoza resigned in November as *Jefe Director* and President Brenes Jarquín appointed Colonel Reyes to that post. The resignation, however, was symbolic only. Somoza dressed in civilian clothes, but continued to occupy his office in the Campo de Marte and to issue all orders for the Guardia, although Reyes now had to sign them.[70] The General also organized a puppet Conservative Party which, of course, nominated him for President, making him the candidate of both the Liberal Nationalist and the Conservative Nationalist Parties.

Preliminary returns yielded the expected landslide victory for Somoza, but the turnout was disappointingly low. On December 11, the totals were announced as 64,000 Liberal Nationalist and 15,433 Conservative Nationalist votes for Somoza against 1,038 Historic Conservative and 162 Constitutional Liberal votes for Argüello. Somehow, by December 18, when the Electoral Commission certified the votes, Somoza's total had grown to 86,258 Liberal Nationalist and 20,943 Conservative Nationalist votes, but Argüello's support had shrunk to only 108 Historic Conservative and 61 Constitutional Liberal votes.[71] Following the lead of its United States-created sister organization in the Dominican Republic, the Guardia had elevated its leader into the nation's highest office.

General Somoza now moved rapidly to reestablish himself as *Jefe Director* of the Guardia Nacional. On December 16, he announced that Rigoberto Reyes would be promoted to Brigadier General and made Minister of War in the incoming cabinet. This created a vacancy in the post of *Jefe Director*. Two days later it was announced that President-elect Anastasio Somoza García had assumed that position.[72] With his inauguration as President, on January 1, 1937, the two positions were combined in the person of one individual, giving him unprecedented power. The rule of the Somozas had officially begun in Nicaragua. It would endure longer than anyone might resonably have predicted.

The action of General Somoza in using the Guardia to elevate himself into the presidency was hardly contemplated in the original American objectives in establishing this force. Much of the credit or blame for the transformation of what was intended to be a nonpolitical organization into, in the words of Arthur Bliss Lane, "the major political power in Nicaragua," must go to Somoza.[73] He had proved himself a shrewd, energetic, skillful and amoral politician, capable of combining diplomacy with force, threats with rewards. His personal charm had influenced a host of important figures. In the final struggle for power even such veteran *caudillos* as ex-Presidents Chamorro and Moncada had proved no match for the Guardia's *Jefe Director*.

The weakness of the Sacasa regime was another important factor in Somoza's rise to power. The administration was riddled with corruption, the President was weak, indecisive, and dominated by a grasping, short-sighted group of relatives.[74] All of this meant that the President's popularity declined constantly during his term of office, costing him much of his potential strength in the ongoing conflict with the Guardia. Finally, it must be remembered that Sacasa himself had worked to convert the Guardia into a partisan, political force. It was only when he realized that this force could be used against him that the President began to call for enforcement of those agreements designed to make the Guardia nonpolitical.

The major share of the responsibility for Somoza's seizure of power, however, must rest with the United States. Such responsibility is due to more than the American influence in Somoza's appointment as *Jefe Director* and the later refusal of the United States to take any responsibility for his actions. Its roots go back to the original concept of creating a supposedly nonpartisan constabulary in Nicaragua. In its drive to ensure political and financial stablity in Nicaragua the United States insisted upon the creation of the Guardia. It was assumed that, by breaking the ties between the political leaders and the military and by giving both officers and men professional training and status, revolutions would be discouraged, fiscal responsibility advanced, and democracy made possible. The United States failed to realize that the traditional army in Nicaragua had developed in response to local conditions and political realities. Any attempt to create an honest, nonpolitical military force without changing the nation's basic social and economic situation was probably impossible. Nicaragua suffered from economic underdevelopment, concentration of wealth, mass illiteracy, strong regionalism, and weak nationalism. The original American conception of the Guardia bore no relationship to any of these realities. As early as 1926, Charles Eberhardt, American Minister to Nicaragua, realized that "the time has not yet come, if it ever will, when a non-partisan constabulary or National Guard, organized under American ideas or ideals will be a success in Nicaragua. It is not wanted."[75]

It was not wanted. The State Department wanted it, foreign investors wanted it, but Nicaragua's politicians did not want it. Sandino's supporters certainly did not want it, and the great majority of the population was completely indifferent to it. Those in power were happy to have a well-trained, disciplined force in place of the old, unreliable political army, but they wanted complete control over the new force, making it an instrument of their political power, just as the old army had been. Those out of power might have wanted a nonpartisan Guardia, but they did not want a strong or efficient one, as that would present too great an obstacle to any future revolution.

Under such circumstances, the change from a nonpartisan to a bipartisan Guardia Nacional was, at least, an effort to bring the Guardia partly into line with Nicaraguan political realities. By making the President and the *Jefe Director* members of the same party, it was thought that the Guardia would at least support the government. Nicaraguan political parties, however, were predominantly vehicles for elevating certain individuals or groups of individuals to power, not unified bodies sharing common ties of loyalty and ideology. Ambitious generals had repeatedly used their troops against an incumbent President. In the past, the President had often won such struggles because of the poor state of the armed forces, but the Guardia was a stronger force than Nicaragua had ever known. Its creation had given the nation its first professional military caste with special interests, separate from those of the nation as a whole. Presidential efforts to control the Guardia often conflicted with these interests, while the *Jefe Director* could usually pose as their defender. To prevent such conflicts during his reign, General Somoza continued as *Jefe Director,* not relinquishing the post until the 1950s when he appointed his own West Point-trained son, Tachito, to succeed him.

The failure of the American effort to create a nonpolitical constabulary in Nicaragua was summarized in a July 1935 letter from Arthur Bliss Lane to Willard Beaulac. Lane characterized the Guardia as a "Nicaraguan-North American hybrid," which constituted the "biggest stumbling block to the progress of Nicaragua." He attacked its absorption of over half of the government revenues and ridiculed the idea that it could guarantee free elections when its commander was an avowed candidate. Lane summed up the problem by saying:

> The people who created the G.N. had no adequate understanding of the psychology of the people here. Otherwise they would not have bequeathed Nicaragua with an instrument to blast constitutional procedure off the map. Did it ever occur to the eminent statesmen who created the G.N. that personal ambition lurks in the human breast, even in Nicaragua? In my opinion, it is one of the sorriest examples on our part of our inability to understand that we should not meddle in other people's affairs.[76]

Lane's basic points were quite accurate. For the Guardia to have worked the way the State Department thought it should, Nicaragua would have had to experience a transformation in its political, economic, and social, as well as its military character. The attempt to impose an American solution on a Nicaraguan problem had destroyed, not promoted, democratic government. Whether it would produce for the United States the stability which it so ardently desired remained to be seen.

NOTES

1. Lane to Hull, May 25, 1934, NA RG 59, 817.00/8054; Lane to Hull, June 22, 1934, *Foreign Relations,* 1934, V, p. 556.

2. Lane to Hull, May 25, 1934, NA RG 59, 817.00/8054; *La Noticia* (Managua), May 31, 1934, p. 1.

3. *La Noticia* (Managua), June 21, 1934, p. 1; Lane to Hull, June 22, 1934, *Foreign Relations,* 1934, V, p. 556.

4. Lane to Hull, June 23, 1934, NA RG 59, 817.00/8076.

5. Lane to Hull, June 22 and 25, 1934; Hull to Lane, June 23, 1934, *Foreign Relations,* 1934, V, pp. 556–58.

6. The American Consul at Matagalpa, Wiley, to Lane, July 15, 1934, NA RG 59, 817.00/8097; Lane to Hull, July 18, 1934, NA RG 59, 817.00/8103.

7. Lane to Hull, July 19, 1934, NA RG 59, 817.00/8104; Lane to Hull, July 21, 1934, NA RG 59, 817.00/8105. Castillo later denied that he ever planned to kill Somoza. (Ternot MacRenato, "Anastasio Somoza: A Nicaraguan Caudillo" [M.A. thesis, University of San Francisco, 1974], p. 109).

8. Lane to Hull, July 18, 1934, NA RG 59, 817.00/8103.

9. Lane to Hull, July 28, 1934, NA RG 59, 817.00/8110.

10. Lane to Hull, August 16, 1934, NA RG 59, 817.1051/874.

11. The American chargé in Nicaragua, Allan Dawson, to Hull, September 14, 1934, NA RG 59, 817.24/283.

12. *La Prensa* (Managua), October 3, 1934, p. 1.

13. Dawson to Hull, September 27, 1934, NA RG 59, 817.24/286.

14. Lane to Hull, September 26, 1934, NA RG 59, 817.1051/940.

15. Dawson to Hull, November 24, 1934, NA RG 59, 817.00/8171.

16. Dawson to Hull, November 17, 1934, NA RG 59, 817.1051/890; Dawson to Hull, November 20, 1934, NA RG 59, 817.00/8168.

17. Lane to Hull, March 6, 1935, 817.1051/908.

18. Memorandum by Beaulac, June 17, 1935, NA RG 59, 817.00/8241.

19. *La Noticia* (Managua), April 25, 1935, p. 1.

20. Interview with Colonel Francisco Mendieta, Managua, December 1963; Lane to Hull, April 22, 1935, *Foreign Relations,* 1935, IV, p. 850; Lane to Hull, April 23, 1935, NA RG 59, 817.1051/915; *La Noticia* (Managua), April 24, 1935, p. 1, and April 25, 1935, p. 1.

21. Lane to Hull, April 25, 26, and 30, 1935, *Foreign Relations,* 1935, IV, pp. 851–54.

22. Lane to Sumner Welles, August 15, 1935, Lane Papers.

23. Lane to Hull, September 9, 1935, NA RG 59, 817.00/8279.

24. Lane to Hull, September 7, 1935, and Memorandum by Beaulac, October 1, 1935, and Memorandum by Wilson, October 16, 1935, *Foreign Relations,* 1935, IV, pp. 877, 882, and 885.

25. Lane to Josephus Daniels, March 4, 1934, Lane Papers.

26. Vladimir Petrov, *A Study in Diplomacy: The Story of Arthur Bliss Lane* (Chicago: Regnery, 1971), pp. 70–72.

27. Lane to Welles, December 16, 1935, Lane Papers.

28. Lane to Hull, January 21, 1936, NA RG 59, 817.00/8358; Memorandum of telephone call from Lane to Welles, January 22, 1936, Lane Papers; Petrov, *Study in Diplomacy,* p. 75.

29. Lane to Welles, February 4, 1936, Lane Papers.

30. Ibid.

31. Lane to Hull, February 1, 1936, NA RG 59, 817.00/8364.

32. Lane to Welles, February 6, 1936, Lane Papers.

33. Lane to Hull, February 11, 1936, *Foreign Relations,* 1936, V, p. 815; Lane to Hull, February 14, 1936, NA RG 59, 817.00/8739; Petrov, *Study in Diplomacy,* pp. 76–77.

34. Lane to Hull, February 11, 1936, *Foreign Relations,* 1936, V, p. 815; Editorials by Juan Ramón Aviles, *La Noticia* (Managua), February 13, 1936, p. 1, and February 16, 1936, p. 1.

35. Lane to Hull, February 16, 1936, NA RG 59, 817.00/8376; Lane to Hull, February 22, 1936, NA RG 59, 817.00/8380.

36. Ibid; Lane to Hull, February 11, 1936, *Foreign Relations,* 1936, V, p. 816.

37. Hull to the American Minister to Nicaragua, Boaz Long, March 28, 1936, *Foreign Relations,* 1936, V, pp. 817–18.

38. Hull to the American Minister in Honduras, April 30, 1936, *Foreign Relations,* 1936, V, pp. 134–36.

39. Sacasa to Somoza, March 21, 1936, printed in Juan Bautista Sacasa, *Cómo y por qué caí del poder,* 2nd ed. (León, Nicaragua: n.p., 1946), pp. 85–86.

40. *La Noticia* (Managua), April 26, 1936, p. 1.

41. Long to Hull, May 7, 1936, NA RG 59, 817.00/8402.

42. Long to Hull, May 8, 1936, NA RG 59, 817.00/8408; Long to Hull, May 28, 1936, NA RG 59, 817.00/8425.

43. Long to Hull, May 12, 1936, NA RG 59, 817.00/8412.

44. Long to Hull, May 19, 1936, NA RG 59, 817.00/8414.
45. Ibid.
46. Chamorro, "Autobiografía," *Revista Conservadora* II (September 1961) 168; Long to Hull, May 22, 1936, NA RG 59, 817.00/8418.
47. Long to Hull, May 28, 1936, NA RG 59, 817.00/8426; Long to Hull, May 29, 1936, NA RG 59, 817.00/8432.
48. "President Sacasa to All Department Commanders of the Guardia Nacional," May 28, 1936, printed in Sacasa, *Cómo y por qué,* p. 97.
49. Sacasa, *Cómo y por qué,* p. 25.
50. Chamorro, "Autobiografía," p. 169; Long to Hull, May 30, 1936, NA RG 59, 817.00/8434.
51. Sacasa to Hull, May 29, 1936, *Foreign Relations,* 1936, V, pp. 825–27.
52. Major Ramón Sacasa to President Sacasa, May 30, 1936, and President Sacasa to Major Sacasa, May 30, 1936, printed in Sacasa, *Cómo y por qué,* p. 104.
53. Long to Hull, May 30, 1936, NA RG 59, 817.00/8438; Somoza to President Sacasa, May 30, 1936, printed in Sacasa, *Cómo y por qué,* p. 107
54. President Sacasa to Somoza, May 30, 1936, printed in Sacasa, *Cómo y por qué,* p. 108; Long to Hull, May 31, 1936, NA RG 59, 817.00/8442.
55. Sacasa, *Cómo y por qué,* p. 91.
56. Hull to Long, May 31, 1936, *Foreign Relations,* 1936, V, pp. 829–30.
57. Long to Hull, June 2, 1936, NA RG 59, 817.00/8452.
58. Memorandum of telephone conversation between Long and Duggan, June 3, 1936, NA RG 59, 817.00/8453½; *La Noticia* (Managua), June 3, 1936, p. 6.
59. Ibid.
60. Chamorro, "Autobiografía," p. 169; Long to Hull, June 2, 1936, NA RG 59, 817.00/8452; memorandum of telephone conversation between Long and Duggan, June 3, 1936, NA RG 59, 817.00/8453½.
61. Long to Hull, June 8, 1936, *Foreign Relations,* 1936, V, pp. 838–39; Chamorro, "Autobiografía," p. 169; Long to Hull, NA RG 59, 817.00/8464.
62. "Message by President Sacasa to the Congreso Nacional," June 6, 1936, printed in Sacasa, *Cómo y por qué,* p. 111; memorandum of telephone conversation between Long and Duggan, June 6, 1936, NA RG 59, 817.00/8482.
63. Memorandum of telephone conversation between Long and Duggan, June 9, 1936, NA RG 59, 817.00/8482.
64. Hull to Long, June 11, 1936, *Foreign Relations,* 1936, V, p. 841.
65. Long to Hull, June 12, 1936, NA RG 59, 817.00/8522.
66. Long to Hull, June 18, 1936, NA RG 59, 817.00/8537; *La Noticia* (Managua), June 28, 1936, p. 1.
67. The American chargé in Nicaragua, Guy W. Ray, to Hull, October 27, 1936, NA RG 59, 817.00/8605.
68. Long to Hull, October 13, 1936, NA RG 59, 817.00/8597;

Memorandum by Duggan, October 22, 1936, *Foreign Relations,* 1936, V, pp. 843–44.

69. Ray to Hull, November 24, 1936, *Foreign Relations,* 1936, V, p. 844.

70. Long to Hull, November 12, 1936, NA RG 59, 817.00/8611.

71. Ray to Hull, December 18, 1936, NA RG 59, 817.00/8629.

72. *La Noticia* (Managua), December 17, 1936, p. 1, and December 19, 1936, p. 1.

73. Lane to Hull, March 8, 1935, NA RG 59, 817.00/8200.

74. Petrov, *A Study in Diplomacy,* p. 64.

75. Eberhardt to Kellogg, April 8, 1926, NA RG 59, 817.1051/99.

76. Lane to Beaulac, July 27, 1935, Lane Papers.

IX

PRESIDENT SOMOZA

In his inaugural address, President Somoza lauded the accomplishments of the Guardia Nacional. He promised to improve its equipment and training, including the training of officers, and to separate the police from the military portions of the Guardia, although both would continue under the same command, that of *Jefe Director* Somoza.[1] A month after his inauguration, he began to act on this program, asking the American Legation for aid in obtaining instructors to help reopen the *Academia Militar.* Since the withdrawal of the Marines there had been no regular means for training new officers and, as a result the force had deteriorated. The State Department was willing to consider Somoza's request for American instructors, but felt that action on this matter should be postponed for the present, until it became clear how the new President was doing in office.[2]

For the first few months, the new President did not seem to be doing at all well. The continuing world depression had badly damaged the Nicaraguan economy. Somoza was forced to devalue the córdoba and this pushed up the cost of living, resulting in worker unrest. Discontent was also reportedly affecting the Guardia. One captain even dared to make a speech highly critical of the President in his presence, accusing him of neglecting the force. This officer was immediately discharged, but many observers saw the incident as a sign that the presidency was too much for Somoza. His former mentor, President Moncada, shared this view, openly stating: "That young man on the hill will not last later than next July."[3]

Hoping to stifle dissent, Somoza began using his armed force to crack down on the opposition. The Guardia raided a Conservative Party gathering ostensibly held to celebrate the birthday of exiled General Emiliano Chamorro, and imprisoned fifty-six of those present. The press was ordered not to mention this incident and, after a day or two, those arrested were released, with a small fine for disturbing the peace.[4] This public display of control over the Guardia and a willingness to use it against political opposition stemmed, for a time, the open plotting against the new administration.

Somoza followed up this advantage rapidly, demonstrating the political skill that helped bring him to power. He obtained Moncada's public support, in return for which he had the government give the ex-President two automobiles and had the National Bank buy up his devalued interest in some Nicaraguan utilities. The press was subject to an informal censorship, maintained largely through the open threat of repression. The Guardia's duties were expanded to include control of internal revenue and the national railroad. It also organized an intelligence service, concentrating its efforts on domestic dissidents.[5] These actions virtually destroyed public opposition, although private resentment over the Guardia's increased power and consequent arrogance probably increased. By July 1937, even Dr. Leonardo Argüello, his opponent in the 1936 "elections," was helping to create a committee to unify the Liberal Party around Somoza.[6]

Guardia functions were continually expanded throughout the year. Control over the postal service and over immigration and emigration was tightened. Military control over all imports of guns and ammunition was firmly established and even commercial companies had to obtain a special Guardia permit to import dynamite for their operations. Finally, the *Dirección General de Sanidad,* the national sanitation service, was placed under military control.[7] The combined effect of these actions was to give the Guardia an awesome amount of power. It was the nation's only armed force, including all police and even customs inspectors within its ranks. It controlled the postal, telegraph, and internal radio services, operated an extensive domestic intelligence service, and controlled the importation and sale of all arms and explosives. No one could enter or leave the country or even start a business without Guardia permission. It was rapidly becoming apparent that as long as he had the support of the Guardia, any effort to overthrow Somoza would probably be an exercise in futility.

As promised in his inaugural address, Somoza had also begun efforts to improve the Guardia's equipment. A major project in this area was his effort to create an air force. He announced plans for a school to train military pilots and purchased four airplanes.

The activities of this miniscule force were badly hampered by a lack of pilots; there was only one man to fly all four aircraft.[8]

The Guardia had a total strength, in 1937, of 201 line officers, 8 medical officers, 2,237 enlisted men, 89 urban police, and 390 *auxiliares.*[9] While this force was large by Central American standards, the Guardia's varied, nonmilitary functions severely limited the force available to meet any revolutionary threat. Somoza's solution to this was to create a Guardia reserve, made up of former Guardia and other politically reliable citizens.[10] In case of conflict, this force could assume police and other nonmilitary duties, freeing large numbers of troops for combat duty.

Throughout 1937, President Somoza had continued to press for American assistance in reopening the *Academia Militar.* By mid-August, the United States had indicated a willingness to make one officer available and to accept $300 per month compensation, $200 per month less than Guatemala was paying for similar services.[11] This offer was suddenly withdrawn in October. A renewal of Nicaragua's border dispute with Honduras caused the State Department to suspend action on the project until the crisis passed.[12]

The border dispute had roots reaching back almost a century. The latest controversy revolved around Nicaragua's issuance of a stamp that showed territory awarded to Honduras in 1906, following arbitration by King Alfonso XIII of Spain, as still disputed. In August, both sides had rushed troops to the border and war was narrowly avoided. Nicaraguan troops remained in the area for the remainder of the year, asserting Nicaraguan claims in the area and preventing illegal immigration from Honduras.[13] The only other significant military operation undertaken by the Guardia in 1937 involved the elimination of Pedro Altamirano, the last of Sandino's generals. Pedrón, as he was popularly known, had increased his activities in 1937, sacking a coffee plantation and briefly seizing the small town of Palpunta on the Coco River.[14] Three Guardia agents and two Managua prostitutes, recruited by the Guardia, managed to infiltrate Pedrón's band. One of the prostitutes persuaded Pedrón to leave his family and spend the night with her. While he was asleep, the Guardia agents cut off his head and brought it back to Managua.[15] This ended, more than ten years after it began, the warfare between the Guardia and the original followers of Sandino.

The year 1938 proved a remarkably peaceful one, at least by

Nicaraguan standards. The elimination of Pedrón meant that there was virtually no active fighting in the nation. Despite continued economic problems Somoza remained firmly in power. For the Guardia, the most significant event in 1938 was probably the founding of the Fuerza Aerea de Nicaragua (FAN) as an integral part of the Guardia Nacional. The previous year two Guardia officers, Captains Guillermo Rivas Cuadra and Rafael Espinosa Altamirano, had gone to Canada for aviation instruction. While there, they purchased two four-passenger Waco biplanes. An attempt to fly these to Nicaragua almost ended in disaster as one of the planes blew a tire and was held up in Belize, while Captain Rivas Cuadra flew the other into a hangar, wrecking the plane, though miraculously not injuring himself.[16] Despite such setbacks, General Somoza persisted in his efforts to develop an air force. He and his wife, who had been proclaimed Godmother of the Air Force, inaugurated permanent headquarters for FAN and seven officers were assigned to aviation duties.[17]

FAN's subsequent career was far from smooth. Several aircraft were destroyed in a variety of mishaps, including one lost when Captain Cuadra landed it without bothering to lower the landing gear. By 1939, the force was in such desperate straits that Somoza considered selling all but one of its planes to a commercial company which, in turn, would train future FAN pilots. This report led the United States to turn down a request for an aviation instructor.[18] The planes were never sold, but shortages of funds limited each plane to about one hour per week in the air and the Guardia was forced to have its pilots trained by serving as copilots with TACA, the Salvadorean national airline.[19] It would take American aid during World War II to make an effective force out of FAN.

For most of the Guardia, the most important event in 1938 was probably the increase in their pay, ranging from 50 percent for privates to 30 percent for higher officers.[20] Somoza was responsible for these increases, which were part of a growing series of paternalistic benefits conferred on the Guardia in return for the force's loyalty and cooperation in maintaining the General in office.

Efforts were even made to start a Nicaraguan navy. A small, fifteen-year-old cutter was purchased from the United States Coast Guard for $1,500. It had no radio and was in rather dubious condition. It was considered delivering it to Nicaragua as deck cargo, but shipping costs would have been three times the purchase price. The Navy finally agreed to tow the craft to Corinto, where it arrived in November 1938.[21] On board was Chief Boatswain's Mate Allan L. Lundquist, whom the Coast Guard had agreed to assign to Nicaragua for six months to train Somoza's navy.[22]

Lundquist's mission was something less than a complete success. He spent more than a year in Nicaragua, during which time the boat left the harbor only four times, cracked a cylinder head, and filled up with cockroaches. By September 1939, the Boatswain was warning that if the boat were not repaired, it might well sink at the dock.[23] Some of Lundquist's problems were due to friction within the Guardia. Somoza was determined that all Nicaraguan armed forces, army, police, air force, and navy, should be part of the Guardia. Some officers disagreed and opposed all plans for a navy. Having little desire to sail out to sea on a cockroach-infested cutter, they refused to cooperate with Lundquist, leading the American Minister to suggest that no more boats be sold to Nicaragua.[24]

His air force might fly into hangars and his navy fill up with cockroaches, but none of this affected Somoza's designs on a long-term career in the *Casa Presidencial.* In 1939 he pushed through Congress a measure calling for a constituent assembly. Delegates were elected in November and met in December, dissolving Congress and assuming the powers of government. The Conservatives boycotted the elections, allowing Somoza to dominate the assembly without resorting to force or fraud.[25] By February the puppet assembly already had an 11,000-word draft to consider and seven weeks later Nicaragua was presented with its "Constitution of 1939." This document provided for a six-year Presidential term with no reelection. A loophole in Article 350, however, exempted the incumbent President from this prohibition.[26]

Articles 335 to 343 dealt with the Guardia Nacional. The Guardia was to be "the sole armed force of the Republic," and any other armed forces in Nicaragua were automatically placed under its jurisdiction. Army members were supposed to be nonpolitical and were not allowed to vote, run for office, or criticize the laws of the nation. Complete control over the Guardia was vested in the President, who, without Congressional approval could issue all laws and regulations for it.[27]

After adopting the Constitution, the assembly became a legislative body, replacing the Congress until May 1, 1947. This new "Congress" then chose Anastasio Somoza G. as President for the period from 1939 to 1947.[28] It was obvious to everyone that the General had moved into the *Casa Presidencial* to stay.

With the Guardia under control and the opposition divided and disorganized, Somoza began to look abroad. Unlike his predecessors, he visited several foreign countries while still in office, even traveling to Honduras despite the continuing border dispute. From both a personal and propaganda viewpoint, the highpoint of his travels came in 1939 when President Franklin D. Roosevelt invited him to visit the United States. Somoza made extensive preparations for this trip. His Minister of War, General Rigoberto Reyes, assumed control over the Guardia and took up residence in the *Casa Presidencial,* along with Colonel Luis Manuel Debayle and General Gustavo Abaunza.[29] Congress was sent on a prolonged vacation, providing still further evidence of the administration's reliance upon and identification with the Guardia Nacional.

In the United States the Nicaraguan dictator received the full red-carpet treatment. He had several long conferences with President Roosevelt and leading figures of his administration. Discussion covered economic matters, proposals for canalization of the San Juan River and Somoza's continued desire to obtain American instructors for the *Academia Militar.*[30] The treatment accorded Somoza produced a storm of protest among Nicaraguan exiles, but this had no observable effect on the United States Government.

The visit ended with an exchange of letters between the two Presidents. Somoza repeated his desire for economic aid in creating a large canal along the San Juan River. He again repeated his request to have an American Army officer detailed "to act as director of the Military Academy." In reply, Roosevelt agreed to have the Army Engineers undertake studies of both canal and highway projects for linking the east and west coasts of Nicaragua and promised that the Army would "assign a qualified officer to act as director of the Military Academy of the Nicaraguan National Guard."[31]

The decision to assign an officer to the *Academia* represented the culmination of long-standing negotiations and was not any new departure in American policy. The previous December, Under Secretary of State Sumner Welles had decided that the

Anastasio Somoza García, founder of the longest-lasting dictatorship in Latin America.

situation with Honduras had quieted sufficiently to allow the United States to provide the *Academia* with a director. The following month the War Department informed the State Department that it would furnish an officer for that position as soon as it received a formal request.[32] Major Charles L. Mullins was selected for this assignment. Before departing for Nicaragua, in the summer of 1939, he called upon the State Department and was told to stay in close touch with the American Legation and be guided by it in his relations with the Nicaraguan government.[33]

The new American director faced immense problems. The building proposed for the *Academia* lacked beds, sanitary facilities, and space for drill instruction and had no offices or library. Furthermore, Somoza was now talking about simply establishing a six-month refresher course, instead of the regular four-year cadet training program that Mullins and the State Department had envisioned.[34] Somoza was finally convinced to set up a regular academy, modeled after the one in Guatemala. By the end of October, Mullins had recevied 250 applications for the 50 spaces in the first class. Classes were to begin on January 20, 1940.[35]

By the end of 1940, General Somoza was already pressing to have Mullins' appointment extended beyond its original two-year term. Pleased with the *Academia's* progress, he had made the American director a brigadier general in the Guardia and was paying him $385 per month in addition to his regular Army salary. Despite some American misgivings, Mullins was reappointed for an additional year and another officer, Captain William Bunker, was sent to join him and give engineering lectures.[36] The *Academia Militar* could now offer a three-year course in basic military subjects, filling the dangerous gap in officer training that had existed since the withdrawal of the Marines.

American efforts to aid in the construction of a barge canal along the San Juan River proved much less successful and, ultimately, this project was abandoned. In its place, the United States proposed to construct a road to Rama, linking the west coast with the headwaters of the Escondido River, which could then be navigated to the east-coast port of Bluefields. Brigadier General Dwight Eisenhower approved this project, estimating its cost at $2,000,000 and declaring that it would be of definite military value in hemispheric defense. His recommendation was adopted but by June 1942 the estimated cost had risen to $4,500,000.[37] Costs continued to rise for over twenty years, until the road was finally completed in the mid-1960s. By then it had become for many a classic case of American mismanagement and poor planning in foreign aid.[38]

A final result of the visit to the United States was the growth of a legend linking Roosevelt and Somoza in a close friendship. Somoza carefully cultivated this legend, expressing his friendship for Roosevelt often and loudly, even declaring a two-day national holiday when the American President was reelected in 1940.[39] He also sent an endless stream of flattering messages to Roosevelt and in 1942 honored the American President's birthday by renaming Managua's main street Avenida Roosevelt.[40] Most Nicaraguans believed that there were close ties between the two Presidents, a belief which undoubtedly inhibited opposition to the dictator. In reality, once he returned to Nicaragua, Somoza was virtually forgotten by Roosevelt, who usually handed his messages of congratulation and friendship over to an aide for reply.[41]

The presidency gave Somoza more than power and prestige. In his first three years in office he accumulated a fortune estimated at from $3 to $4 million, a record no previous Nicaraguan President had even approached. He had even taken $185,000 for "expenses" during his visit to the United States. Somoza had become wealthy in a variety of ways. He demanded a tribute of one-and-a-half cents per pound on exported cattle. Contributions were exacted from various industries such as mining and textiles. All government employees were forced to contribute 5 percent of their salaries to the Liberal Party. General Somoza then drew upon these funds as if they constituted a personal bank account.[42] Much of this new wealth was invested in acquiring property in Nicaragua. The General almost never "stole" land, preferring to "buy" it from the legal owner. The dictator would simply drive up to a house and offer the owner a price, usually about half the real value, for his land. Often the owner would accept the offer, finding discretion the better part of valor, or would even offer it as a gift to Somoza, hoping to gain some political reward in return. Any owner who did not want to sell found himself faced with a campaign of harrassment, tax increases, and similar measures until he finally gave in.[43] The General also bought up underdeveloped land, then had the government build a road to it or dredge out a new harbor in its vicinity.[44] Using such techniques, he soon became the wealthiest man in Nicaragua's history.

Graft was common in Nicaragua, but Somoza refined and systematized it. Emboldened by the example of their leader, the officers and men of the Guardia used their positions, especially in customs, immigration, and police, to enrich themselves. They even engaged in wholesale cattle smuggling. The corruption extended from the Minister of War, General Reyes, to the private on the street who would demand, "pay me five córdobas or be arrested."[45] The rural population came to fear the Guardia, claiming that the local soldiers, who were also the rural police, could simply walk into their homes and take anything, leaving them no possible redress.[46] All of this alienated the Guardia from the civilian population, making them a separate military caste, loyal only to their own leader, not to the nation as a whole. They did manage to maintain a high degree of internal order and stability, but the average citizen found himself paying an ever-increasing price for these benefits.

The preoccupation with graft cut sharply into efficiency and by March 1940 the American Legation felt that only the two companies of presidential guards had any potential for combat. Alarmed by this, Somoza began to seek possible American aid for a total reorganization of the Guardia. The American Minister informed the State Department that if we wanted "to maintain Somoza in power," or to "avoid the outbreak of revolution shortly within Nicaragua," we would have to provide such services.[47] The State Department, however, was not anxious to bolster the Nicaraguan dictator's sagging prestige and instructed the American Legation to avoid "any intimation that such appointments would be desired by the United States."[48]

Failing to secure American aid, Somoza set out to reorganize the Guardia on his own. In the fall of 1940, when General Reyes went to Washington to attend a meeting of Western Hemisphere Chiefs of Staff, the shakeup began. Somoza burst into the Campo de Marte, searched various officers' desks, and transferred most of the arms in the Campo to the Presidential Palace. The General Staff was overhauled with Colonel Medina, hurriedly promoted from Major, replacing Reyes as Chief of Staff. Eight officers were arrested, four discharged, and twenty others suddenly transferred.[49] General Reyes knew nothing about the affair until his return from Washington. He was met at the Managua airport by the Chief of Police. Somoza demanded and obtained his prompt resignation from the Guardia, reportedly telling Reyes that he should be court-martialed and shot.[50] The dictator offered a variety of explanations for his actions, including charges that Reyes had tapped his phones, had failed to carry out orders, was influenced by pro-Nazi elements, and was guilty of graft and corruption, a rather odd charge for Somoza to make against anyone else.[51]

These actions revealed two Somoza tactics which, with considerable success, he would employ repeatedly in coming years. First, any officer whose popularity or power made him seem a potential threat was quite likely to find himself suddenly transferred, retired, or discharged. Those who accepted this treatment without protest often found themselves later restored to a measure of favor.[52] Prison and death were generally reserved for those who actually attempted to overthrow the President. The other tactic was the identification of all opposition, actual or potential with whatever foreign threat currently preoccupied the United States. In the 1940s, this was the Nazi movement; later it would be the Communists.

Throughout 1941, United States concern over the defense of the Western Hemisphere continued to increase. An October 1941 lend-lease agreement promised Nicaragua $1,300,000 in military equipment from the United States at a deferred cost of $900,000.[53] Even before this agreement was signed, General Somoza had submitted a detailed request for the $300,000 worth of equipment promised for the coming year. He asked for 100 machine guns, 15 BARs, 15 submachine guns, 100 rifles, 1 Waco airplane, 125 fragmentation bombs, and large quantities of supplies and ammunition.[54] Colonel Mullins strongly endorsed this request. As early as June 1941, he had been urging American aid to the Guardia so that "neither expatriate Nicaraguans nor resident Nazis make any kind of diversion for the United States in this country," and pointing out that the "needs in Nicaragua are immediate if we are to get this army in condition to be of any material assistance."[55] Nicaragua's armed forces never fired a single shot against the Axis armed forces, but Lend-Lease would provide them enough equipment to ensure their continued domination of the domestic political scene.

Nicaragua declared war on Japan on December 9, 1941, and on Germany and Italy two days later. During the war an American naval base was constructed at Corinto and an air base was also built in the Republic.[56] A seaplane base and a Coast Artillery unit were established at Corinto and Nicaragua's tiny navy received several small patrol boats from the United States and took over some patrol duties along its coasts. The Guardia's air arm was also built up, receiving numerous new aircraft under the Lend-Lease Agreement. FAN claimed a total of almost forty aircraft by the end of the conflict. These were used in coastal patrols and in flying American and Nicaraguan officers around the nation.[57]

General Somoza used the war as an excuse for declaring a state of siege and suspending constitutional guarantees. Under these conditions, the Conservatives were barred from holding any political meetings on the pretext that such activities "didn't promote Nicaragua's interests" during the war.[58]

During the war, there was at least one significant dispute between General Somoza and the American military. This involved Colonel Mullins, the *Academia Militar's* director, who had grown increasingly disillusioned with Somoza's rule. When, in May 1942, the President sent the Colonel a bill for C$3,336 which he claimed the *Academia* owed for electricity, Mullins returned a check for the amount made payable to Somoza, clearly implying that the *Jefe Director* would pocket the money.[59] The Nicaraguan dictator immediately asked that Mullins be replaced and the request was granted. Colonel Fred Cruse became the *Academia's* new director.[60] In December 1943 he was replaced by Colonel Leroy Bartlett. Under Colonel Bartlett the *Academia's* cadets began the practice, continued ever since, of traveling to Panama to spend their senior year receiving instruction from American officers at Fort Gulick.[61]

By the end of 1943 General Somoza had already begun considering ways of altering the constitution to permit his reelection in 1947. These efforts led to a split in the January 1944 Convention of the Liberal Party. A large faction, led by General Carlos Pasos, opposed any plan for reelection, but the dictator used the Guardia to confine the dissidents to their homes and push his plans through the Convention.[62] The opposition then formed their own political party, the Partido Liberal Independiente.

Encouraged by the fall of the long-standing dictatorships of Generals Martínez in El Salvador and Ubico in Guatemala, Nicaraguan university students and opposition political groups began to demonstrate against Somoza in the summer of 1944. The Guardia remained loyal, but many Liberal Party leaders, including ex-President Moncada, were alarmed by the strength of the opposition and began to urge the President to renounce all plans to succeed himself.[63] Instead, Somoza closed the National University, and this precipitated the protest resignation of his

Minister of Education.[64] In an effort to enlist American support for his sagging regime, General Somoza announced plans to stage a military parade, ostensibly in honor of the United States, on July 4, and asked American permission to deliver a speech from the Embassy's balcony. The State Department turned down the request to use the balcony, but could not prevent Somoza from making further efforts to identify his regime with the United States.[65] A few days later, when his opponents attempted to launch a general strike, a tactic which had played a key role in the fall of Ubico and Martínez, the President succeeded in having Colonel Lindberg, the American president of the *Junta de Control de Precios y de Comercio,* sign an order announcing that any establishment that closed its doors would be seized, have its goods sold, and be "denied the right again to engage in business." Any foreigner who joined the strike would be subject to deportation.[66] The threatened strike collapsed, but Somoza's difficulties were far from over.

Pressures against Somoza's reelection continued to mount during July. An exile publication from El Salvador devoted considerable space to attacking Somoza's corruption of the Guardia, declaring that Somoza had replaced *Academia* graduates with political supporters, refused to punish the military for any crimes against civilians, and given control of gambling and other illegal activities to Guardia officers.[67] Student agitation increased, opposition from within the Liberal Party also grew, and even some Guardia officers began to express doubts about the wisdom of the General's plans for his own reelection. The puppet Congress ignored these protests and passed an amendment legalizing reelection, but fearing that the continued protests might lead to his own overthrow, Somoza reluctantly vetoed this measure.[68] Agitation continued for another month until the President also agreed to amnesty for those arrested in earlier demonstrations. With these concessions, General Somoza managed to avoid the fate of Generals Ubico and Martínez. His control over the Guardia had been shaken by these events, however, and by November even his most loyal supporters were reporting discontent, especially among the enlisted men.[69]

In an effort to strengthen his position, Somoza began early in 1945 a campaign for increased aid and support from the United States. In addition to requesting arms and supplies, he invited several American officers to Nicaragua, presented them with medals, and even made them honorary members of the

Nicaraguan Air Force.[70] A conversation between the American chargé in Managua and one of these officers, Brigadier General Luther G. Smith, Chief of the Military Missions Section of the Caribbean Defense Command, revealed American motives for participating in such ceremonies. The chargé pointed out the crucial role of the Guardia in Nicaraguan politics, noting that Somoza would "doubtless be interested in improving his National Guard by any and every means at his disposal." He added that Somoza would probably remain in command of the Guardia even if he stepped down as President after the next elections, then concluded by urging the Army not to "burden the country with armaments." General Smith in reply voiced the War Department's determination "that military missions from foreign countries in the Americas should be avoided at all costs," adding that the War Department wanted to "modernize the Nicaraguan Guard . . . so that it might be easily integrated into the American Army in case of need."[71]

Despite these sentiments, Somoza encountered considerable difficulty in obtaining the arms he desired. Evidence of the importance he attached to this matter was provided by the person he selected to handle negotiations in this matter, his eldest son, Luis Somoza Debayle. Luis had graduated from Louisana State University, then been given a commission as a captain in the Guardia. All of the dictator's efforts proved unavailing, since the State Department intervened to block the proposed arms sales. Concern over Central American conditions was one factor in this decision, but more important were the renewed indications that Somoza was once again seeking some means to perpetuate himself in power beyond 1947. The Department feared that "Any arms which we might ship him at this time could only be taken by him, by the Nicaraguan public, and by the other Republics of Central America and of the hemisphere as a demonstration of our complete support for his plans. This impression would not only be erroneous, but extremely embarrassing."[72]

Renewed efforts by President Somoza to find some means for manipulating his own reelection had begun early in 1945. In an effort to broaden his base of support he courted Nicaragua's infant labor movement, pushing through the Congress a new Labor Code with provisions which were, by Central American standards, remarkably progressive. New unions, operating under government sponsorship, were also created.[73] In an effort to make Nicaraguans believe that his ambitions had American support, he had his Ambassador in Washington, son-in-law, Guillermo Sevilla Sacasa, spread reports that the United States wanted him to stay in office beyond 1947. Such efforts further angered the State Department, which believed that "his determination to continue in control, if not in power, will bring a rising opposition," especially since Somoza was continuing to expand "his widespread commercial activities."[74]

The succession of Harry Truman to the American Presidency and his appointment of James F. Byrnes as Secretary of State produced a change in United States policy toward Nicaragua. While still paying lip service to the idea of noninterference in internal affairs, the State Department now began active efforts to block Somoza's plans for reelection.[75] On August 1, Assistant Secretary of State Nelson Rockefeller called in the Nicaraguan Ambassador and bluntly informed him that "should Somoza run for reelection it might create difficulties for him which would seriously affect relations between the two countries."[76]

Informed of this conversation, the dictator sought to soften American opposition. He informed the American Ambassador that "the whole business of his running for election is a big game," and that he had not authorized the proclamations of his candidacy that were being made. He claimed that he had not repudiated these efforts because, if he did, Guardia officers would begin to seek the presidency for themselves and "the Guardia Nacional would get out of control." In addition, the President asserted that, by allowing his own candidacy to remain a possibility until the last minute, he would be in a position to select as his successor an individual who would "serve patriotically and loyally the interests of Nicaragua and the United States." Claiming that he neither wanted nor intended to run for reelection, he invited the American Ambassador and the State Department to join him in selecting his successor, a proposal the Department quickly declined.[77]

Despite Somoza's protestations, the State Department continued to believe that he sought reelection and continued to oppose any such course. Ambassador Warren informed the Department that the size of his investments in Nicaragua made the President unwilling to even consider the possibility of allowing anyone hostile to his interests to obtain the presidency.[78] The key to the situation remained the Guardia. The State Department noted that, while Somoza had promised free elections, there was "nothing in his record to warrant belief in this promise" and added that his control over the Guardia put him "in a position to ensure his own reelection."[79]

As predicted, opposition to the proclamation of Somoza's candidacy grew steadily during 1945. By the end of October an unexpected boost was given to this opposition when both his wife and his eldest son urged him to quit at the end of his term. His wife even wanted him to step down from his post as *Jefe Director* as well, something the General was totally unwilling to consider.[80]

Far from giving up, the Nicaraguan dictator simply increased his efforts to build up his military strength in order to ensure his continued rule. Unable to obtain warplanes from the United States Government, he tried to obtain commercial aircraft from American suppliers. Ambassador Warren urged the State Department to block any such sales, noting that the "Nicaraguan govt is already experimenting with mounting machine guns on BT-13's," and adding that "Any planes we supply Nicaragua at this time will be considered by a good proportion of the populace (perhaps an overwhelming majority) as aid given to present govt to suppress its own people."[81] Blocked in the United States, Somoza attempted to obtain planes from British or Canadian sources, but was again opposed by the State Department which, in addition to its concern over the use to which such planes might be put, was now also angry over Nicaraguan default on its Lend-Lease repayments.[82]

By November, elements within the Guardia were growing restive over the reelection efforts. There were even some officers who suggested that the President should "be bumped off." The American Ambassador believed that the Guardia was ready "to assist in the removal of Somoza or to take advantage of

Papa Somoza and his two sons, "Tachito" and Luis, have been the key figures in Nicaragua's forty-year-old nightmare.

his removal to forward individual or group interest." Ambassador Warren concluded that "if Somoza plans to oppose the revolution with Guardia, he will not have the discipline, obedience or support he expects."[83] While the State Department was trying to discourage the reelection campaign, it evidently felt that murder was too extreme a measure to employ in accomplishing this end and Warren was urged to "use your influence . . . with the Guardia to avoid the assasination of President Somoza."[84]

The younger officers were especially restive, a situation that did not escape the General's attention. He blamed much of this on the American Military Attaché, Colonel Judson, whom he accused of telling these officers that the "Guardia should be nonpolitical," a stance that was equated with disloyalty to Somoza, and that "political appointees in the Guardia should be kicked out." Furthermore, the attaché had told the officers that the Guardia "could not expect planes, arms, ammunition or related material" until the crisis caused by the President's campaign to succeed himself was resolved. Somoza demanded Judson's immediate recall, a course which the Ambassador, despite strong efforts, was unable to alter.[85] To avoid publicizing the incident, it was announced that Judson was taking an extended leave and no replacement was named for some time.

Despite the continued opposition of the United States and the unrest within the Guardia, Somoza was still reluctant to abandon his candidacy. In an effort to soften American opposition, he even threatened to pull his younger son, Anastasio Somoza Debayle, known as Tachito, out of West Point. He also tried persuasion, arguing that the Guardia looked on him "almost as a father, in other words . . . [it] holds personal allegiance to him," and saying that, if he were reelected this time, he would then train the Guardia "so that it will be prepared to accept the next President."[86] None of these arguments moved the State Department, nor did they do anything to curb the growing divisions within the Guardia. Motivated by institutional self-interest and concern over possible successors to Somoza as *Jefe Director,* many officers applied increasing pressure on the General to abandon his efforts. Colonel Luis Manuel Debayle, a brother of the President's wife, even resigned from the Guardia in protest over the reelection campaign, and told the American Ambassador that he was debating between trying to lead a Guardia movement against the President or simply leaving the country.[87] The Colonel's defection may have been the last straw for on

November 29, 1945, Somoza promised the State Department that he would withdraw his candidacy within thirty days. He even put his promise into writing and also pledged to end the state of siege and release all political prisoners.[88] While the actual public renunciation did not come until early in January 1946, this action marked an end to the General's efforts to retain the presidency. It did not, however, signal any willingness on his part to abandon his power.

Control of the Guardia remained the key to power in Nicaragua and Somoza was determined to retain that at any cost. He had General Camilo González approach the United States Embassy with the idea of his retaining the post of *Jefe Director* after he left the presidency, an idea that Ambassador Warren bluntly declared would prove unpalatable in Nicaragua and abroad.[89] Such sentiments had no visible effect on Somoza, who made no secret of his intention of continuing as *Jefe Director*. The effect of all this was summed up by Warren in early 1946 when he wrote:

> Somoza realizes that in the last analysis his strongest card is the Guardia Nacional. He has played, as only an expert can, on the loyalty, allegiance and feelings of the Guardia. Today there is confusion, due largely to Somoza, in the ranks of the Guardia. He wants both officers and men to look to him as the benevolent and beneficent father of the organization, to whom the organization owes everything. He is right in thinking that many hold this impression. He has managed to arouse feeling between civilians and Academy trained officers. The impression left with them is that only Somoza can manage that both groups continue in the Guardia. The feeling is that without Somoza the Guardia will be politically purged and reduced to an inefficient police force. The result is that now many of the Guardia consider that Somoza must continue in the Presidency or that a Somoza-selected man, in whom the Guardia has confidence, must succeed him. In other words . . . the most important issue in Nicaragua is not Somoza, but the Guardia Nacional.[90]

To the surprise of many, Somoza not only renounced his own candidacy, but actually took some steps toward restoring freedoms in Nicaragua. On January 30 a massive anti-Somoza parade, with estimates of participation ranging up to 100,000 was allowed in Managua. The Guardia remained in their barracks and a group of ex-soldiers took part, carrying signs with such slogans as, "We want professional and not political chiefs," and, "For a Guardia Nacional serving the Republic and not one man."[91] When the opposition united behind the candidacy of Dr.

Enoc Aguado, Somoza reluctantly allowed the Liberals to nominate his rival in the 1936 election, Dr. Leonardo Argüello, finding him the most popular candidate he could accept and evidently believing that his advanced age would make it possible to control him once he took office.[92]

A surprising amount of freedom was allowed during the campaign. The press began to attack Somoza directly and Dr. Aguado was able to campaign throughout the nation.[93] There were limits to this freedom as the Guardia was occasionally used to harass opponents and break up some of their meetings. Of greater import was Somoza's complete control over the electoral machinery, assuring that, with his administration counting the votes and with the Guardia supervising the polling places, the Liberals' candidate would have no problem winning in the official returns if not in the actual voting.

The election was held on February 2, 1947. Voters were required to stand in separate lines according to their voting choice, but despite the obvious hazards of standing in Dr. Aguado's line it was soon clear that at least in Managua, the majority of the votes were going to Aguado.[94] By nightfall, lines of voters for Argüello were nonexistent, but, in part due to official harrassment, long lines of people were still waiting to vote for Aguado. At this point the Guardia dispersed the crowds and rushed the ballots, under heavy guard, to the National Palace to be counted. The following day, Somoza announced that Dr. Argüello had won the election.[95] The opposition charged fraud and the defeated candidate even flew to the United States to argue against recognition of the Argüello administration.[96] These efforts accomplished nothing and Argüello was inaugurated, as scheduled, on May 1, 1947.

General Somoza had made elaborate plans to ensure his continued power after he left the presidency. A new residence for the *Jefe Director,* designed along lines similar to a medieval castle and known as La Curva, was built on La Loma, dominating the road from Managua to the President's residence. The ammunition formerly stored under the *Casa Presidencial* was transferred to La Curva and Somoza moved into that new residence before Argüello's inauguration. Command of the Guardia's First Batallion, which garrisoned La Loma, was given to Major Anastasio Somoza D., the General's younger son, who had recently graduated from West Point. Shortly after the inauguration, it became apparent that these preparations alone were not sufficient to maintain Somoza's position.

Two months before his inauguration, the new President had privately indicated to the American Ambassador his determination to remove Somoza from the Guardia, even if he had to use force to do so. Argüello claimed promises of support for this from many Guardia officers. Ambassador Warren gave some credence to this, observing that "although Somoza is the cleverest político in Nicaragua and knows thoroughly the Guardia Nacional, I am convinced that he does not have the control over the Guardia that he once had. I believe that there are those in the Guardia who for personal gain or, in rare cases, through patriotism might desert him."[97] Somoza had no intention of leaving the Guardia voluntarily. He felt that Argüello would be unable to control the force without him and that his supporters would "be able to take care of any movement directed toward his removal from the Guardia."[98]

Once in office, the new President wasted no time in trying to curb Somoza's power. Declaring that he did not have to consult the General on military appointments, Argüello announced several changes in Guardia assignments. Most notable of these were the removal of Major Anastasio Somoza D. as commander of the First Battalion, transferring him to León and also removing him from his other post as Guardia Inspector General, and replacing the Pro-Somoza Chief of Police in Managua with Colonel Alberto Baca, one of his own supporters.[99]

These actions infuriated Somoza, who attempted to intimidate Argüello by parading the Guardia's three tanks in front of the *Casa Presidencial.*[100] This failed to impress Argüello, who proceeded to appoint a cabinet composed largely of opponents of the General. He then discharged hundreds of government employees whose duties evidently consisted of work on privately owned Somoza properties. The *Jefe Director,* in response, reduced the First and Second Companies of the First Battalion (Presidential Guard) from 400 to less than 100 men. The men removed from these companies were added to the Third Company, described by the American chargé as "Somoza's personal guard," and were assigned to the General's properties, to La Curva, and to the Campo de Marte.[101]

Undeterred, Argüello called Somoza and informed him that he had "deliberately by-passed the office of the Jefe Director" in making Guardia assigments "to demonstrate to Somoza as well as to the people of Nicaragua that he is actually in command."[102] Without consulting Somoza, Argüello had Colonel Medina, the Guardia's new Chief of Staff, and Colonel Policarpo Gutiérrez invite officers to a banquet in the President's honor. Argüello was convinced that the Guardia was abandoning Somoza and that he would be able to get rid of the General without even having to resort to force.[103] This would prove to be a fatal misconception.

While continuing to issue protestations of loyalty, even asking the American Embassy to transmit to the President a guarantee that the Guardia, under Somoza, would not revolt, the General busied himself with preparations for deposing his own, hand-picked successor.[104] He retained control of Congress and, over the President's strong objections, had that body select three of his supporters as Presidential Designates, putting them in line to succeed Argüello. He also sent two circular telegrams to all Guardia Department Commanders, instructing them to obey only orders issued by the *Jefe Director* and to arrest any officer whom the President might send to replace them.[105]

The crisis came on the night of May 25-26. The President had sent for Somoza the previous night, intending to demand his resignation then, but Somoza had pleaded illness as an excuse for not keeping the appointment. The following day the President informed Somoza that he would have to leave the country, following which his resignation as *Jefe Director* would be announced. The General appeared to accept this decision, asking only that he be allowed a few days to arrange his affairs, a request the President foolishly granted. Somoza immediately began active coup preparations. He made unsuccessful overtures to the Conservative and Independent Liberal Party leaders, offering them posts in the cabinet, Congress, and local government in return for their cooperation in the planned coup. After some deliberations, this offer was turned down, but the opposition refrained from communicating any word of the General's actions to the government.[106]

At 2 A.M. on the morning of May 26, the Guardia struck. They seized the Campo de Marte, the Palacio Nacional (which housed the Congress and most government ministries), and the Managua police barracks, and cut off all communications with the Presidential Palace. Argüello's supporters were apparently taken by complete surprise and the coup was carried off without bloodshed. Several Guardia officers loyal to Argüello were arrested, others took refuge in the *Casa Presidencial.* Somoza refrained from directly attacking the President, preferring to starve him out if necessary. Meanwhile, reinforcements poured into Managua and soldiers were stationed at key points throughout the city.[107] Argüello refused demands for his resignation, but on May 27 he and eleven officers took refuge in the Mexican Embassy.[108] Congress was then ordered to meet and was informed that Argüello had tried to split the Guardia, murder the *Jefe Director,* and dissolve Congress so that he could rule as a dictator. Coming from Somoza, the last charge sounded a bit strange, but surrounded by Guardia bayonets, the members of Congress were in no position to appreciate the irony. They did as they were told, removing Argüello and installing Benjamín Lacayo Sacasa as provisional President.[109]

The coup had succeeded for Somoza, but it produced major consequences. Taking their cue from the United States, none of the other American Republics would recognize the new regime. The United States also took action aimed directly at the Guardia, demanding the return of all ammunition belonging to the military mission, halting all material and instructional aid, and withdrawing the American director from the *Academia Militar.* This led Somoza to appoint his own son as the first Nicaragua director of that institution.[110]

In an effort to regain American support, Somoza called a new constituent assembly and included in his new Constitution strong anti-Communist provisions, plus provisions making it easier to allow the United States to establish military bases in Nicaragua. In addition, the assembly selected Victor Román y Reyes, an uncle of Somoza's as President.[111] The State Department was unmoved by these efforts and continued to withhold recognition and military aid.

Opposition political parties also refused, despite repeated overtures, to cooperate with Somoza. In early September, led by Nicaragua's perennial revolutionary, Emiliano Chamorro, they attempted to overthrow the government. As usual, the plans were discovered before the uprising. The Guardia was ready, and, aided by the use of the Lend-Lease-equipped FAN to strafe the rebels, put down the uprising with only a reported fifteen Guardia casualties. Chamorro, under the protection of the American Embassy, left for exile in Mexico, while hundreds of other opposition leaders were arrested in an impressive show of Somoza's strength.[112]

This abortive uprising represented the last real threat to the new regime. By the end of the year the diplomatic boycott had begun to break down as both Costa Rica and the Dominican Republic recognized the Román y Reyes administration.[113] In January 1948, the new Constitution was proclaimed. In addition to outlawing the Communist Party, it contained provisions placing all transfers, troop movements, and promotions under the control of the *Jefe Director,* eliminating the possibility of any future President adopting Argüello's tactics.[114] The United States continued to withhold recognition until after the Inter-American meeting of Foreign Ministers at Bogotá in April 1948. At that meeting a resolution was adopted urging the continuity of diplomatic relations among hemispheric nations. In conformity with that resolution, the United States announced plans to reestablish relations with Nicaragua.[115]

Reestablishment of relations was complicated by a revolution that had broken out in March in neighboring Costa Rica. Defeated in presidential elections, the government of President Teodoro Picado had annulled the elections, leading to an uprising led by José Figueres and supported by a collection of exiles and soldiers of fortune from various Latin American nations known as the Caribbean Legion.[116] Somoza, who reportedly developed a profitable cattle-smuggling business with officials of the Picado administration, denounced the uprising as Communist-dominated and hurriedly dispatched aid to Picado.[117] The General reportedly even offered to fly 1,000 Guardia into San José, but even Picado was not willing to have his regime preserved by Nicaraguan bayonets and the offer was declined.[118] Somoza did send several hundred Guardia across the border, allegedly with Picado's permission, claiming that they were being used only to repel planned attacks upon Nicaragua. They reported one major clash with a column of Costa Rican revolutionaries, but their intervention, remote from the center of power and population, had no influence on the outcome of the struggle.[119] The revolution triumphed and Picado and ex-President Calderón Guardia sought refuge in Nicaragua.

Figueres' triumph only deepened the antipathy between the Costa Rican leader and Somoza. Despite United States opposition, the Nicaraguan strongman had purchased additional arms for his troops, including B-24 bombers from Brazil, for possible use against Costa Rica.[120] In December a force of Costa Rican exiles, armed and equipped by the Guardia and, according to some reports, including Guardia fighting out of uniform, invaded Costa Rica. Somoza evidently hoped this might lead to an open conflict between Nicaragua and Costa Rica, but the rapid defeat of the exiles, combined with United States pressure to limit the conflict, prevented this from happening.[121]

In 1949, Somoza turned his attention back to domestic considerations. General Chamorro was allowed to return from exile and he and Somoza negotiated a compromise political agreement. Announced early in 1950, this provided for calling another constituent assembly and holding simultaneously a new presidential election. The minority party was guaranteed at least one-third of the seats in Congress and various other government posts, including a seat on the Supreme Court.[122] Elections were held in May 1950, with Somoza the Liberals' candidate and Chamorro, now in his late seventies, running for the Conservatives. President Román y Reyes died two weeks before the election and Congress unanimously chose Somoza to succeed him. Two weeks later, the newly appointed President won reelection by a margin of over 100,000 votes.[123]

With Somoza back in the presidency the Guardia enjoyed continued growth and prosperity. From the 1949–1950 fiscal year to the 1953–1954 fiscal year the force's budget nearly doubled, but the personnel assigned to combat units actually declined. There were large increases in the Police and Air Force contingents. United States aid to the Guardia, motivated in part by preoccupation with the alleged Communist influence on the Guatemalan government, increased greatly. In 1952 an Air Force mission was sent to Nicaragua, the following year an agreement establishing an Army mission was signed, and in 1954 a Military Assistance Program was begun.[124] All of this made it even more unlikely that any attempt to remove Somoza could succeed without the acquiescence, if not the support, of the Guardia.

By 1954, the United States had determined to overthrow the Arbenz government in Guatemala. Large quantities of American arms were flown into Nicaragua, some of which were turned over to Guatemalan exiles, preparing for a CIA-sponsored invasion of their homeland.[125] Most, however, remained in control of the Guardia, for General Somoza had other plans for their use.

In 1954, another attempt had been made on Somoza's life. A group of conspirators, financed by General Chamorro and encouraged by the Costa Rican government of President Figueres had planned to ambush Somoza when he returned from a visit with the American Ambassador, but as usual word of the plot leaked and the conspirators were hunted down. Somoza showed a special vindictiveness toward several former Guardia officers involved in the plot, offering a special C$10,000 reward for them and shooting any who fell into his hands.[126]

Angered by Costa Rican support for this plot, the Nicaraguan dictator now sought to overthrow the Figueres regime. In preparation for a possible conflict, he purchased twenty-five P-51 fighters from Sweden, making FAN Central America's largest air force. The Guardia's ground combat capability had already been enhanced by United States aid in equipping and training a battalion of troops, the *Batallón de Combate Somoza,* at a reported cost of $600,000.[127] Open conflict began in January 1955, when another force of Costa Rican exiles, supported by some Guardia troops fighting out of uniform and aided by a few of the P-51s, evidently piloted by Costa Rican exiles, crossed the border and attempted to march on San José. Despite Somoza's claims that the Costa Rican government was aiding Communist plots in Central America, the United States was determined to halt this conflict. Navy planes from the Canal Zone were sent to help prevent direct Guardia intervention in the fighting and the Organization of American States (OAS) condemned the participation of "foreign forces" and asked Nicaragua to close its border to further supplies for the rebels. Ultimately, Costa Rican forces managed to defeat the invaders and an uneasy peace was restored.[128]

This dispute was Somoza's last serious external conflict. By the time it ended, he had less than a year to live. Late in 1955, he had announced his determination to serve another term in office and, in September 1956, he traveled to León to receive the inevitable nomination of his liberal Nationalist Party. He took even greater than usual security precautions for the trip, but these were to prove ineffective. On September 20 he was officially nominated and the following night he attended a reception at the *Casa del Obrero* in León. Without warning, a young poet, Rigoberto López Pérez, pulled a revolver and fired four shots at point-blank-range into the Nicaraguan President. An instant later Pérez was riddled by shots from Somoza's bodyguards.[129]

The wounded dictator was rushed to Managua by helicopter. Then, through the personal intercession of Thomas Whelan, the American Ambassador and a personal intimate of Somoza's, he was flown to Gorgas Hospital in the Canal Zone. Several prominent American physicians, including the commander of the Walter Reed Army Hospital, were sent by President Eisenhower to treat the wounded General, but despite this array of medical talent Somoza never fully regained consciousness, expiring in the early morning hours of September 29, 1956.[130] An era in Nicaraguan history had come to an abrupt end.

NOTES

1. General Anastasio Somoza García, *Mensaje Inaugural del Excomo. Señor Presidente de la República, General Anastasio Somoza G., al honorable Congreso Nacional* (Managua: Talleres Nacionales, 1937); pp. 13–14.

2. The American chargé in Nicaragua, Gerald Drew, to Hull, February 1, 1937, NA RG 59, 817.20/26; memorandum of conversation between the Nicaraguan chargé, Dr. Henri DeBayle and Laurence Duggan, Chief of the Division of Latin American Affairs, October 10, 1936, NA RG 59, 817.20/26.

3. Long to Hull, April 7, 1937, NA RG 59, 817.00/8644.

4. Long to Hull, May 14, 1937, NA RG 59, 817.00/8653.

5. Long to Hull, July 19, 1937, NA RG 59, 817.00/8657.

6. *Novedades* (Managua), July 18, 1937, p. 1, and July 20, 1937, p. 1.

7. *Memoria de la Secretaría de Guerra, Marina y Aviación–1937* (Managua: Talleres Nacionales, 1937), pp. 9, 11, 119–24, 127–129, and 134.

8. Ibid., pp. 8 and 211.

9. Unsigned, undated memorandum from Headquarters, USMC, Vogel Papers.

10. *Memoria de la Secretaría de Guerra, Marína y Aviación–1937,* p. 12.

11. Memorandum from O'Donoghue to Duggan, August 17, 1937, NA RG 59, 817.223/12.

12. Memorandum by O'Donoghue, October 14, 1937, NA RG 59, 817.20/28.

13. Adolfo Reyes Huete, *ETAPAS del Ejército* (Managua: Talleres Nacionales, n.d.), pp. 73–74.

14. Long to Hull, May 3, 1937, NA RG 59, 817.00/8646; Long to Hull, November 23, 1937 NA RG 59, 817.00/8664.

15. Interview with Major Salvador d'Arbelles, Corinto, Nicaragua, December 1963; Long to Hull, December 6, 1937, NA RG 59, 817.00/8666; Long to Hull, December 14, 1937, NA RG 59, 817.00/8667; Reyes Huete, *ETAPAS,* p. 104.

16. Naval Attaché Report, October 28, 1937, NA RG 59, 817.284/45;

the American Vice Consul at Belize, William G. Rupprecht, to Hull, March 8, 1938, NA RG 59, 817.248/50.

17. *Revista de la Fuerza Aérea de Nicaragua,* February 1959 (pages not numbered).

18. Memorandum from Ellis Briggs to Sumner Welles, January 30, 1939, NA RG 59, 817.20/37.

19. The American Minister to Nicaragua, Nicholson, to Hull, September 16, 1939, NA RG 59, 817.248/73.

20. Long to Hull January 7, 1938, NA RG 59, 817.00/8669.

21. Memorandum from Duggan to Welles, June 28, 1938, NA RG 59, 817.34/43; memorandum by Gerald Drew, November 24, 1938, NA RG 59, 817.34/54.

22. The Nicaraguan Minister to the United States, Leon DeBayle, to Hull, August 6 1938, NA RG 59, 817.30/1; Adolf Berle to Leon DeBayle, September 13, 1938, NA RG 59, 817.30/1.

23. Nicholson to Hull, September 6, 1939, NA RG 59, 817.34/73.

24. Ibid.

25. Nicholson to Hull, November 18, 1938, NA RG 59, 817.00/8701.

26. Russell H. Fitzgibbon, " 'Continuismo' in Central America and the Caribbean," *The Inter-American Quarterly* II (July 1940) 69–70.

27. "The Nicaraguan Constitution of 1939," quoted in Reyes Huete, *ETAPAS,* pp. 91–95.

28. Fitzgibbon, "Continuismo," p. 70.

29. Nicholson to Hull, April 28, 1939, NA RG 59, 817.00/8715.

30. There is a great deal of material covering this trip in the NA RG 59, 817.00 file and in the papers in the Franklin D. Roosevelt Memorial Library, Hyde Park, New York. (Cited hereafter as Roosevelt Papers.)

31. President Somoza to President Roosevelt, May 22, 1939, and Roosevelt to Somoza, May 22, 1939, *Foreign Relations,* 1939, V, pp. 725–30.

32. Memorandum of a conversation between Welles and the Nicaraguan Ambassador to the United States, December 1, 1938, NA RG 59, 817.20/34; memorandum from Ellis Briggs to Welles, January 30, 1939, NA RG 59, 817.20/37.

33. Memorandum by Briggs, June 21, 1939, NA RG 59, 817.20/55.

34. Nicholson to Hull, August 18, 1939, NA RG 59, 817.20/57.

35. The American chargé in Nicaragua, La Verne Baldwin, to Hull, October 28, 1939, NA RG 59, 817.20/60.

36. Nicholson to Hull, January 18, 1941, NA RG 59, 817.20/76; Baldwin to Hull, March 24, 1941, NA RG 59, 817.20/80; Hull to Nicholson, August 26, 1941, NA RG 59, 817.20/85a; memorandum by Phillip Bonsal, August 9, 1941, NA RG 59, 817.223/27; memorandum from S. Morris to Bonsal, August 16, 1941, NA RG 59, 817.223/27.

37. Welles to President Roosevelt, April 3, 1942, Roosevelt Papers; memorandum from Harold D. Smith, Budget Director, to Roosevelt, Roosevelt Papers.

38. For the history of this project, see J. Frank Rippy, "State Department Operations: The Rama Road," *Inter-American Economic Affairs* IX (Summer 1955) 17–32.

39. John Gunther, *Inside Latin America* (New York: Harper 1941), pp. 137–38.

40. Somoza to Roosevelt, January 30, 1941, January 30, 1942, and March 9, 1942, Roosevelt Papers.

41. Nearly all of Somoza's letters to Roosevelt, now found in the Roosevelt Library, were treated in this manner. On one occasion Somoza signed his letter, "Su Afmo. Amigo, A. Somoza G.," and the routine reply was addressed to "President Afmo. Amigo Somoza."

42. The American chargé in Nicaragua, LaVerne Baldwin, to Hull, December 2, 1939, NA RG 59, 817.00/8736.

43. Several accounts of cases such as these were told to me during interviews in Nicaragua in 1963, 1966, 1970, and 1975. One such case was reported by the American chargé, Bernbaum, to the State Department, on September 2, 1947, NA RG 59, 817.00/9-247.

44. Nicholson to Hull, April 19, 1940, NA RG 59, 817.00/8762.

45. Baldwin to Hull, December 2, 1939, NA RG 59, 817.00/8736.

46. Confidential interviews in Nicaragua, 1963 and 1970; the American Ambassador to Nicaragua, Fletcher Warren, to Secretary of State Byrnes, July 9, 1946, *Foreign Relations,* 1946, XI, p. 1071.

47. Nicholson to Hull, March 15, 1940, NA RG 59, 817.00/8753.

48. Welles to Nicholson, April 16, 1940, *Foreign Relations,* 1940, V, pp. 1069–71.

49. Ildefonso Solórzano, *La Guardía Nacional de Nicaragua: Su trajectoria y incógnita, 1927–1944* (Granada, Nicaragua: El Centro-Americano, 1944), p. 37; Nicholson to Hull, October 19, 1940, November 5, 1940, and November 7, 1940, NA RG 59, 817.00/8876, 817.00/8879, and 817.00/8882.

50. Nicholson to Hull, November 15, 1940, NA RG 59, 817.00/8884.

51. Nicholson to Hull, November 5, 1940, and November 7, 1940, NA RG 59, 817.00/8889, and 817.00/8882; Solórzano, *La Guardia Nacional,* p. 37; Gunther, *Inside Latin America,* p. 142.

52. Reyes accepted his dismissal without public protest and was later restored to favor, being given a seat in the Nicaraguan Senate, a seat which he still held, though rarely filled, in 1975. He also subsequently served as Minister of Public Works, but never again was given command of troops.

53. Lend-Lease Agreement between the United States and Nicaragua, October 16, 1941, *Foreign Relations,* 1941, VII, pp. 410–13.

54. Memorandum from Orme Wilson, Liaison Officer, to Major Johnson, War Department, October 2, 1941, NA RG 59, 817.24/434A.

55. Colonel Mullins to the Assistant Chief of Staff, G-2, U.S. Army, June 17, 1941, and Mullins to Colonel C.B. Moore, office of the Assistant Chief of Staff, G-2, U.S. Army, June 18, 1941, Records of the War

Department General and Special Staffs, Record Group 165, National Archives, Washington, D.C. (hereafter cited as NA RG 165).

56. Gustavo Alemán-Bolaños, *Los probres diablos* (Guatemala: Editorial Hispania, 1947), p. 87.

57. Interviews with Major Salvador d'Arbelles, Corinto, Nicaragua, December 1963, and with Colonels Guillermo Rivas Cuadra and Rafael Espinosa Altimirano, Managua, December 1963.

58. The American Ambassador to Nicaragua, James Stewart, to Hull, November 7, 1942, NA RG 59, 817.00/8951.

59. The American chargé in Nicaragua, William Cocharan, to Hull, June 1, 1942, NA RG 59, 817.20/100.

60. Hull to Cocharan, May 19, 1942, NA RG 59, 817.20/105; Cocharan to Hull, June 1, 1942, NA RG 59, 817.20/114.

61. *Academia Militar de Nicaragua, 1947* (Managua: Talleres Nacionales, 1947), p. 17.

62. Solórzano, *La Guardia Nacional,* pp. 48–51.

63. Ibid., pp. 55–66.

64. *La Nueva Prensa* (Managua), July 6, 1944, pp. 1 and 2.

65. Stewart to Hull, June 29, 1944, and Hull to Stewart, June 30, 1944, *Foreign Relations,* 1944, VII, pp. 1394–95.

66. Stewart to Hull, July 7, 1944, *Foreign Relations,* 1944, VII, p. 1396.

67. *Nicaragua under Somoza: To the Governments and People of America* (San Salvador, El Salvador: Imprenta Fanes, 1944), pp. 24–25.

68. *La Noticia* (Managua), July 25, 1944, p. 1 and August 9, 1944, p.1; *La Nueva Prensa* (Managua), July 27, 1944, p. 1.

69. Report by Lieutenant Colonel Frederick Judson, U.S. Military Attaché in Nicaragua, November 11, 1944, NA RG 165, Mil. 350.5 Nic.

70. Harold Finley, chargé in Nicaragua, to Secretary of State Stettinius, February 26, 1945, *Foreign Relations,* 1945, IX, pp. 1196–98.

71. Ibid.

72. Director, Office of American Republics Affairs, to the American Ambassador to Nicaragua, Fletcher Warren, August 20, 1945, *Foreign Relations,* 1945, IX, pp. 1205–08.

73. John Morris Ryan et al., *Area Handbook for Nicaragua* (Washington: Government Printing Office, 1970), p. 261; Rosa Argentina Correa Muñiz and Maria del Tránsito Flores Mena, *Breve diagnóstico del sindicalismo Nicaragüense* (Managua: Universidad Nacional de Nicaragua, 1975), pp. 37–38.

74. William Cocharan to Finley, February 23, 1945, NA RG 59, 817.00/2–2345.

75. The State Department documents on this subject printed in *Foreign Relations,* 1945, IX, are in a section under the somewhat contradictory title "Efforts to Discourage President Somoza's Bid for Reelection in 1947, while Maintaining a Policy of Non-Interference in Nicaragua's Internal Affairs."

76. Acting Secretary of State Grew to Warren, August 7, 1945, *Foreign Relations,* 1945, IX, pp. 1213–14.

77. Warren to Secretary of State Byrnes, August 10, 1945, and August 29, 1945, Byrnes to Warren, August 31, 1945, *Foreign Relations,* 1945, IX, pp. 1214–18.

78. Warren to the Secretary of State, July 24, 1945, NA RG 59, 817.00/7–2445.

79. Memorandum from Cocharan to Rockefeller, July 25, 1945, NA RG 59, 817.00/7–2545.

80. Warren to Assistant Secretary of State Braden, October 30, 1945, NA RG 59, 817.00/10–3045.

81. Byrnes to Warren, November 9, 1945, and Warren to Byrnes, November 15, 1945, *Foreign Relations,* 1945, IX, pp. 1210–11.

82. Warren to Byrnes, November 21, 1945, and Byrnes to Warren, November 27, 1945, *Foreign Relations,* 1945, IX, pp. 1212–13.

83. Warren to Byrnes, November 7, 1945, NA RG 59, 817.00/11–745.

84. Byrnes to Warren, November 15, 1945, NA RG 59, 817.00/11–1545.

85. Warren to Byrnes, November 12, 1945, NA RG 59, 817.00/11–1245.

86. Warren to Byrnes, November 15, 1945, NA RG 59, 817.00/11–1545.

87. Warren to Byrnes, November 20, 1945, and November 27, 1945, NA RG 59, 817.00/11–2045 and 817.00/11–2755.

88. Warren to Byrnes, November 29, 1945, *Foreign Relations,* 1945, IX, pp. 1225–27.

89. Interview with General Camilo González, Managua, December 1963; Warren to Byrnes, December 6, 1945, NA RG 59, 817.00/12–645.

90. Warren to Byrnes, January 14, 1946, NA RG 59, 817.00/1–1446.

91. Warren to Byrnes, January 30, 1946, NA RG 59, 817.00/1–3046.

92. Pedro Joaquín Chamorro C., *Estirpe sangrienta: los Somozas* (Buenos Aires: Editorial Triángulo, 1959), p. 70; Emiliano Chamorro, "Autobiografía," *Revista Conservadora* II (September 1961) 173; *New York Times,* February 2, 1947, p. 16, and February 3, 1947, p. 1; Alejandro Cole Chamorro, *Desde Sandino hasta los Somozas* (Granada, Nicaragua: Editorial El Mundo, 1971), pp. 246–48; Mariano Fiallos Oyanguren, "The Nicaraguan Political System: The Flow of Demands and the Reactions of the Regime" (Ph.D. dissertation, University of Kansas, 1968), p. 38.

93. *New York Times,* February 4, 1947, p. 11. Proof of this relative press freedom becomes clear when one reads the violently anti-Somoza articles published in *La Prensa* (Managua) during this time.

94. Pedro Joaquín Chamorro, *Estirpe sangrienta,* p. 70; *New York Times,* February 2, 1947, p. 16.

95. *New York Times,* February 3, 1947, p. 1.

96. The Acting Secretary of State to Warren, April 8, 1947, *Foreign Relations,* 1947, VIII, p. 846. Even the Nicaraguan Ambassador to the United States, Somoza's son-in-law, Guillermo Sevilla Sacasa, admitted that Dr. Aguado had won in Managua. See the memorandum by the Chief of the Division of Central American and Panamanian Affairs, February 14, 1947, *Foreign Relations,* 1947, VIII, pp. 843–844.

97. Warren to Secretary of State Marshall, March 3, 1947, NA RG 59, 817.00/3–347.

98. Memorandum of a conversation between General Somoza and Ambassador Warren, March 25, 1947, NA RG 59, 817.00/3–647.

99. Bernbaum to Marshall, May 6, 1947, NA RG 59, 817.00/5–647; *La Prensa* (Managua), May 4, 1947, p. 1.

100. Bernbaum to Marshall, May 5, 1947, NA RG 59, 817.00/5–547.

101. Bernbaum to Marshall, May 7, 1947, NA RG 59, 817.00/5–747.

102. Bernbaum to Marshall, May 9, 1947, *Foreign Relations,* 1947, VIII, p. 848.

103. Bernbaum to Marshall, May 14, 1947, and May 20, 1947, NA RG 59, 817.00/5–1447, and 817.00/5–2047.

104. Memorandum by Lieutentant Colonel Harry Towler, U.S. Military Attaché in Nicaragua, May 19, 1947, NA RG 59, 817.00/5–2047.

105. Bernbaum to Marshall, May 20, 1947, and June 6, 1947, NA RG 59, 817.00/5–2047, and 817.00/6–647.

106. *La Prensa* (Managua), May 25, 1947, p. 1, and May 28, 1947, pp. 1 and 4; Bernbaum to Marshall, May 26, 1947, May 27, 1947, and June 5, 1947, NA RG 59, 817.00/5–2647, 817.00/5–2747, and 817.00/6–547.

107. Bernbaum to Marshall, May 26, 1947, NA RG 59, 817.00/5–2647.

108. Bernbaum to Marshall, May 27, 1947, NA RG 59, 817.00/5–2747.

109. *New York Times,* May 28, 1947, p. 11; *La Prensa* (Managua), May 28, 1947, pp. 1 and 4; Bernbaum to Marshall, May 28, 1947, *Foreign Relations,* 1947, VIII, pp. 860–863.

110. Bernbaum to Marshall, May 28, 1947, NA RG 59, 817.00/5–2847; Bernbaum to Marshall, June 26, 1947, and July 1, 1947, *Foreign Relations,* 1947, VIII, pp. 858–59.

111. Bernbaum to Marshall, January 20, 1948, NA RG 59, 817.00/1–2048; Bernbaum to Marshall, August 7, 1947, *Foreign Relations,* 1946, VIII, pp. 864–66. Somoza's efforts to achieve United States recognition at times bordered on the absurd. Besides offering military bases and proclaiming himself the object of numerous "Communist plots," Somoza even claimed to have secret information showing that Secretary of State Marshall had advance knowledge of the attack on Pearl Harbor, information which he would withhold if Lacayo were granted recognition. (Memorandum by Mr. Reid, October 14, 1949, NA RG 59, 817.00/10–1449.)

112. Bernbaum to Marshall, September 8, 1947, September 9, 1947,

September 10, 1947, September 27, 1947, and October 3, 1947, NA RG 59, 817.00/9–947, 817.00/9–1047, 817.00/9–2747, and 817.00/10–347.

113. Acting Secretary of State Lovett to United States Diplomatic Representatives in the American Republics except Costa Rica, the Dominican Republic, and Nicaragua, December 31, 1947, *Foreign Relations,* 1947, VIII, p. 880.

114. *Constitución Política y Leyes Constitutivas de Nicaragua* (Managua: Talleres Nacionales, 1948).

115. Marshall to United States Diplomatic Representatives in the American Republics except Nicaragua, May 30, 1948, *Foreign Relations,* 1948, IX, p. 108.

116. For a detailed account of the Costa Rican revolution, see John Patrick Bell, *Crisis in Costa Rica* (Austin: University of Texas Press, 1971).

117. John D. Martz, *Central America: The Crisis and the Challenge* (Chapel Hill: University of North Carolina Press, 1959), pp. 181–82. Somoza's charge was patently absurd since Vanguardia Popular, the Costa Rican Communist Party, was a major supporter of the Picado regime.

118. Bell, *Crisis,* 146–47; Marshall to United States Diplomatic Representatives in the American Republics, March 22, 1948, *Foreign Relations,* 1948, IX, p. 499. There were several serious controversies between the United States and Nicaragua during the time centering around Somoza's efforts to obtain warplanes and other combat material in defiance of United States laws. See Bernbaum to Marshall, April 29, 1948, NA RG 59, 817.00/4–2948.

119. Bernbaum to the Secretary of State, April 17, 1948, memorandum of a long-distance telephone conversation by the Chief of the Division of Central American and Panamanian affairs, Newbegin, May 19, 1948, and Bernbaum to Marshall, April 19, 1948, *Foreign Relations,* 1948, IX, pp. 517–21.

120. Bernbaum to Marshall, March 3, 1948, *Foreign Relations,* 1948, IX, pp. 103–07.

121. The United States Ambassador to Nicaragua, Shaw, to Marshall, December 12, 1948, *Foreign Relations,* 1948 p. 539; W. Tapley Bennett, Jr., "The Costa Rica–Nicaragua Incident: Effective International Action in Keeping the Peace," *Bulletin of the Department of State,* June 5, 1949, pp. 707–708; Martz, *Central America,* p. 183.

122. Roberto Gutiérrez Silva, "Revelaciones íntimas de la mediación política de 1950 entre Chamorro y Somoza," *Revista Consevadora* VII (September 1963) 13–17; Adán Selva, *Política de los come-patos* (Managua: Editorial Asel, 1961).

123. *New York Times,* May 7, 1950, p. 106; May 8, 1950, p.11; and May 29, 1950, p.3.

124. The text of the agreement establishing the Army mission is printed in Edwin Lieuwen, *Arms and Politics in Latin America* (New York: Praeger, 1960), pp. 263–71. The text of the other agreements may be

found in the U.S. Treaty Affairs Staff, Office of the Legal Advisor, Department of State, *Treaties in Force: A List of Treaties and Other International Agreements in Force on January 1, 1958* (Washington, D.C.: Government Printing Office, 1958), p. 121.

125. *New York Times,* May 25, 1954, p. 1; Mario Rosenthal, *Guatemala* (New York: Twayne Publishers, 1962), p. 254; Lieuwen, *Arms and Politics,* p. 93.

126. Martz, *Central America,* p. 186; *La Prensa* (Managua), April 6, 1954, p. 1, and April 23, 1954, p. 2.

127. *Hispanic American Report* VII (December 1954) 16; Senator Allen Ellender, *Review of United States Government Operations in Latin America* (Washington: Government Printing Office, 1959), p.113.

128. Martz, *Central America,* pp. 193–96; Thomas W. Palmer, Jr., *Search for a Latin American Policy* (Gainesville: University of Florida Press, 1957), pp. 72–75.

129. Martz, *Central America,* p. 201.

130. Pedro Joaquín Chamorro, *Estirpe sangrienta,* p. 173; Martz, *Central America,* pp. 201–02.

X

GUARDING THE DYNASTY

The assassination failed to end Somoza rule in Nicaragua. Even before their father was shot, his two legitimate sons, Luis and Anastasio (Tachito), had moved into position to succeed him. After a brief military career, Luis had entered politics, serving in the Congress. Earlier in 1956 he had been made President of Congress and selected as First Designate to succeed to the presidency.[1] His brother, Anastasio, graduated from West Point in 1946 and had immediately been given high commands in the Guardia, leading to the half-humorous observation that he was the only cadet in the Academy's history to receive an army as a graduation present. At the time of his father's death he was Acting *Jefe Director* of the Guardia Nacional and Commander of the Nicaraguan Air Force (FAN).[2] An illegitimate son of the dictator, José Somoza, had entered the Guardia as an enlisted man in 1933, had been made an officer in 1940, and was serving as a Major in 1956. While other family members flew to Panama to be near the mortally wounded President, the sons remained in Managua to maintain control of the government.

During the days following the shooting, Nicaraguan and foreign journals printed optimistic reports of General Somoza's condition.[3] Belief in the President's eventual return to office undoubtedly helped the brothers retain control. During this period Colonel Gaitán, the Minister of War, played a key role in preventing uprisings within the Guardia. A veteran of more than twenty years' service and a graduate of the initial class from the Marine-operated *Academia Militar,* Gaitán was loyal to the President, but contemptuous of his sons. Believing that the wounded dictator would recover, he kept the Guardia under tight control. By the time news of the General's death reached Nicaragua, the sons had entrenched themselves in power. To eliminate any potential opposition within the Guardia, some officers were dismissed or retired and Colonel Gaitán was hurriedly appointed Ambassador to Argentina and sent to his new post with orders never to return. He remained there for more than a decade, returning to Nicaragua only a few months before his death.[4]

On September 30, 1956, the Nicaraguan Congress formally selected Luis Somoza to fill the remainder of his father's unexpired term. Less than two weeks later, the Liberal Party Convention reassembled and obediently nominated the new President for reelection.[5] Meanwhile the younger brother, in his capacity as *Jefe Director* of the Guardia, was rounding up hundreds of persons, many of whom were beaten and held for weeks without formal charges. Among those arrested were former presidential candidate, Dr. Enoc Aguado, General Emiliano Chamorro, and Pedro Joaquín Chamorro, outspoken young editor of *La Prensa,* Nicaragua's leading opposition newspaper. Many were soon released, but others, including Pedro Joaquín Chamorro and Dr. Aguado, were tried and convicted by military courts on a mixture of circumstantial and manufactured evidence.[6] They were released shortly before the 1957 "elections," but Dr. Aguado's health was permanently damaged by the brutal treatment he had endured.[7] Others were even less fortunate. The three defendants most closely linked with the assassin remained in Guardia custody until 1960 when they were all shot, supposedly while trying to escape.[8]

The imprisonment of its leaders, limitations on press freedom, and continued Somoza control of the Guardia and the electoral machinery all led the Conservative Party's leadership to decide to boycott the 1957 elections. To provide Luis with an opponent the puppet Conservative Nationalist Party was revived and then overwhelmingly defeated in the February 1957 elections.

As President, Luis Somoza made some gestures toward liberalizing the regime. He announced that he would serve only one term and, in 1959, restored the constitutional articles prohibiting immediate reelection or succession to the presidency by any relative of the incumbent.[9] He attempted to inaugurate some programs of economic modernization and to broaden the regime's base of support. The role of the military was played down and in 1958 its budget was actually reduced by nearly $1.5 million.[10] Freedom of the press increased and new opposition publications, such as the *Revista Conservadora,* appeared. By the end of Luis' term it was even possible to print and sell such books as Dr. Clemente Guido's *Noches de Tortura,* an exposé of Guardia tortures following General Somoza García's murder. Freedom of expression, however, did not imply freedom of action and the new President was no more willing to tolerate real threats to the family's power than his father had been. Four of his five years in office were conducted under martial law.[11] In 1957 a conspiracy between civilian opposition leaders and some Guardia officers was uncovered and promptly crushed.[12] A more serious threat developed in June 1959. Known as *el movimiento de Olama y Mollejones,* this effort to unseat the Somoza dynasty involved a land attack from Costa Rica and the airlifting of two plane loads of rebels into Nicaragua. These forces were led by the Independent Liberals' perpetual revolutionary, Enrique Lacayo Farfán, and by *La Prensa's* editor, Pedro Joaquín Chamorro. Their plans went badly astray, as the two planes landed almost 100 kilometers (60 miles) apart and one of their aircraft was promptly destroyed on the ground by FAN. An attempted general strike failed and the people in the area of the invasion proved apathetic, dashing hopes for a popular uprising. This made it relatively easy for the Guardia to capture 112 of the 114-man force and to shoot the other 2.[13] Chamorro and his followers were court-martialed and imprisoned, but by late 1960 most of them were back at work in Managua.

Fidel Castro's successful revolution in Cuba produced additional problems for the Somoza dynasty. As early as June 1959, Luis Somoza publicly charged Cuba with supporting efforts to overthrow him.[14] Another abortive uprising, in November 1960, intensified the regime's anxieties. In this effort a group of young rebels, drawn largely from new, militant Conservative Party members, strongly influenced by Christian Democratic ideology, seized the Guardia headquarters in the coffee centers of Jinotepe and Diriamba. Others tried to invade Nicaragua from Costa Rica, but that nation made a determined effort to close the frontier, an effort given added incentive when the commander of Costa Rica's Civil Guard was killed by a Nicaraguan rebel.[15] This left the insurgents in Jinotepe and Diriamba isolated and surrounded by an estimated 1,000 Guardia and they soon surrendered.

Shortly thereafter, President Eisenhower ordered the United States Navy to prevent any "Communist led" invasions of Central America.[16] At the same time Nicaragua began to participate actively in preparations for the ill-fated 1961 Bay of Pigs invasion of Cuba. Indeed, most of the troops and many of the air attacks involved in this operation would operate from Nicaraguan bases.[17] Besides aiding Cuban exiles, the Guardia was also involved for the remainder of Luis Somoza's term with a host of minor exile plots and internal student disturbances. One source claims that Nicaragua experienced twenty-three different uprisings in the period from mid-1959 through 1961.[18] None of these, however, came close to succeeding.

The year 1962 was an eventful one in Nicaragua. Keeping his promise to step down after one term, Luis Somoza imposed the selection of René Shick as the Liberal Party's candidate for President in the February 1963 elections, shoving aside the supporters of the more popular, and therefore potentially dangerous, candidacy of Minister of Gobernación Julio Quintana.[19] The Conservatives nominated Dr. Fernando Agüero Rocha, but his increasingly personalist approach to the campaign alienated many younger party members influenced by Christian Democratic ideology. More radical elements rejected electoral politics altogether. Led by Carlos Fonseca Amador and drawing both moral inspiration and material support from the Cuban Revolution, they founded in 1962 the Frente Sandinista de Liberación Nacional. Their objective was to overthrow the Somozas through guerrilla warfare.[20] Initial efforts in this area were notably unsuccessful, but confident Guardia reports of the movement's virtual extinction were to prove quite inaccurate.

The 1963 elections were again little more than a farce. Knowing that Somoza control of the electoral machinery ensured his defeat, Agüero demanded that the OAS supervise the elections. When the Somozas dismissed his proposal as a violation of national sovereignty, Agüero, carrying a pistol, led a small protest march in Managua. He was promptly placed under house arrest until after the elections.[21] The Conservatives then announced a boycott of the elections and the Somozas were forced to again resurrect the farcical Nicaraguan Conservative Party, better known as the Zancudo (Mosquito) Party, to provide some semblance of opposition. The elections were held in an atmosphere of overwhelming apathy, and the official returns, which in some areas showed more voters than the total adult population, gave Shick a victory margin of better than ten to one.[22]

The early years of René Shick's term were relatively peaceful. The Guardia, under General Anastasio Somoza Debayle, maintained internal order and, aided by United States military aid and by the presence of both American Army and Air Force missions, built up its equipment and improved its training. Several TV-2 jet trainers were purchased from the United States, giving Nicaragua the largest force of jet aircraft in Central America.[23]

Nicaragua also received direct military aid from the United States. In 1963 this was valued at $1,600,000, eleventh highest among the American republics, and included trucks, engineering equipment, communication equipment, an M-62 wrecker, and a C-47 for FAN.[24] The effect of this equipment buildup combined with the severe defeat that the young Frente Sandinista had suffered at the hands of the Guardia in 1963 helped ensure relative tranquility for most of Shick's tenure in office.

While the Somozas remained the dominant force in Nicaragua, disputes between the brothers, centering around Luis's efforts to improve the regime's image, left some maneuvering room for President Shick. In 1964 he was twice able to limit Guardia power. In January three individuals who had been charged with creating agitation among peasants near Chinandega were found murdered. Evidence clearly linked this crime to the area Guardia commander, Colonel Juan López. Despite strong opposition from within the Guardia, the Colonel was eventually tried by court-martial, convicted, and imprisoned. President Shick, supported by Luis Somoza, evidently played a major role in bringing this about.[25] In July, Carlos Fonseca Amador, leader of the Frente Sandinista, was arrested. Shick again intervened to ensure that he survived to stand trial, then after his conviction changed his sentence from imprisonment to exile.[26] Such triumphs, however, proved short-lived. As Shick's term progressed, Anastasio Somoza D., from his position as *Jefe Director,* began increasingly to exert controls over the entire administration in preparation for his own "election" as President in 1967 and the prevailing political joke in Nicaragua centered around the possibility that President Shick might attempt a *golpe de estado* and take over the government. Increasingly depressed by this situation, Shick reportedly began to drink heavily and his health failed rapidly.

Important internal changes took place in the Guardia during 1965 and 1966. In 1965, the United States extracted a partial repayment for its military aid by requesting and obtaining the participation of a force of Guardia troops in the intervention in the Dominican Republic. Commander of this contingent was Julio Gutiérrez, previously commander of the Guardia's small armored battalion and one of the most popular officers in the military. Somoza used his absence from the country to remove him from all internal military posts, replacing him with Colonel Alfonso Pérez as commander of the armored battalion and assigning Guttiérez to the post of military attaché to Salvador and

Guatemala. He was later transferred to the post of attaché in Washington, promoted to Brigadier General, and then retired while still absent from the country. *La Prensa* praised Colonel Gutiérrez in terms rarely used by the opposition when referring to the Guardia, and reported considerable unhappiness among junior officers over his transfer.[27] General Somoza Debayle, however, was obviously determined that no officer should ever be in a position to rival his own popularity.

Further internal changes took place in 1966. In a general command shakeup, Colonel José Somoza, illegitimate half-brother of Luis and Anastasio, was placed in command of the Guardia's Third Company, the *Batallón de Combate Somoza,* Nicaragua's only fully reliable combat unit.[28] Changes were made in several other Guardia posts to ensure the full support of the force for Anastasio's election to the presidency. In addition, Guardia units engaged in two major counterinsurgency exercises held in conjunction with other Central American armed forces during the year. Within a few months this experience was to prove quite valuable.

On August 1, 1966, the Liberal Party, as predicted, nominated Anastasio Somoza Debayle for President. Since the Constitution prohibited any candidate from holding an active military post, the General announced that his powers as *Jefe Director* would be assumed by the President, but in reality Somoza continued to fill the post, residing in La Curva and issuing all orders for the Guardia. President Shick's term as even nominal head of the Guardia was to prove the briefest in history. On August 3, he died suddenly, apparently of natural causes, and was promptly replaced as President by an even more compliant Somoza puppet, Minister of the Interior Lorenzo Guerrero.[29]

In an effort to oppose Somoza's candidacy the major opposition parties, the Conservatives, the Christian Democrats, and the Independent Liberals, had united in a National Opposition Union (UNO) behind the candidacy of Dr. Fernando Agüero. From the start, their campaign efforts encountered opposition and harrassment from the Guardia and from a paramilitary group, AMOROCS (Asociación Militar de Officiales Retirados, Obreros y Campesinos Somocistos). Since the issuance of all permits to carry arms was a Guardia function, AMOROCS had no problem in obtaining such permits, while the opposition naturally found it impossible to arm themselves legally. Several UNO supporters were shot or beaten during the course of the campaign by AMOROCS and Guardia, but despite such actions, Agüero rallies continued to draw larger crowds than did those organized in favor of Somoza.[30]

The growing electoral violence reached its climax on January 22. Dr. Agüero, Pedro Joaquín Chamorro, and other opposition leaders, convinced that Somoza's control of the electoral machinery made it impossible for them to win, hoped to use a major political rally in the capital to incite a revolt. For weeks they had been calling upon their supporters to come to Managua for the demonstration, urging them not to forget their "little packages of food," a thinly veiled suggestion that they bring arms with them. A crowd estimated at between 40,000 and 60,000 gathered in Managua on January 22 and began calling for a Guardia revolt to overthrow Somoza. The Guardia ignored this plea and when the opposition began a march on the Presidential Palace, firing broke out. In the ensuing panic more than 40 demonstrators were killed and at least 100 more wounded. A Guardia officer and two enlisted men also lost their lives. Opposition leaders sought refuge in the Gran Hotel, using foreigners staying there as hostages. After prolonged negotiations they surrendered and the leaders, including Pedro Joaquín Chamorro, were imprisoned.[31] The total failure of this effort made the results of the elections, held a few days later, a foregone conclusion. The government announced that General Somoza D. had won, gaining a reported 70 percent of the popular vote.[32]

The Frente Sandinista also engaged in an unsuccessful effort to end the Somoza dynasty in 1966–1967. An effort was made to create a guerrilla base in the mountains of the Department of Matagalpa. Finances for this effort were to be provided by urban assaults on banks. In contrast to the 1963 effort, the guerrillas, some of whom had been trained in Cuba, made a conscious effort to enlist the support of the local peasantry and to recruit them for the movement. From the start, however, they encountered massive difficulties. The local population proved apathetic, the Guardia's active counterguerrilla patrolling kept them constantly on the run, and even the outlawed Nicaraguan Communist Party (PSN) refused to support them, viewing their efforts as premature adventurism. In August and again in October, the Frente was badly beaten in combat with the Guardia and by the end of October most of the would-be guerrillas were dead or had gone into hiding.[33] Somoza was so confident of his ability to handle the situation that he brought most of the troops back to Managua and offered to send a contingent to Vietnam in support of United States efforts there.[34] This offer, which was never accepted, served to underline the links between the Guardia and the United States.

Two other developments in 1967 were important for the future of the Guardia and of Nicaragua as a whole. A few days before the end of his term, President Guerrero clearly acting on the incoming President's directions, released the previously convicted Colonel López and absolved him of all guilt in the murders, though his previous discharge from active Guardia service remained in effect.[35] This indicated a clear return to earlier policies of virtual immunity for any offenses committed by officers against opponents of the regime. The other event was the sudden death of Luis Somoza in April 1967. The two brothers had reportedly often engaged in heated disputes about the future political tactics that the family should pursue, with Luis arguing for a more moderate, civilian-oriented approach and Anastasio preferring a harder line dependent upon Guardia support. Their mother had evidently served as a mediating influence, preventing these disputes from developing into an open break.[36] The death of Luis removed the major restraint upon the new President's actions as well as depriving the Somozas of the most politically astute member of the family.

The influence of these events became apparent early in General Somoza Debayle's administration. Once elected, he had followed his father's example and resumed the post of *Jefe Director* of the Guardia, combining in his own hands the highest political and military posts in the nation. Following the death of Luis, he began increasingly to use his half-brother, José Somoza, to help maintain control of the Guardia, promoting him to Brigadier General in 1967 and giving him command of the Guardia's armor as well as the vital Third Company.[37] He also gave increasing power to lower-ranking officers who gained his trust to enrich themselves through their Guardia positions and to use their authority to intimidate any potential opposition. The pages of *La Prensa* soon became filled with complaints against Guardia abuses, with the names of two officers who were quite close to the President, Majors José Ivan "Pepe" Alegrett, Director of Immigration, and Oscar Morales, popularly known as "Moralitos," executive officer of the Third Company, figuring especially prominently in such reports.[38] A major public scandal developed in April when two brothers, David and René Tejada, suspected of "subversive activ-

American Ambassador to Nicaragua Thomas E. Whelan *(extreme right)* ***with "Tachito"*** *(in dark glasses)* ***and Luis*** *(in suit)* ***after the death of their father in 1956. Whelan played a key role in the consolidation of dynastic rule in Nicargua.***

ities," were turned over to Major Morales for interrogation. David Tejada was a former Guardia lieutenant and this evidently aroused a special wrath in the Major, who proceeded to slowly beat him to death, then attempted to dispose of the body by throwing it into the Santiago volcano.[39] Under considerable public pressure, Somoza was forced to agree to a military trial of his erstwhile protégé. The Guardia itself seemed divided by the issue. The prosecutor, Major José Ramón Silva Reyes, displayed surprising skill and zeal in prosecuting the case, and critical testimony against Moralitos was supplied by the Third Company's Medical Officer, Captain Fernando Cedeño.[40] The trial dragged on for months, finally resulting in a conviction for the Major, but on charges of neglect of duty and bringing discredit on the Guardia Nacional as an institution, not on murder.[41] An eight-year sentence was handed down, but due to various appeals and reviews it was not finally confirmed until March 1969. Throughout this period Moralitos was supposedly under house arrest, but continued to dress as an officer and was occasionally reported traveling freely in a Guardia jeep.[42] The confirmation of the sentence resulted in a brief disappearance from public view of the Major, but it was far from the end of the entire affair.

The Moralitos case was not the only difficulty plaguing Somoza's term in office. His efforts to run the nation like an extension of the Guardia produced resentments within the Liberal Party as well as from the opposition, resentment that was heightened by his evident determination to retain power beyond the expiration of his term. As President, Tachito also concentrated on expanding his financial holdings and on installing relatives and cronies from the Guardia in as many lucrative public positions as possible. Retired Guardia General Montiel was installed as Finance Minister. Somoza's brother-in-law, Guillermo Sevilla Sacasa, continued to serve as Ambassador to the United States, his uncle, Luis Manuel Debayle, was given control of ENALUF, the government-owned national electric company, and a cousin, Noel Pallais, served as his personal secretary and also ran INFONAC, the National Development Bank. Resentment within the Liberal Party surfaced in September 1968 when another Somoza relative, Education Minister Ramiro Sacasa, having previously declared that the President should not try to amend the Constitution to provide for his own reelection, announced his own intention of seeking the Liberals' nomination in 1970.[43] The one bright spot during the administration was the relatively rapid economic growth, spurred on by Vietnam war-era high prices for some Nicaraguan exports. From 1968 through 1971 Nicaragua's GNP per capita, measured in 1970 dollars, increased over 8 percent. The most rapid growth came in the manufacturing sector, which grew by just under 10 percent annually, a rate second only to that of Brazil in Latin America.[44] Much of this growth, however, was illusory as it came in inefficient Somoza-owned or -controlled industries whose growth was made possible by massive, unsecured government loans.

While traditional politicians grumbled about the regime and attacked it in print, the Frente Sandinista resorted to more direct methods. Having failed at rural guerrilla tactics, they turned to urban assaults, robbing a bank in Managua, assaulting other commercial establishments in the capital, and reportedly netting over $600,000 in their activities.[45] In July 1969, the Guardia, under the direction of the ruthless new Director of Internal Security, Colonel Samuel Genie, crushed the Managua unit of the Frente. Seven members had taken refuge in a house in the Las Delicias section of the capital. The Guardia assaulted their hideout with tanks, automatic weapons, and tear gas, killing five of the guerrillas and capturing the remaining two at the cost of two Guardias killed. One of those killed, Julio César Buitrago, was the reputed head of the urban guerrilla movement and had served as an FSLN delegate to the Organization of Latin American Solidarity meeting in Cuba.[46]

With the destruction of their urban base, the focus of Frente activities shifted briefly to Costa Rica. In September 1969, FSLN leader Carlos Fonseca Amador was captured and imprisoned in that nation on a charge of bank robbery. Numerous efforts by his compatriots to secure his release, including threats on the Costa Rican embassy in Managua and even an assault on his jail in Costa Rica failed. Finally, in October 1970, a Costa Rican airliner, with four United States citizens aboard, was hijacked and returned only after Fonseca Amador and three fellow FSLN members were released from Costa Rican jails and flown to Cuba.[47] While the FSLN leader had been languishing in Costa Rica, the Guardia had been busily engaged in stamping out the last remnants of Frente activity in rural Nicaragua and, by mid-1970, had apparently eliminated the guerrillas as a significant force within the nation.[48]

Despite the military success, all was far from well within the

Guardia during late 1969 and 1970. Increasing resentment by younger officers over the lack of professional ability and gross corruption of the senior officers, dislike among *Academia* graduates for the preference given nongraduates such as José Somoza, a major drug scandal involving the Guardia's chief of immigration, and increasing personal arrogance, reportedly coupled with family problems and heavy drinking, by President Somoza, all took a toll on morale. Somoza's own confidence in the Guardia evidently diminished. He tried to exercise tighter controls over Guardia ammunition supplies and troop movements, especially those involving FAN, which found it increasingly difficult to obtain new equipment.[49] In an effort to appease some of the younger officers, the entire First Promotion of the *Academia Militar* was retired in March 1970, with most of the officers receiving high posts in government or in Somoza industries as compensation.[50]

The greatest blow to Guardia discipline and unity was provided in April with a dramatic revival of the Moralitos case. *La Prensa* had been complaining for some time that far from being imprisoned, Major Morales was frequently seen in Managua, often riding in a Guardia jeep.[51] He had also been voicing threats on those who had testified against him, notably Captain Fernando Cedeño and Major Silva Reyes. An attempt had even been made on Silva Reyes' life when a group of men in a Toyota fired into his house.[52] In April, Moralitos was again riding around Managua in a jeep with a Guardia "escort." They passed a car carrying Captain Cedeño and Major Morales pulled a revolver from the holster of one of his companions and killed the Captain.[53] The result was a national scandal and an uproar within the Guardia. Killing civilians, even if one had been a former officer, was of only limited internal concern to the Guardia, but the public murder of a fellow officer on active duty was a much more serious matter. Somoza could no longer protect his protégé and was forced to have him imprisoned, with considerably fewer privileges. How long Moralitos would have remained in jail under ordinary circumstances will never be known. In the confusion following the 1972 earthquake he was allowed to escape, reappearing in Honduras, where he maintains a comfortable living supported by regular infusions of funds from Nicaragua.[54]

The impact of this case upon the Guardia continued for months. Some officers, including such personal henchmen of the dictator as FAN commander Colonel Orlando Villalta defended

Moralitos, while others condemned the entire episode and, at least indirectly, blamed Somoza for it. The scandal reached its height in September 1970 with an open, pistol-waving confrontation between Villalta and Silva Reyes in the Campo de Marte.[55] By the end of 1970 Somoza's power base, even within the Guardia, seemed to have eroded badly and his plans for reelection in 1971 appeared to be in considerable jeopardy.

As had happened in the past, the Somoza dynasty was again saved, at least in part, through the intervention of the United States, this time operating through the new Ambassador, Turner Shelton. A trip to the United States, including a private dinner with President Richard Nixon, and a public meeting with United Nations Secretary General U Thant was arranged. Nixon remembered that Nicaragua was one Latin American country which had not greeted him with hostile demonstrations during his 1958 tour of Latin America and he considered Somoza a firm American ally, deserving of all possible support.[56] The renewed evidence of American support helped strengthen the dictator's position and, with further encouragement from Shelton, negotiations designed to prolong Somoza's power beyond 1971 were begun with the political opposition. In March 1971, Somoza and his former presidential rival, Fernando Agüero, concluded an agreement providing for the dissolution of Congress, the calling of a constituent assembly, and the appointment of a three-member ruling junta, made up of Agüero and two Somoza appointees, to govern the nation from May 1972 to December 1974. Elections for a new President were to be held in 1974.[57] While other opposition leaders including dissident Liberal Ramiro Sacasa and the leaders of the Christian Democrats, opposed the pact, they were unable to block its implementation.

Nixon-Shelton support was also instrumental in promoting the interests of Howard Hughes in Nicaragua. Hughes established residence in an entire floor of Managua's new Inter-Continental Hotel, purchased a 25 percent interest in Lanica, the Somoza-controlled national airline, and reportedly was considering several other major investment possibilities in Nicaragua before the 1972 earthquake disrupted all such plans.[58]

While United States support helped limit opposition from traditional political groups and from within the Guardia, it had little effect on other sectors. Unrest among students and among labor groups, fueled by rampant inflation, increased throughout 1972. These groups found an unexpected ally that year with the appearance of an open rupture between Somoza and the Roman Catholic Church, led by Managua's new archbishop, Miguel Obando Bravo. In an effort to give the appearance of Church support for his agreement with the Conservatives to call a constituent assembly and to turn over nominal power to the three-man junta, Somoza had arranged for three bishops, two without dioceses, to witness the signing of the agreement. In February 1972, Archbishop Obando and Bishop Manuel Salazar of León issued statements supporting Christian Democratic Party protests over the agreement, denying that the pact had any official Church sanction and, in the case of the Archbishop, indicating that he might abstain from voting in the next election because of the current political situation. Somoza responded by withdrawing Guardia units from the traditional men's procession at the cathedral and forbidding the Liberal radio stations to broadcast the event.[59]

The breach widened still further in late April. Not one bishop attended the ceremony that supposedly transferred power to the triumvirate. Instead, the Nicaraguan episcopacy issued a joint pastoral letter highly critical of existing social conditions and declaring Church support for the creation of "a completely new order."[60] This letter marked the end of thirty-seven years of acquiescence, if not support, by the Church for the rule of the Somozas.

The conflict with the Church weakened the triumvirate's already shaky claim to political legitimacy, but this did not seem to alarm the nation's real ruler. Somoza continued as *Jefe Director* of the Guardia, giving him control over all real power in Nicaragua. To further solidify his support within the force, he instituted major salary raises for all ranks, averaging just under 50 percent for officers, for whom, at least at the rank of major and above, the official salary represented only a small percentage of their actual income, and ranging up to 150 percent or more for privates, whose opportunities for supplementing their salaries were, of course, much less.[61] While the triumvirate exercised nominal power, the Liberal majority ensured that all real decisions were made by Somoza. Tachito even continued to represent Nicaragua at meetings of heads of state.

It was, however, the sudden release of natural rather than political tensions which was to violently disrupt this situation. At 12:34 A.M., on December 23, 1972, Managua was hit with a major earthquake. The damage caused by this quake and its aftershocks and by the resultant fire, which swept through much of the city's center, reduced most of Nicaragua's capital to a heap of rubble. Between 8,000 and 10,000 inhabitants were killed, many more injured, and hundreds of thousands left homeless as more than 50,000 homes were destroyed. Over 80 percent of the capital's commercial establishments were destroyed, including all major hotels except the new Inter-Continental, which was severely damaged. In addition, 118 commercial establishments, over 35 percent of those in the city, were pillaged after the earthquake.[62] The *Palacio Nacional,* housing Congress and most government ministries, survived with limited damage, but both the *Casa Presidencial* and La Curva on La Loma were so badly damaged that they had to be razed. Fortunately, most of Nicaragua's industrial capacity was located in suburban areas and suffered less severe damage.

In the aftermath of the earthquake the Guardia Nacional virtually disintegrated. Most soldiers left their posts to take care of their families or to try to salvage personal belongings. Others, often led by officers, occupied themselves with massive looting, at times using Guardia vehicles to remove the stock from damaged stores. For nearly two days, Somoza was unable to muster even a company of troops. As a result, his prestige and that of the Guardia had sunk to an all-time low and the nation seemed on the verge of anarchy.[63]

Once again the United States, personified by Ambassador Turner Shelton, came to Somoza's rescue. The American Embassy was destroyed by the quake, but Shelton's lavish residence in the suburbs was virtually undamaged. From there the Ambassador conferred regularly with the Nicaraguan strongman, encouraging him to seize total power, allowing him to regroup his troops and other supporters under the United States flag, and even suggesting that United States troops be brought in to help restore order.[64] This last suggestion, was not followed by the State Department, but most of the others were. The pretense of a ruling triumvirate was shoved aside and Somoza ruled by decree. When the junta's Conservative member, Dr. Agüero, protested, he was suddenly removed and replaced by a complete puppet, again reportedly at Shelton's suggestion.[65]

The widespread destruction removed some traditional areas of graft for the Guardia, but the massive amounts of foreign aid, from both government and private sources, which flowed into Nicaragua during 1973 more than made up for this. Initially, the Guardia profited by selling looted goods on the black market;

later, sales of relief supplies and of smuggled luxuries provided major sources of income. In addition, Guardia families got first priority on those relief supplies which were distributed, with second priority going to other employees of the government and lowest priority being given to the public at large.[66]

Shortly after the earthquake, the entire downtown area was sealed off by barbed wire and Guardia patrols. Approximately a quarter of a million of the city's inhabitants were evacuated to other Nicaraguan towns and hundreds of thousands of others were housed in temporary tent cities around the edges of the capital. Military courts took over some of the judicial functions within Managua. Despite widespread opposition and considerable evidence that the center of the city was permanently subject to the threat of further quakes, Somoza announced his determination to rebuild the capital on the original site.[67] A number of reasons were advanced for this decision, but it was generally accepted that it was major, land-owning interests of the Somozas and of Guardia officers in the Managua area that doomed all proposals for relocation of the capital.[68]

The earthquake destroyed more than property and human lives. It eliminated many traditional sources of Guardia graft and badly damaged the reputation of that force's strength and reliability within Nicaragua. Somoza could do little to counteract the increased public contempt and hostility that surfaced in the months following the earthquake, but he could and did strive to restore Guardia cohesion and loyalty through additional pay raises, expansion of the force, and opening up of opportunities to profit from the diversion of relief supplies.[69] As usual, Guardia were given first priority in home repairs or in the construction of new homes. If officers needed materials for construction, they often simply took them from relief supplies, transporting them in military vehicles. Enlisted men were seldom free to employ such direct methods, but their interests were also carefully looked after with José Somoza, popularly known as "Papa Chepe," often dealing directly with them in the traditional patron-client relationship.

As the work of reconstruction progressed, the Somozas and higher-ranking officers increasingly found ways to use the disaster as a means of increasing their own wealth. Bribes for guarding damaged property, for issuing new construction permits, or for obtaining import licenses, or even for obtaining food, the distribution of which was for a time a government monopoly, all

U. S. trained and equipped soldiers of the Guardia Nacional de Nicaragua on maneuvers on the shore of Lake Managua.

offered lucrative possibilities. General Noguera, the Guardia's Chief of Staff, demonstrated exceptional foresight in this area, concentrating his efforts on obtaining and developing a monopoly over the vital new bus routes between the huge emergency housing development known as "Las Americas," located on the fringes of the city, and the industrial and new commercial areas, located miles away, where desperately needed employment was available. This concentration on individual and family needs, to the neglect of national priorities, severely hindered recovery efforts.[70]

Adverse publicity resulting from the post-earthquake corruption further damaged Somoza's internal and international prestige. In the spring of 1973 a telegraphed message from the Nicaraguan dictator to El Salvador's President, urging him to instruct his delegation to the OAS to oppose lifting sanctions against Cuba, drew a sarcastic reply, inquiring if Somoza was making the request on his own or acting on the instruction of his North American masters.[71] Mounting press criticism, both foreign and domestic, was also a source of growing concern to the regime. Foreign critics were generally beyond Somoza's reach, but domestic critics were not and, in October 1973, new laws, imposing fines up to $16,000 for writers or commentators who defamed the government, went into effect.[72] Somoza also found himself faced with renewed activity by the Frente Sandinista, but prompt Guardia countermeasures managed to keep these limited until late 1974.

Early in 1974 a new Constitution was adopted for Nicaragua and General Somoza deceitfully announced his retirement from active military duty, supposedly to remove the constitutional barrier preventing any officer on active duty from running for political office. However, the constitutional barrier was not removed because all Somoza did, in fact, was to drop his title, but not the functions, of *Jefe Director* while retaining his other title of Supreme Chief of the Armed Forces *(Jefe Supremo).* In typical Somoza logic this farcical maneuver was supposed to allow Somoza to retain the prerogatives of *Jefe Director* as a civilian.[73] Despite its grandiose overtones, vaguely reminiscent of nineteenth-century Paraguay, the title of *Jefe Supremo* evidently appealed to the Nicaraguan strongman and the sycophants who surrounded him soon learned to address him in that way.

While the legal political opposition was unable to offer much opposition to Somoza's plans to officially install himself once again as President by means of the September 1974 elections, increasing pressures were brought to bear upon him from other sources. Despite government threats, violence, and imprisonment, the Marxist-controlled CGT won a series of major victories in several strikes, notably those involving the construction trades, in 1973 and 1974. The damaged prestige of his close ally, American Ambassador Turner Shelton, whose always low prestige in the State Department had been still further eroded by his post-earthquake actions, and the decline and fall of President Nixon, a strong advocate of American support for Somoza, still further weakened the dictator's image.[74] This process was given further impetus in November when Secretary of State Kissinger presented the American Foreign Service Association's Rivkin Award to James Richard Cheek, a mid-career Foreign Service officer, in recognition of his determined dissent from Ambassador Shelton's reports on conditions in Nicaragua. The official citation noted that "Cheek was the first to recognize, seek out, and report on the new socio-political forces in Nicaragua. . . . In the process, he differed strongly with his superiors and others on the Country team. He persevered, challenging the conventional wisdom . . . submitted through the Dissent Channel critical, but balanced analyses of the issues."[75] Cheek's reports had been highly critical of Somoza's post-quake actions, including his efforts at censorship and his handling of labor disputes, and his award was an open rebuke to Ambassador Shelton and his uncritical support of the dictator.

Within Nicaragua problems for Somoza and the Guardia continued throughout 1974. Despite stepped-up military efforts, small bands of FSLN guerrillas continued to stage occasional raids in the Department of Matagalpa. A group of twenty-seven prominent citizens, including Pedro Joaquín Chamorro and Ramiro Sacasa, from nine different political and labor organizations published a document stating that since Tachito Somoza and his puppet opposition candidate were unconstitutional candidates, there really were no candidates for whom to vote. Somoza decreed that these twenty-seven citizens were the ones who had violated the Constitution and they were consequently arrested, charged with urging a boycott of the presidential election, tried, and sentenced to a loss of their political rights.[76] A more difficult problem was presented in August when Nicaragua's bishops signed a joint pastoral letter, highly critical of repressive and unrepresentative politics and declaring that "no one could be compelled to vote to benefit a particular group."[77] Publicly, the dictator claimed to agree with the sentiments of the pastoral letter, but privately he began a campaign to discredit the Archbishop and to brand him as a dangerous radical.

The September elections, producing the predictable overwhelming Somoza victory over a handpicked puppet opponent, did not end the conflict with the Church. In November the Bishops' Conference refused to participate in Somoza's inauguration as President and, at the same time, criticized the regime's economic and tax policies.[78] Opposition political leaders also boycotted the ceremony and announced the formation of a united opposition front, the Unión Democrática de Liberación (UDEL), to coordinate their struggle against the Somozas. This coalition embraced everyone from Pedro Joaquín Chamorro and Remiro Sacasa to the Christian Democrats and even included the CGT and the Moscow-oriented and officially illegal Communist Party (PSN).[79]

A much more dramatic expression of discontent occurred on the night of December 27, 1974. An FSLN assault group attacked the house of former Agriculture Minister José María Castillo, where a party in honor of Ambassador Shelton was being held. The American Ambassador had already departed, but the guerrillas captured several prominent Nicaraguan politicians, including Minister of Foreign Relations Alejandro Montiel A., Managua's Mayor, Dr. Luis Valle Olivares, and two members of the Somoza family, Guillermo Sevilla Sacasa, the President's brother-in-law and Nicaragua's Ambassador to the United States, and Noel Pallais Debayle, Somoza's cousin and head of the National Development Institute. During the attack on the house Dr. Castillo, two Guardia enlisted men, and a private bodyguard were killed. Somoza was out of Managua when the assault occurred, but returned immediately. The house had already been surrounded by heavily armed Guardia and the dictator reportedly wanted to have them storm the guerrillas, an action that would undoubtedly have cost the lives of his advisors and relatives who were being held hostage. With considerable difficulty he was dissuaded from this violent course of action and persuaded to allow Archbishop Obando Bravo to act as a negotiator. Negotiations dragged on until the morning of December 30. Somoza finally agreed to allow the guerrillas free passage to Cuba, along with fourteen other members of the Frente who were to be released from Nicaraguan jails. A ransom of $5 million was also paid and a lengthy Frente communiqué, denouncing Somoza and the United States and calling on the Nicaraguan people to overthrow the dynasty, was read on Nicaraguan radio and published in *La Prensa.* The guerrillas, who were to be accompanied to Cuba by the Papal Nuncio and the Spanish and Mexican Ambassadors, agreed in return to release the hostages and dropped several other demands, including one calling for an increase in the salary of Guardia privates to 500 córdobas monthly.[80] A *New York Times* editorial commenting on the affair rubbed further salt into Somoza's wounds by observing that his regime "deserved the humiliation it suffered."[81]

Reacting furiously to the guerrillas' safe escape, Somoza ordered a state of siege throughout the country, placed all publications under strict censorship, set up a special military tribunal to investigate FSLN, and in a lengthy New Year's Eve broadcast, sought to blame the attack on Pedro Joaquín Chamorro.[82] The Frente meanwhile accelerated their activities in rural areas, gaining increasing prestige and support from the December raid.

The year 1975 was, in almost every way, a bad one for Somoza. The economy, which had done quite well in 1974, cooled off considerably in 1975, with virtually no growth in the GNP per capita.[83] Somoza's younger son, Julio, dropped out of West Point. Following two highly critical columns by Jack Anderson, Ambassador Shelton was recalled, over Somoza's anguished protests, and replaced with a conservative academic specialist on Latin America, Dr. James Theberge.[84]

As his difficulties piled up, the dictator's responses became increasingly erratic. He resisted pressure from domestic opposition and business leaders to ease the censorship and state of siege and efforts from the American Embassy to have him pursue a more moderate course. Instead he announced that the state of siege would be continued indefinitely and proceeded to try anyone suspected of complicity in the December raid before drumhead Guardia courts. The fact that most of the accused had to be tried in absentia did nothing to add to the Guardia's prestige.[85] Neither did the continuing campaign against the FSLN in the Department of Matagalpa. Since Somoza's criterion for promotion to high Guardia ranks eliminated most competent and popular officers from high positions and since total loyalty rather than combat ability was the prime requisite for being given command of troops, these operations were entrusted to Colonel J. Gonzalo Evertsz, whose main tactics have evidently been to brutalize local peasantry. An American missionary priest reported that in one case Guardia simply rounded up the men in a rural village and shot twenty of them.[86] When the Archbishop protested these murders, Somoza's only response was to extend the censorship decree to include Church radio broadcasts and publications.[87] The Frente did not confine its protests to verbal or written assaults. The guerrillas began to take reprisals against those who cooperated with the military.[88]

August 1975 was a particularly bad month for Somoza. Coinciding with the arrival of the new American Ambassador, another storm of adverse publicity descended on the increasingly nervous dictator. Articles by Alan Riding, criticizing Somoza and reporting on the increase in guerilla activity, appeared in the *Financial Times* of London and in the *New York Times*. Even more devastating were a series of three columns by Jack Anderson, labeling Somoza "the world's greediest ruler," and detailing much of his stranglehold over the national economic as well as political scene.[89] The beleaguered dictator lashed out in all directions, blaming Pedro Joaquín Chamorro for the columns and reportedly threatening to have him killed, denouncing Anderson, and established additional restrictions upon Nicaraguan dissent. Anderson was attacked as a paid character assassin, and threatened with libel suits. Ambassador Sevilla Sacasa even wrote a long letter to the *Washington Post* attacking the columns, but offering little in the way of evidence to refute the major charges.[90]

The bad publicity from abroad was accompanied by further erosion of support at home. While the press remained muzzled, Nicaraguans of virtually all social levels were increasingly outspoken in their denunciations of the President and the Guardia Nacional, volunteering bitter attacks on their incompetence and corruption without any questioning or encouragement. Symptomatic of this was the ability of the Frente, in late August 1975, to paint slogans on the walls of scores of consecutive houses in one of Managua's poorer barrios in a single night without a single resident notifying the Guardia.[91] Some evidence of fear and unrest appeared within the Guardia, with many officers expressing concern at the possibility that the change of Ambassadors and the Anderson columns might signal a shift of United States support away from Somoza.[92] Early in 1976, when additional unfavorable publicity resulted in his failure to obtain a major loan from the Inter-American Development Bank that he had sought, it appeared to many observers that the dynasty's days might at last be numbered. Such speculation had, however, arisen before and had always proven false. The key in all past cases had been the family's ability to maintain control of the Guardia Nacional and to convince Washington that Somoza's type of "law and order" is better for the United States than the possibility of a nationalistic regime that might not be as favorable to United States interests.

It is obvious that in the months to come Somoza will continue to do everything to maintain control over what has become the world's largest personal bodyguard, the Guardia Nacional de Nicaragua. His success in this endeavor will be at least partially dependent on his ability to convince the Guardia that the United States is still firmly behind him.

NOTES

1. *New York Times,* September 25, 1956, p. 2.
2. *Nicaragua, A Country on the March* (New York: Las Americas Publishing Co., 1961), p. 20; *New York Times,* September 25, 1956, p. 20.
3. The comments in *La Prensa* (Managua), *Novedades* (Managua), and the *New York Times* were all highly optimistic.
4. *New York Times,* November 24, 1956, p. 11; confidential interviews, Managua, December 1963 and August 1970.
5. Mariano Fiallos Oyanguren, "The Nicaraguan Political System" (Ph.D. dissertation, University of Kansas, 1968), p. 101.
6. Pedro Joaquín Chamorro, *Estirpe sangrienta: los Somozas* (Buenos Aires: Editorial Triángulo, 1959), pp. 60 and 99; Clemente Guido, *Noches de Tortura,* 2nd ed. (Managua: Artes Gráficas, 1963).
7. Interview with Dr. Enoc Aguado, November 1963; Fiallos Oyanguren, "Nicaraguan Political System," p. 136.
8. *Hispanic American Report* XIII (July 1960) 304.
9. Franklin D. Parker, *The Central American Republics* (New York: Oxford University Press, 1964), p. 232.
10. Charles W. Anderson, "Nicaragua: The Somoza Dynasty," in Martin Needler, ed., *Political Systems of Latin America,* 2nd ed. (New York: Van Nostrand Reinhold, 1970), p. 116.
11. Mario Rodriguez, *Central America* (Englewood Cliffs, N.J.: Prentice-Hall, 1965), p. 42.

12. Fiallos Oyanguren, "Nicaraguan Political System," p. 104; Luis Somoza D., *El Presidente de la República informa la pueblo sobre su labor* (Managua: n.p., 1962), p.76.

13. *Hispanic American Report* XII (August 1959) 316; interview with Pedro Joaquín Chamorro C., Managua, November 1963. For details, see Pedro Joaquín Chamorro, "Diario de un preso," *Revista Conservadora* II (June-August 1961) 1–48.

14. *New York Times,* June 17, 1959, p. 16.

15. *Hispanic American Report* XIII (January 1961) 780–81.

16. *New York Times,* November 18, 1960, p. 1.

17. In February 1963, Luis Somoza openly admitted Nicaraguan participation in the Cuban invasion attempt during an interview for the NBC News Special, "Nicaragua." For details on the Nicaraguan role in the invasion, see Haynes Johnson et al., *The Bay of Pigs: The Leader's Story of Brigade 2506* (New York: Norton, 1964).

18. Lester Velie, "New Time Bomb in the Caribbean," *Readers Digest,* January 1962, p. 206.

19. Institute for the Comparative Study of Political Systems, *Nicaragua Election Factbook, February 5, 1967* (Washington, D.C.: Institute for the Comparative Study of Political Systems, 1966), p. 24.

20. The earliest evidence of Frente activity I have uncovered is an anonymous February 1962 pamphlet entitled "Homenaje de J.P.N. a Sandino."

21. Institute for the Comparative Study of Political Systems, *Nicaragua Election Factbook,* p. 30.

22. Ibid., p. 31; Fiallos Oyanguren, "Nicaraguan Political System," pp. 115–22; Ronald H. McDonald, *Party Systems and Elections in Latin America* (Chicago: Markham Publishing Co., 1971), p. 232.

23. *Hispanic American Report* XV (June 1962) 312; interview with Colonel Mansfield, Las Mercedes, Nicaragua, December 1963.

24. Agency for International Development and Department of Defense, *Proposed Mutual Defense and Development Programs,* FY 1965, p. 200; interview with Colonel Murray, Managua, November 1963; interview with Colonel Mansfield, Las Mercedes, Nicaragua, December 1963.

25. Fiallos Oyanguren, "Nicaraguan Political System," pp. 140–41.

26. Ibid., pp. 141–42; confidential interviews, Managua, February 1966.

27. *La Prensa,* (Managua), July 7, 1965, p. 1, and July 9, 1965, p. 1.

28. Ibid., June 21, 1966, p. 1; *Revista de la Guardia Nacional,* June 1970, p. 10.

29. *La Prensa* (Managua), August 4, 1966, p. 1; Fiallos Oyanguren, "Nicaraguan Political System," p. 127.

30. Fiallos Oyanguren, "Nicaraguan Political System," pp. 126–29; *La Prensa* (Managua), April 21, 1966, p. 1; May 23, 1966, pp. 1 and 12; October 10, 1966, p. 1; November 15, 1966, pp. 1 and 5; November 19,

1966, p. 2; November 29, 1966, p. 1; December 6, 1966, p. 1; and January 13, 1967, pp. 1 and 5.

31. Fiallos Oyanguren, "Nicaraguan Political System," pp. 129–30; confidential interviews, Managua, September 1970; Msgr. Donald Chávez Núñez, *Una ventana abierta* (Managua: Editorial Union, 1974), pp. 149–55.

32. Fiallos Oyanguren, "Nicaraguan Political System," p. 130; *New York Times,* February 7, 1967, p. 14.

33. *La Prensa* (Managua), October 3, 1967, p. 1, and October 10, 1967, p. 1; *New York Times,* August 21, 1967, p. 27, and October 12, 1967, p. 22; Carlos Fonseca Amador, "Zero Hour in Nicaragua," *Tricontinental,* October-November 1969, pp. 34–40; Anonymous, "Sandinist Front: Peoples' War in Central America," *Tricontinental,* June-July 1970, p. 93; Richard Gott, *Guerrilla Movements in Latin America* (New York: Doubleday, 1972), p. 484.

34. *La Prensa* (Managua), October 28, 1967, p. 1; *St. Louis Globe Democrat,* October 30, 1967, p. 1.

35. Fiallos Oyanguren, "Nicaraguan Political System," p. 141; *La Prensa* (Managua), March 3, 1967, p. 10.

36. This is based on numerous confidential interviews in Nicaragua during September 1968, September 1970, and August 1975.

37. *Revista de la Guardia Nacional,* May 1970, p. 10.

38. *La Prensa* (Managua), May 3, 1967, p. 5; June 16, 1967, p. 1; June 17, 1967, p. 1; October 27, 1967, p. 1; November 6, 1967, p. 1; November 7, 1967, p. 1; December 27, 1967, p. 1; December 31, 1967, p. 5b; April 16, 1968, p. 1.

39. *Latin America* (London) II (June 21, 1968) 199; *La Prensa* (Managua), April 16, 1968, p. 1; April 17, 1968, p. 1; and April 21, 1968, pp. 1 and 7.

40. *La Prensa* (Managua), April 18, 1968, p. 1; April 25, 1968, p. 1; April 26, 1968, p. 1; and April 30, 1968, p. 1; confidential interviews, Managua, September 1970.

41. *La Prensa* (Managua), July 7, 1968, pp. 1 and 12.

42. Ibid., October 3, 1968, p. 1; March 19, 1969, p. 1; and March 27, 1969, p. 1.

43. *Latin America* (London), II (September 20, 1968), p. 304.

44. Inter-American Development Bank, *Economic and Social Progress in Latin America: Annual Report, 1972,* pp. 388 and 393.

45. *La Prensa* (Managua) September 20, 1968, p. 1; September 21, 1968, p. 1; and March 31, 1969, p. 1.

46. Ibid., July 17, 1969, p. 1. At the meeting a huge portrait of Sandino was given equal honors with portraits of Lenin, Che, and Martí.

47. Ibid., September 1, 1969, p. 1; September 9, 1969, p. 1; and December 24, 1969, p. 1; *New York Times,* October 28, 1970, p. 18.

48. *La Prensa* (Managua), August 6, 1969, p. 1; November 11, 1969, p.

1; January 17, 1970, p. 1; January 24, 1970, p. 1; February 17, 1970, p. 1; February 18, 1970, p. 1; and April 21, 1970, p. 1.

49. Numerous confidential interviews in Nicaragua, August and September 1970, and September 1972.

50. *La Prensa* (Managua), February 27, 1970, pp. 1 and 12; and March 1, 1970, p. 1.

51. Ibid., January 29, 1970, p. 1.

52. Ibid., April 15, 1970, pp. 1 and 12.

53. Ibid., April 14, 1970, p. 1.

54. Confidential interviews, Nicaragua, August and September 1970; September 1972; August and September 1975.

55. Confidential interviews, Managua, September 1970.

56. Confidential interviews, Washington, D.C., April 1973, and March 1975.

57. *Latin America* (London), V (March 26, 1971) 104; James Budd, "Nicaragua Plans on Somoza Forever," *Copley News Service,* July 27, 1971.

58. Susanne Jonas, "Nicaragua," *NACLA's North American and Empire Report* X (February 1976) 21.

59. L. P. News Service release, February 11, 1972.

60. Ibid., April 28, 1972; *Latin America* (London), VI (May 26, 1972) 161–62.

61. For exact figures, see the 1970 and 1973 editions of the *Presupuesto General de ingresos y egresos de la República de Nicaragua* (Managua: Ministerio de Hacienda y Crédito Público, 1975).

62. *La Nación* (San José, Costa Rica), December 23, 1973, p. 6; *La Prensa* (Managua), March 24, 1973, p. 1.

63. Confidential documents and interviews, Washington D.C., April 1973, and Managua, August 1975.

64. Ibid.

65. *Latin America* (London) VI (December 29, 1972) 409; VII (January 5, 1973) 8; (January 12, 1973) 16; (March 9, 1973) 80; and March 30, 1973) 104. The new member of the triumvirate was Edmundo Paguada Irias.

66. Confidential interviews, Washington, D.C., April 1973, March 1975, and June 1975; confidential interviews, Managua, August and September 1975; *Latin America* (London) VII (February 9, 1973) 42 and 44.

67. *La Nación* (San José, Costa Rica), January 23, 1973, pp. 4 and 6, December 23, 1973, p. 6; *La Prensa* (Managua) March 31, 1973, pp. 1, 9, and 10.

68. Robert W. Kates et al., "Human Impact of the Managua Earthquake," *Science* CLXXXII (December 7, 1973) 988.

69. The contrast between the responses of the Nicaraguan and Guatemalan armies to the problems posed by each nation's recent massive earthquakes has been striking. The Guatemalan military has evi-

dently limited corruption in relief supplies and has concentrated on national reconstruction. Somoza's main concern has evidently been retaining his own power base and rebuilding the army, a process which has been aided by his willingness to tolerate or encourage wholesale theft of relief supplies by the Guardia.

70. Kates et al., "Impact of Earthquake," pp. 985–89.

71. I was shown the President's message to Somoza in 1973. While the source must remain confidential, the authenticity was unquestionable.

72. *Latin America* (London), VII (October 19, 1973) 336.

73. Ibid., VIII (March 8, 1974) 80.

74. Ibid., VIII (May 3, 1974) 136; confidential interviews, Managua, August 1975.

75. "Program: 7th Annual Awards Luncheon, American Foreign Service Association," Washington, D.C., November 11, 1974.

76. *Latin America* (London) VIII (July 12, 1974) 216, and (August 30, 1974) 265.

77. Nicaraguan Episcopal Conference, "El Hombre, la Iglesia y la Sociedad," Pastoral Letter issued by seven bishops, August 1974.

78. Bishop Manuel Salazar Espinosa, Secretary, Nicaraguan Episcopal Conference, to the Junta Nacional de Gobierno, November 20, 1974.

79. Jonas, "Nicaragua," pp. 29–31.

80. Laszlo Pataky, *Llegaron los que no estaban invitados* (Managua: Editorial Pereira, 1975), is a dramatic account of the kidnappings, written by one of the hostages. Most of the major documents relating to the incident and a detailed account of the negotiations are contained in Miguel Obando Bravo, *Golpe Sandinista* (Managua: Editorial Union, 1975).

81. *New York Times,* December 31, 1974.

82. Jonas, "Nicaragua," p. 29; Obando Bravo, *Golpe Sandinista,* p. 107; *New York Times,* January 3, 1975, p. 3.

83. United States Embassy in Nicaragua, "Nicaragua: Economic Performance in the First Half of 1975," mimeographed document, July 1975.

84. Jack Anderson and Les Whitten, *Washington Post,* March 20, 1975, p. F25, and *New York Post,* March 31, 1975; *New York Times,* August 11, 1975, p. 3.

85. *Latin America* (London) IX (June 18, 1975) 224, and (December 5, 1975) 384; confidential interviews, Managua, August 1975.

86. *Our Sunday Visitor* (Huntington, Indiana), July 13, 1975.

87. *National Catholic Reporter,* July 18, 1975, p. 17.

88. Unión de estudiantes de Carazo, "23 de Julio," mimeographed, illegal publication, issued summer 1975. It contains a list of claimed FSLN actions from May 1974 through June 1975.

89. Jack Anderson and Les Whitten, *New York Post,* August 18, 1975,

August 19, 1975, and August 22, 1975; Allan Riding, *The Financial Times* (London), August 13, 1975; Allan Riding, *New York Times,* August 6, 1975.

90. Letter from the Nicaraguan Ambassador to the United States, Guillermo Sevilla Sacasa, *Washington Post,* August 29, 1975, p. A29.

91. I saw these painted slogans myself the next morning. Hostile attitudes toward Somoza and the Guardia were expressed openly to me in Nicaragua in August and September 1975 by dozens of Nicaraguans in response to a simple inquiry as to "How are conditions here now?" Not a single Nicaraguan who was not a government employee expressed any positive sentiments concerning the Guardia or the Somozas during my last visit.

92. Confidential interviews, Managua, August and September 1975.

XI

THE GUARDIA TODAY—AND TOMORROW

In 1976 Nicaragua was clearly a nation occupied by its own army. Far from producing a professional, nonpolitical force, United States influence had helped create one of the most totally corrupt military establishments in the world, a force that functions more as the guardians of the Somoza dynasty than as the protectors of Nicaraguan sovereignty and freedom. Part of the responsibility for this situation falls upon the American military, which created the Guardia and which in subsequent decades has helped train, equip, and support this force, while rarely, if ever, questioning the uses to which this training and equipment were put. The impact of this aid has been crucial. In terms of dollars, the Guardia has received over $20 million since 1941, with the greatest amounts coming in the late 1960s.[1] This exceeds the amount of aid given any other Central American nation except Guatemala.[2] American officials like to stress that in recent years none of this aid has been combat arms, but rather has been training and medical equipment, logistical and engineering supplies, and similar material. While this is true, it is also obvious that such aid frees up funds for other areas. In addition to direct grants, it should also be noted that credit and surplus sales of United States equipment have been vital in developing the Guardia's combat capacity. A key case in point would be the Guardia's purchase, in the early 1960s, of Navy jet trainers (TV-2), a purchase that greatly increased the combat capacity of FAN.[3]

Aid for training has been at least as important as aid for equipment. The Guardia's only reliable combat unit, the Third Company, was trained and equipped through American military aid in the 1950s.[4] United States Army and Air Force missions have been maintained in Nicaragua for nearly a quarter of a century.

Even more important has been training provided outside of Nicaragua. General Somoza likes to boast that a higher percentage of his officers and men have been trained abroad, by the United States, than those of any other Latin American army. Most of this training has been in the School of the Americas in the Canal Zone. By mid-1975, 4,252 Nicaraguan officers and men had been trained there, a greater number than those from any other Latin American nation.[5] Without all this training and support it is unlikely that the Guardia could have maintained its monopoly over Nicaraguan politics.

Greater responsibility, however, must rest upon overall United States policy in Latin America. This policy has generally equated verbal opposition to America's current enemies, be they Fascist, as they were up until 1945, or Communist as they have been since, with a convergency of interests and, consequently, has led to American nurture, support, and defense of the Guardia and the Somozas on repeated occasions. The real nature of the Guardia's role in Nicaraguan politics has long been appreciated by many State Department officials. In 1946 a message from the American Ambassador in Nicaragua described the average citizen of that nation as "intimidated by the repressive and uncontested rule of the Guardia Nacional."[6] From FDR's gala reception for General Somoza García's visit to Washington up through Ambassador Shelton's patronizing of the dynasty in the period following the 1973 earthquake, American diplomats and policymakers have usually supported the Somozas and discouraged or actively opposed efforts to remove them. While not all American ambassadors have been as open in their support as Shelton or Thomas Whelan, whose affinity for General Somoza García earned him the nickname of "Somoza's shadow," the dynasty has been remarkably successful in equating opposition to their rule with opposition to the United States.[7]

The bulk of the responsibility for the current status of the Guardia, however, probably rests with the upper classes and the traditional opposition political leaders. They have repeatedly allowed concern with their personal interests and fear of any basic change in the nation's social and economic structures to outweigh their dislike of the Somozas and have supported, compromised with, or at least muted their opposition to the dynasty's rule. For a system such as that maintained in Nicaragua by the Somozas to succeed, there must be great numbers of those willing to be corrupted as well as a dominant family willing to do the corrupting.

The results of forty years of acquiescence in Somoza rule can be seen in every facet of Nicaraguan life. While the economy has seen considerable growth in recent decades, the benefits of this growth have largely been absorbed by the Somozas, their close supporters, and members of the traditional oligarchy. Aided by the Central American Common Market, some industrial development has occurred, but much of this is foreign-owned and a good deal of the remainder is dominated by the Somoza family and often serves more as a subsidized and protected agency for the employment of relatives and retired Guardia officers than as any real contribution to the national economy. Agriculture, especially that designed for export, notably cotton, cattle, and coffee, continues to dominate the national economy. Here the trend toward concentration of the best land in the hands of a few families, most notably the Somozas, has accelerated in recent years.[8]

The Somozas' stranglehold on the national economy extends beyond industries, including those which produce cloth and shoes for the Guardia, and agriculture. They own the national airline, Lanica, and the only national shipping company, Mamenic Lines. They have extensive interests in banking, hotels and real estate, fishing, radio, television, and newspapers. They even control Managua's parking meters and trash collection. In addition, they are now engaged in exporting blood and importing Mercedes Benz automobiles, which coincidentally are used exclusively by the Managua police detachment of the Guardia.[9]

While the supporters of the dynasty prospered, the average Nicaraguan suffered. As usual, poverty was accompanied by chronic malnutrition, disease, and lack of health care facilities. Gastroenteritis and other diarrhea diseases remained the leading cause of death in the 1970s, accounting for 23.6 percent of all deaths. Over 90 percent of these deaths occurred among children under five.[10] The Nicaraguan who managed to survive beyond that age had other problems to contend with. Nicaragua has the world's highest homicide rate, an extremely high rate of accidental deaths, and the highest rate of chronic alcoholism in Central America.[11]

The key to maintaining this system of exaggerated social and economic inequality has been and continues to be control over the

Guardia Nacional. This control is maintained in a number of ways, many of which have already been detailed. Every higher post in the Guardia reportedly has its price tag, representing the amount of money, over and above his salary, which an officer can reasonably expect to make, through graft, "gifts," and similar perquisites. Loyalty to Somoza is the major requirement for appointment to any potentially lucrative post. Officers are expected to endure years of relatively low-paying posts, supplemented by special allowances, gifts, duty-free imports, and income from subsidiary jobs, while waiting to get a post in immigration, customs, or, best of all, command of a department. Frontier or port areas, such as Bluefields or Rivas, are real prizes here, but even the less desirable posts allow a colonel to accumulate enough money to live comfortably for the rest of his life. To keep the system moving, Somoza has recently been retiring entire classes of the *Academia Militar*. Those retired continue to draw full Guardia salaries. In addition, they usually land lucrative positions with the government or with Somoza industries or, taking advantage of their Guardia ties to avoid taxes and gain protection, go into business for themselves. All of this represents a major, invisible cost to the national economy.

Since so much of the Guardia's real cost to Nicaragua is outside of the official budget, it is possible to keep the budgeted costs at a relatively reasonable level. In 1975 these amounted to approximately $28 million or under 11 percent of total government expenditures. About $18,700,000 represented the budget of the Ministry of Defense, another $7,500,000 came from the costs of the Guardia's police units, included under the Ministry of Gobernación, a further $1,500,000 could be found in the Ministry of Hacienda (Treasury) for control of contraband, and a final $200,000 comes from the military officials assigned to the budget of the presidency and to the Ministry of Foreign Relations, where they serve as military attachés.[12] Modest as these figures seem, they represent, as Steve Ropp and Neal Pearson pointed out in 1974, a cost per man almost twice that of neighboring Honduras.[13]

The increasing internal opposition to the Somoza dynasty and the consequent increasing reliance on the Guardia to maintain the status quo have been clearly reflected in recent Guardia budgets. Besides authorizing rapid increases in pay scales, especially those of enlisted men, the government has recently considerably expanded the army component of the Guardia. The

Turner B. Shelton, American Ambassador to Nicaragua in the early seventies, shown here with his close friend, Anastasio Somoza Debayle.

army component consisted of 488 officers and 1,627 enlisted men in 1970. By 1975 this had grown to a force of 630 officers and 2,478 enlisted men. Among the officers the most notable increases were in the higher ranks with the 1970 budget providing for 4 generals and 48 colonels and lieutenant colonels while the 1975 budget included 9 generals and 72 colonels and lieutenant colonels.[14] During this same period the personnel assigned to the police and Treasury Guard components of the Guardia remained virtually unchanged, totaling 63 officers and 3,262 enlisted men in 1970 and rising only to 64 officers and 3,434 enlisted men by 1975.[15] The Air Force (FAN) also showed little change in this period, providing for 103 officers and 201 enlisted men in 1970 and 110 officers and 198 enlisted men in 1975.[16]

Another area of the Guardia's budget which has increased rapidly in recent years has been that allocated for intelligence. This almost doubled, increasing from C$510,600 in 1970 to C$945,840 in 1975.[17] This increased concern with internal security and military force, however, has not produced any rapid increase in spending for military hardware. From 1965 through 1974 Nicaragua bought only $9 million worth of arms from abroad, over half of that total coming in 1975. This was less than that spent by any other Central American nation.[18]

Preoccupation with internal security is reflected in Guardia publications and training and in the attitudes of cadets from the *Academia Militar.* A study of cadet attitudes in the early 1970s revealed a "monomaniacal concern with internal security." Compared to cadets from neighboring Honduras, those from Nicaragua exhibited an overwhelming preoccupation with controlling internal dissent and combating possible insurgent efforts. One cadet even suggested that those engaged in such activities should be burned in public plazas in order to discourage their fellow citizens from supporting such efforts.[19]

This obsessive fear of opposition from within Nicaragua, coupled with the institutionalized corruption of both officers and enlisted personnel, helps keep the force isolated and alienated from the population as a whole and therefore totally dependent upon the support and favors of the Somozas. Everything possible is done to increase this sense of separateness. As previously noted, Guardia members and their families were singled out for special preference in terms of post-earthquake aid, loans, and services. In more normal times Guardia families benefit from their own system of medical care, schooling, and housing, and their food and clothing are obtained with the aid of government subsidies.[20] Crimes committed by Guardia personnel against civilians are rarely tried in civil courts and officers are not usually subject to the same taxes and duties as ordinary citizens.

The Guardia's alienation from the rest of Nicaraguan society and their consequent dependency on the Somozas has made them constantly available to support the dynasty's interests in times of crisis. This has recently been amply demonstrated as the nation has been under martial law since the December 1974 FSLN kidnappings. This suspends constitutional rights, gives vast powers to Guardia commanders of any "military operations, provides for detention without trial, and even gives the Guardia the right to use any personal property throughout the nation." Under these conditions more than 500 persons were reportedly arrested for political offenses by late 1975.[21]

Prospects for any substantial change in the nature and role of the Guardia Nacional within the near future are not very good. Such change, however, might conceivably come about in several ways. A widespread conspiracy among senior Guardia officers could lead to a revolt, but this hardly seems likely without considerable pressure from outside events. The entire system of Guardia promotions and duty assignments works against this possibility. Officers are constantly transferred from post to post and any whose popularity seems threatening or whose loyalty is questioned are likely to be retired or sent abroad as attachés or on "study" assignments. The Somozas have always been most careful in selecting those who will exercise direct command over potential combat units. First preference for such assignments goes to members of the family. In addition, arms and ammunition are strictly controlled. This is clearest in the case of FAN, where the possibility of anti-Somoza action has at times appeared significant. In recent years they have acquired no new combat aircraft and have seen their current inventory actually decline because of mechanical and maintenance problems. While the army component of the Guardia has been expanding, the number of enlisted men assigned to FAN has declined slightly. In addition, ammunition and bombs are tightly controlled by non-FAN personnel and even the training as well as operational flights are strictly regulated.[22]

Under such circumstances senior Guardia officers may complain, but they have never engaged in any concerted effort to change the rules of the game. If they believed that the regime was on the verge of total collapse and that United States support had been withdrawn, they might then move to give the dynasty its coup de grâce, but until such time as conditions reach that stage, it is highly doubtful that they will ever have the requisite motivation, unity, or courage to revolt.

Chronic discontent has long existed among some elements of the Guardia's junior officers. In earlier years, this element was involved in numerous plots within the Guardia, often growing out of resentment over preferences given to non-*Academia Militar* graduates for higher posts. Elements of this discontent remain today, but the constant retirement of senior officers, the command structure, which keeps real power out of the hands of junior officers, and the efficiency of Somoza's intelligence operations within the Guardia have all combined to keep the unhappiness of junior officers at a subdued, verbal level. Many do have a sense of nationalism, a desire to see the Guardia develop a more honorable and professional image, and some have even expressed interest in and admiration for the social role being played by the Peruvian military.[23] Like their senior counterparts, the junior officers might be more inclined to move against the regime if they were convinced that United States support had been withdrawn and internal dissent had reached the point where collapse was imminent. But under present conditions little concrete action can be expected from this group.

The prospects that civilian opposition can provide the necessary conditions for a Guardia revolt are limited. Despite considerable and growing popular support, especially among student groups, FSLN guerrilla activities have remained confined to remote areas of the country and the movement has been unable to provide a major military threat to the regime. While much of the population gains at least some emotional satisfaction from the continuing embarrassment for the Somozas caused by Frente activities, fear, apathy, and preoccupation with personal survival help prevent any translation of this sympathy into concrete support. The guerrillas face serious problems of leadership and supplies and have continuing problems in gaining effective local support in their zones of operation.[24] By themselves, they seem to

With the Guardia Nacional and the U. S. State Department firmly behind him, "Tachito" Somoza has reason to enjoy life.

have little chance of taking power, but their continued survival does exacerbate tensions within the Guardia and within Nicaraguan society as a whole.

Outside of the FSLN, potential internal opposition to the dynasty remains largely ineffective. The union of opposition political factions into UDEL seems a repetition of a tactic that has proven unsuccessful time and time again in the past forty years. The recent death of Manolo Morales, leader of the Christian Democrats, coupled with the health problems of Ramiro Sacasa and the repeated past failures of Pedro Joaquín Chamorro, all illustrate the limited leadership potential of this alliance. The lack of effective leadership also militates against the possibility of any mass uprising or general strike, such as those which overthrew Presidents Ubico in Guatemala and Martínez in El Salvador in 1944. Such an effort might strain Guardia loyalties to the breaking point, but at present it seems only a remote possibility.

The role of the United States remains pivotal in any assessment of the future of the Somozas, the Guardia Nacional, and Nicaragua itself. In recent months some American officials have become increasingly critical of Somoza's government, reacting to his increasingly arbitrary use of power, the massive misappropriation of earthquake relief funds, the inability to eliminate the Frente, and the growing influence of the CGT. Adverse publicity in the United States, especially that related to the Anderson columns, the June 1976 House of Representatives hearings on the violations of human rights, and the conflict with the Catholic Church, have also contributed to this climate of disenchantment. Lack of viable, non-Marxist political alternatives and fear of the potential consequences of any abrupt change in the Nicaraguan political order, however, have combined to limit the translation of this concern into concrete actions. While United States support is not as total as it was in the time of Ambassador Shelton, it is clearly still present. As in so many other cases, fear and inertia are again major aids to Somoza in maintaining his position. A continued deterioration of the regime's support combined with increased success for radical opposition groups might lead to a major reassessment of American options vis-à-vis the Nicaraguan situation, but even then the final result might be to increase, rather than decrease, support for the existing regime. It is somewhat ironic that the recent revelations of CIA covert operations may ultimately prove to benefit Somoza since they certainly diminish the possibility that the United States might ultimately resort to the same tactics in Nicaragua that were used to remove Trujillo from power in the Dominican Republic.

For the immediate future, it seems likely that Somoza control over the Guardia Nacional and thus control over Nicaragua will continue. All of this could change, of course, especially if Anastasio Somoza Debayle were to be removed from the scene, either through a random act of individual violence, such as that which took the life of his father, or through natural causes, such as those which caused the death of his brother, Luis. In such a case the Somoza dynasty would in all probability come to an end, as no other member of the family seems currently to possess either the ability or the influence to maintain control. What type of regime would then take power is impossible to predict, but it is obvious that the Guardia would play a critical role in determining the new order of power. As long as the Somozas rule, however, the Guardia Nacional will remain not guardians of the Nicaraguan people, but rather the crucial and effective guardians of the dynasty.

NOTES

1. Steve C. Ropp, "Goal Orientations of Nicaraguan Cadets," *Journal of Comparative Administration* IV (May 1972) p. 110; Suzanne Jonas, "Nicaragua," *NACLA's North American and Empire Report* (February 1976), p. 24.

2. Jaime Wheelock R., *Imperialismo y dictadura* (Mexico, D.F.: Siglo Veintiuno, 1975), p. 135.

3. *Hispanic American Report* XV (June 1962) 312; interview with Colonel Richard M. Mansfield, Chief of U.S. Air Force Mission to Nicaragua, Las Mercedes, Nicaragua, December 1963.

4. Interview with Colonel Marrag, Managua, 1963.

5. Data furnished to author by the School of the Americas, Fort Gulick, Canal Zone, September 1975.

6. Ambassador Fletcher Warren to Secretary of State Byrnes, July 9, 1946, *Foreign Relations,* 1946, XI, p. 1071.

7. The only significant exceptions to this policy have been the United States opposition to General Somoza Garcia's coup against President Argüello in 1947 and the relative coolness of Ambassador Aaron Brown

to the Somozas during the Presidential term of René Shick. Because of the Guardia's police functions some United States aid for the force has been arranged directly by the State Department or the President without the involvement of the American military. An example of this was the assignment of Gunter Wagner by AID to help "develop" the Nicaraguan police in the late 1960s. When Congress forced an end to such AID projects, Wagner remained in Nicaragua, ostensibly under private contract to the Nicaraguan government.

8. John Morris Ryan et al., *Area Handbook for Nicaragua* (Washington: U.S. Government Printing Office, 1970), p. 221; Wheelock R., *Imperialismo,* pp. 32–49; Edmundo Jarquín C., "Reflexiones sobre la situación actual," (Managua: n.p., 1975), pp. 7–29. For a detailed description of the organization and operations of the dominant interest groups within the Nicaraguan economy, see Harry W. Strachan, "The Role of Business Groups in Economic Development: The Case of Nicaragua" (DBA dissertation, Harvard University, 1973).

9. Data based upon a confidential inventory of Somoza family holdings and interests prepared in Nicaragua in 1975. A summary of some of this material, though containing a few minor errors (for example, the hotel building owned by the Somozas is that of the Gran Hotel in San Salvador, not the Inter-Continental in Managua), can be found in the Jack Anderson and Les Whitten columns of August 18, 19, and 22, 1975, in the *Washington Post* and numerous other newspapers. See also the *National Catholic Reporter,* July 4, 1975, p. 2.

10. B. Holland, J. Davis and L. Gangloff, *Syncresis: The Dynamics of Health,* IX, *Nicaragua* (Washington: Dept. of Health, Education, and Welfare, 1973), pp. 11 and 15.

11. Ibid., pp. 15–16; Norris and Ross McWhirter, eds., *The Guinness Book of World Records,* 17th ed. (London: Guinness Superlatives Limited, 1970), p. 200; Harry Goethels, "Know Your Hemisphere," *Copley News Services,* June 3, 1971.

12. See Ministerio de Hacienda y Crédito Público, Dirección General del Presupuesto, República de Nicaragua, *Presupuesto General de ingresos y egresos de la República* (Managua: Ministerio de Hacienda y Crédito Público, 1975). Cited hereafter as Nicaragua, *Presupuesto* and year.

13. Steve C. Ropp and Neale J. Pearson, "Attitudes of Honduran and Nicaraguan Junior Officers toward the Role of the Military in Latin America," unpublished manuscript, prepared for the March 1974 meeting of the Southwestern Political Science Association, p. 21.

14. Nicaragua, *Presupuesto,* 1970, pp. 445, 475, and 503; 1975, p. 503.

15. Nicaragua, *Presupuesto,* 1970, pp. 347, 351, and 400; 1975, pp. 395, 398–99, and 450.

16. Nicaragua, *Presupuesto,* 1970, pp. 446, and 1975, pp. 503–504. The Guardia budget for 1975 also provided for 17 officers and 96 men assigned to the Band, 4 officers assigned to the Coast Guard, 96 officers and 259 men, plus a host of contract personnel, assigned to the Medical

Department, 62 officers and 306 men assigned to Radio, and 120 cadets in the *Academia Militar.* In addition the Guardia also has several thousand civilian personnel.

17. Nicaragua, *Presupuesto,* 1970, pp. 341, 351, and 400; 1975, pp. 389, 399, and 450. An additional C$4,042,000 is allotted to confidential salaries of agents outside of Nicaragua in the 1975 budget.

18. United States Arms Control and Disarmament Agency, *World Military Expenditures and Arms Transfers, 1965–1974* (Washington: U.S. Government Printing Office, 1976), pp. 67 and 76. Reports of new purchases in 1975, notably in helicopters, if confirmed, might substantially alter this picture.

19. Ropp, "Goal Orientations," p. 111; Ropp and Pearson, "Attitudes of Honduran and Nicaraguan Junior Officers," pp. 8–9.

20. Ryan et al., *Area Handbook,* p. 347.

21. Report of Pedro Joaquín Chamorro to the Inter-American Press Association, 1975.

22. Confidential interviews, Managua, September 1970 and August 1975.

23. Confidential interviews, Managua, September 1970, September 1972, and August 1975.

24. For the FSLN's leadership's own views of some of these problems, see the document they issued on October 16, 1975, "Exposición a los compañeros de la dirreción sobre algunos problemas urgentes de nuestro movimiento y nuestra posición antes las decisiones tomadas en relación a dichos problemas." Copy in possession of the author.

APPENDIX

BIBLIOGRAPHICAL NOTE

The nature, availability, and reliability of source material for a history of Nicaragua's Guardia Nacional varies widely depending on the time period involved. Material is most plentiful and studies of related areas most adequate for the period of the Guardia's development under United States Marine Corps direction. Research problems become progressively more difficult as one moves toward the present.

Because of the dominant American influence exercised over the creation and development of the Guardia Nacional, the State Department records concerning Nicaragua, contained in Record Group 59 in the National Archives, provide a major source of information as to that organization's early history. Decimal File 817.1051 deals specifically with the Guardia, but much relevant material is found in other files, notably 817.00, which deals with political developments. Many of the major documents were later published by the State Department in *Papers Relating to the Foreign Relations of the United States* and whenever possible reference has been made to these documents. For the period of his 1927 mission to Nicaragua and for his 1929–1933 tenure as Secretary of State, the diary of Henry L. Stimson, now in the Yale University Library, offers valuable insights. A small collection of the papers of Ambassador Matthew B. Hanna, included among the Managua consular records in the National Archives, proved valuable in understanding the problems involved in the Guardia's transition from United States to Nicaraguan control.

Marine records concerning the Guardia Nacional were taken to the United States in 1933 and divided into two major collections. The most valuable of these, formerly housed in the Marine Corps Historical Library at the Navy Annex, Arlington, Virginia, is now at the Federal Records Center in Suitland, Maryland. The other collection is included with the Marine Corps Records, Record Group 127, housed in the National Archives. These collections include documents covering the pre-1927 history of the Nicaraguan military, reports on combat operations, including detailed reports on combat operations, including detailed reports on training, medical developments, and police activities, and a host of additional information covering virtually every facet of the Marines' development and command of the Guardia.

Private papers of several important military figures involved in the American interventions helped fill in many gaps in the official records and gave a more personal view of the conflicts involved in developing the Guardia. The Manuscripts Division of the Library of Congress has the collections of Major General Frank McCoy, head of the 1928 Electoral Mission to Nicaragua, of Admiral David Foote Sellers, Commander of the Special Service Squadron, and of Major General John A. Lejeune, Commandant of the Marine Corps. A wide variety of Marine papers and materials relating to Nicaragua can be found in the office of the Marine Corps Museums in the Washington Navy Yard. Formerly housed in the Marine Corps Museum at Quantico, Virginia, these include the private papers of such notable figures as Lieutenant Generals Clayton B. Vogel and Julian C. Smith and Major General Smedley Darlington Butler. The collection also includes a fascinating group of photographs taken during interventions.

Virtually all Nicaraguan records from this period were destroyed in the 1931 earthquake. Newspaper files and a few official documents can be found in Nicaragua's Archivo Nacional in Managua, where the small staff's dedicated efforts to provide assistance make up, at least in part, for the lack of materials.

Personal interviews with such figures as the late Lieutenant General Julian C. Smith, ex-Nicaraguan President Emiliano Chamorro, former Foreign Minister Dr. Carlos Cuadra Pasos, and Ambassadors Dana G. Munro and Willard Beaulac also provided major material for this period of the Guardia's history. Tape recordings were made of many of these interviews and these, along with several very valuable letters from Ambassador Munro, remain in my possession.

There are a number of important published sources available for the period up through 1932. Two volumes by Dana G. Munro, *Intervention and Dollar Diplomacy in the Caribbean, 1900–1921* (Princeton, N.J.: Princeton University Press, 1964) and *The United States and the Caribbean Republics, 1921–1933* (Princeton University Press, 1974), helped fit the events of the Nicaraguan interventions into overall United States policy. The best detailed account of the diplomatic side of the intervention can be found in William Kammen's *A Search for Stability: United States Diplomacy Toward Nicaragua, 1925–1933* (Notre Dame, Ind.: University of Notre Dame Press, 1968). Still of considerable value are Isaac Joslin Cox's scholarly *Nicaragua and the United States* (Boston: World Peace Foundation, 1928) and Harold Norman Denny's journalistic account, *Dollars for Bullets* (New York: Dial Press, 1929).

By far the best account of the conflict with Sandino is Neill Macaulay's *The Sandino Affair* (Chicago: Quadrangle Books, 1967). There are a multitude of works on Sandino in Spanish, the best of which is probably Gregorio Selser's two-volume *Sandino, General de los hombres libres* (Buenos Aires: Editorial Triángulo, 1958), which includes a host of Sandinista documents. General Anastasio Somoza García's ghost-written *El verdadero Sandino* (Managua: Tipografía Robelo, 1936) also contains numerous documents, but its overwhelming anti-Sandino bias limits its value.

There are two books dealing specifically with the Guardia during this period. Julian C. Smith et. al., *A Review of the Organization and Operations of the Guardia Nacional de Nicaragua; by Direction of the Major General Commandant of the United States Marine Corps* (United States Marine Corps, no date) is an invaluable compilation of documents along with a summary account of the Marines' development of the Guardia. Marvin Goldwert's *The Constabulary in the Dominican Republic and Nicaragua: Progeny and Legacy of United States Intervention* (Gainesville: University of Florida Press, 1962) is brief and based largely on secondary sources.

There are a host of magazine and journal articles written by actual participants in the events of this period which are essential sources for any study of the Guardia. Many of these can be found in the pages of Nicaragua's *Revista Conservadora del Pensamiento Centroamericano,* including autobiographical articles by General Emiliano Chamorro and Dr. Carlos Cuadra Pasos. Marine officers contributed a host of articles relating to the intervention and the Guardia to the pages of the *Marine Corps Gazette* during the late 1920s and early 1930s. Major Calvin B. Carter's "Kentucky Feud in Nicaragua," *World's Work* LIV (July 1927), provides important material on Nicaragua's first constabulary.

There are numerous unpublished studies dealing with the pre-1933 period in Nicaraguan history. Early aspects of United

States-Nicaraguan relations are covered in John Ellis Findling's "The United States and Zelaya: A Study in the Diplomacy of Expediency" (Ph.D. dissertation, University of Texas, 1971) and in Virginia L. Greer's "Charles Evans Hughes and Nicaragua, 1921–1925" (Ph.D. dissertation, University of New Mexico, 1954). Specialized aspects of the second intervention are covered in Thomas J. Dodd, Jr.'s "United States in Nicaraguan Politics: Supervised Elections, 1927–1932" (Ph.D. dissertation, George Washington University, 1966) and in John Milton Wearmouth's "The Second Marine Intervention in Nicaragua" (M.A. thesis, Georgetown University, 1952).

Documentation on the period from 1933 till 1956, during which the Guardia was dominated by General Anastasio Somoza García, is often difficult to obtain. State Department records, which have been opened through 1948, remain a prime source. A valuable supplement to the official record is provided by the Arthur Bliss Lane Papers at Yale University. A limited amount of material was also found in the reports of American military attachés to Nicaragua, but much of this material, which is housed in the National Archives, remains closed to public examination. There are also a few valuable documents available among the Franklin D. Roosevelt papers in the Roosevelt Library, Hyde Park, New York.

Government restrictions rather than earthquake destruction prevents access to most Nicaraguan government documents covering this period. Some material can be found in the newspaper collections and files of published government documents housed in Nicaragua's Archivo Nacional.

As documentary evidence became more scarce, interviews became increasingly important. A host of Nicaraguans cooperated in this, notably two former members of the Guardia's General Staff, General Camilo Gonzáles and Major Alfonso Gonzáles Cervantes. Former United States Ambassador Gerald Drew also provided considerable valuable information. The identity of several other valuable informants for this period must, for various reasons, remain confidential.

Published material covering this period is limited and often heavily biased. Ildo Sol's *La Guardia Nacional de Nicaragua: Su tragectoria y incógnita, 1927–1944* (Granada, Nicaragua: El Centro-Americano, 1944) provides an interesting, but undocumented account of the Guardia's early years. Adolfo Reyes Huete, *ETAPAS del ejército* (Managua: Talleres Nacionales, no date), is a compilation of pro-Guardia articles and documents prepared by the Nicaraguan government.

Some data on the conflict between Somoza and Sandino and the consequent death of Sandino can be found in the previously cited works by Macaulay and Selser. An inside view of these tragic events is provided by Salvador Calderón Ramírez, *Ultimo días de Sandino* (Mexico, D.F.: Ediciones Botas, 1934). Domingo Ibarra Grijalva has provided a poorly written, but at times valuable account in *The Last Night of General Augusto César Sandino* (New York: Vantage Press, 1973).

There are no books in English covering the Somoza presidency. Some material can be found in John Martz, *Central America: The Crisis and the Challenge* (Chapel Hill: University of North Carolina Press, 1959). Among the host of bitter, undocumented attacks upon General Somoza García which have been published in Spanish the works of Gustavo Alemán-Bolaños, *Los pobres diablos* (Guatemala City: Editorial Hispania, 1947) and *Un lombrosiano: Somoza, 1939–1944* (Guatemala City: Editorial Hispania, 1945), of Pedro Joaquín Chamorro Cardenal, *Estirpe sangrienta, los Somozas* (Buenos Aires: Editorial Triángulo, 1959), and of Ramón Romero, *Somoza, asesino de Sandino* (Mexico, D.F.: Editorial Patria y Libertad, 1959), probably deserve special mention. Alejandro Cole Chamorro's *Desde Sandino hasta los Somoza* (Granada, Nicaragua: Editorial El Mundo, 1971) provides perhaps the most dispassionate view of Nicaraguan politics during this period. A valuable, though hardly objective account of Somoza's accession to the Nicaraguan presidency can be found in ex-President Juan Bautista Sacasa's *Cómo y por qué caí del poder* (León, Nicaragua, n.p., 1946).

Except for a few interesting accounts in the *Revista Conservadora,* notably those in General Chamorro's autobiography, and occasional brief pieces in such sources as *Time* and *Newsweek,* there is an almost total lack of worthwhile articles on this period of Nicaraguan history. The only ones worth citing are probably James L. Busey's "Foundations of Political Contrast, Costa Rica and Nicaragua," *Western Political Science Quarterly* XI (September 1958), and my own "Anastasio Somoza García: Fundador de la dinastía Somoza en Nicaragua," *Revista Estudios Centroamericanos* XXX (December 1975).

Unpublished scholarly studies are equally rare. Of great value as an introduction to Somoza's career is Ternot MacRenato's "Anastasio Somoza: A Nicaraguan Caudillo" (M.A. thesis, University of San Francisco, 1974), but unfortunately this study concludes with the General's assumption of the presidency at the start of 1937. Mariano Fiallos Oyanguren's "The Nicaraguan Political System: The Flow of Demands and the Reactions of the Regime" (Ph.D. dissertation, University of Kansas, 1968) does provide some valuable insight into both the rule of General Somoza and that of his sons.

The problem of available sources becomes even more severe for the post-1956 period. No archival resources are available. In some cases I was able to see official documents, but this was usually under circumstances which made note taking or citation virtually impossible. A few United States Government documents relating to military aid, the establishment and functioning of military missions and economic conditions, are available. A useful, if generally uncritical compilation of data on contemporary Nicaragua is available in the *Area Handbook for Nicaragua,* prepared for the Army by John Morris Ryan et. al. and published by the U.S. Government Printing Office in 1970.

In Nicaragua, I was able to obtain copies of the Guardia's official Escalafón, listing all officers and their assignments, various other Guardia publications, and budget data for the period. I also managed to obtain some illegal opposition publications, including several from the Frente Sandinista. The newspaper files in the Archivo Nacional continued to be of considerable value, although the Somozas' habit of suppressing the opposition press, notably *La Prensa,* during times of crisis was the cause of considerable frustration.

There are few published works of any value dealing with recent Nicaraguan history. A passionate critique of the regime can be found in Jaime Wheelock R.'s *Imperialismo y dictadura* (Mexico, D.F.: Siglo Veintiuno, 1975). The North American Congress on Latin America (NACLA) devoted the February 1976 issue of its *North American and Empire Report* to Nicaragua. Charles W. Anderson's chapter on "Nicaragua: The Somoza Dynasty," in Martin Needler, ed., *Political Systems of Latin America,* 2nd ed. (New York: Van Nostrand Reinhold, 1970) is quite perceptive. These three publications, along with the previously cited works by Cole Chamorro and Fiallos Oyanguren represent the only attempts to present a comprehensive examination of the functioning of the Somoza dynasty.

Several valuable special studies do exist. Thomas W. Walker has published a brief monograph, *The Christian Democratic Move-*

ment in Nicaragua (The University of Arizona Comparative Government Studies, 1970). The Institute for the Comparative Study of Political Systems produced the *Nicaragua Election Factbook, February 5, 1967* (ICOPS, 1967). The December 1974 kidnappings produced two interesting accounts, Laszlo Pataky's personal reminiscences, *Llegaron los que no estaban invitado* (Managua; Editorial Pereira, 1975) and a combination of documents and narrative by Archbishop Miguel Obando Bravo, *Golpe Sandinista* (Managua: Editorial Union, 1975). Richard Walter Oscar Lethander's "The Economy of Nicaragua" (Ph.D. dissertation, Duke University, 1968) provides an overview of the economic system while Harry W. Strachan's "The Role of Business Groups in Economic Development: The Case of Nicaragua" (D.B.A. dissertation, Harvard University, 1973) gives details as to the dominant elements within that system. Of greater relevance to this study are Steve Ropp's "Goal Orientations of Nicaraguan Cadets," *Journal of Comparative Administration* IV (May 1972), and Ropp and Neale Pearson's "Attitudes of Honduran and Nicaraguan Junior Officers Toward the Role of the Military in Latin America" (unpublished ms. prepared for the March 1974 meeting of the Southwestern Political Science Association). While it contains some useful statistics relating to military aid to Nicaragua, Donald Etchison's *The United States and Militarism in Central America* (New York: Praeger, 1975) is based largely on published sources and contains little new information.

The data gleaned from sources such as those listed above have been complemented by accounts in Nicaraguan and United States newspapers, by articles in the British newsletter, *Latin America,* and by bits and pieces gleaned from a host of other sources. Without the aid of scores of individuals, Americans and Nicaraguans, including military and civilian officials, church leaders, journalists, scholars, and even Managua's market women and taxi drivers, the last section of this study would have been virtually impossible. Among those interviewed during the course of this project were several United States Ambassadors to Nicaragua, numerous high-ranking Guardia officers including General José Somoza, and even President Anastasio Somoza Debayle, himself. The most valuable information was, however, received from individuals whose identity cannot be revealed. Only accounts which could be substantially verified were used in this study, but such verification often depended upon the position of the individual in question and on documentary evidence which I am not free to cite. Recently, however, an impressive amount of evidence supporting many of the charges made against the Guardia and the Somoza regime has become available, notably in the two volumes of evidence produced by the June, 1976 Congressional Hearings on Human Rights in Central America. Should any readers wish a fuller listing of sources used in this book they might consult the lengthy, though now somewhat dated bibliography that accompanied my 1966 University of New Mexico Ph.D. dissertation, "The History of the Guardia Nacional de Nicaragua, 1925–1965."

INDEX